Globalisation and Poverty

Is globalisation making the poor poorer, or is it the most effective factor in global poverty reduction? The consequences of globalisation for the world's poor are uncertain and fierce rhetoric is dividing its supporters and detractors.

During the last two decades, bilateral and multilateral donors' policy advice to developing countries has been centred on greater market openness and better integration into the global economy – a process that characterises globalisation. This advice is based on the premise that globalisation enhances growth and faster growth reduces poverty. But many analysts doubt whether globalisation is necessarily pro-poor.

This book provides a systematic analysis of the impact of globalisation on poverty, using simulation methods and rich empirical evidence to try to establish directions and magnitudes of effect to inform policy response. The book features detailed case studies on Colombia, Ghana, India, Nepal, Bangladesh and Vietnam. The studies show that a 'one-size-fits-all' policy prescription is a bad idea and that country-specific circumstances combined with domestic policies and other factors are co-determinants of the final poverty outcome.

Written by a team of experts in the field, this book will be invaluable for students and researchers in the field of development, economics and politics.

Maurizio Bussolo is Senior Economist at the World Bank and formerly of the OECD Development Centre, Paris. **Jeffery I. Round** is Reader in the Department of Economics, University of Warwick.

Routledge/Warwick Studies in Globalisation

Edited by Richard Higgott and published in association with the Centre for the Study of Globalisation and Regionalisation, University of Warwick.

What is globalisation and does it matter? How can we measure it? What are its policy implications? The Centre for the Study of Globalisation and Regionalisation at the University of Warwick is an international site for the study of key questions such as these in the theory and practice of globalisation and regionalisation. Its agenda is avowedly interdisciplinary. The work of the Centre will be showcased in this new series.

This series comprises two strands:

Warwick Studies in Globalisation addresses the needs of students and teachers, and the titles will be published in hardback and paperback. Titles include:

Globalisation and the Asia-Pacific
Contested territories
Edited by Kris Olds, Peter Dicken, Philip F. Kelly, Lily Kong and Henry Wai-chung Yeung

Regulating the Global Information Society
Edited by Christopher Marsden

Banking on Knowledge
The genesis of the global development network
Edited by Diane Stone

Historical Materialism and Globalisation
Edited by Hazel Smith and Mark Rupert

Civil Society and Global Finance
Edited by Jan Aart Scholte with Albrecht Schnabel

Towards a Global Polity
Edited by Morten Ougaard and Richard Higgott

New Regionalisms in the Global Political Economy
Theories and cases
Edited by Shaun Breslin, Christopher W. Hughes, Nicola Phillips and Ben Rosamond

Routledge/Warwick Studies in Globalisation is a forum for innovative new research intended for a high-level specialist readership, and the titles will be available in hardback only. Titles include:

1. **Non-State Actors and Authority in the Global System**
   Edited by Richard Higgott, Geoffrey Underhill and Andreas Bieler

2. **Globalisation and Enlargement of the European Union**
   Austrian and Swedish social forces in the struggle over membership
   Andreas Bieler

3. **Rethinking Empowerment**
   Gender and development in a global/local world
   Edited by Jane L. Parpart, Shirin M. Rai and Kathleen Staudt

4. **Globalising Intellectual Property Rights**
   The TRIPs agreement
   Duncan Matthews

5. **Globalisation, Domestic Politics and Regionalism**
   The ASEAN Free Trade Area
   Helen E. S. Nesadurai

6. **Microregionalism and Governance in East Asia**
   Katsuhiro Sasuga

7. **Global Knowledge Networks and International Development**
   Edited by Diane Stone and Simon Maxwell

8. **Globalisation and Economic Security in East Asia**
   Governance and institutions
   Edited by Helen E. S. Nesadurai

9. **Regional Integration in East Asia and Europe**
   Convergence or divergence?
   Edited by Betrand Fort and Douglas Webber

10. **The Group of Seven**
    Finance ministries, central banks and global financial governance
    Andrew Baker

11. **Globalisation and Poverty**
    Channels and policy responses
    Edited by Maurizio Bussolo and Jeffery I. Round

Globalisation and Poverty
Channels and policy responses

Edited by Maurizio Bussolo
and Jeffery I. Round

Taylor & Francis Group

LONDON AND NEW YORK

0231582484

First published 2006
by Routledge
2 Park Square, Milton Park, Abingdon, Oxon, OX14 4RN

Simultaneously published in the USA and Canada
by Routledge
270 Madison Ave, New York NY 10016

Routledge is an imprint of the Taylor & Francis Group

Transferred to Digital Printing 2008

Typeset in Times by
HWA Text and Data Management, Tunbridge Wells

British Library Cataloguing in Publication Data
A catalogue record for this book is available from the British Library

Library of Congress Cataloging in Publication Data
Globalisation and poverty : channels and policy responses / edited by
    Maurizio Bussolo and Jeffery I. Round
  p. cm. – (Routledge/Warwick studies in globalisation ; 11)
  Includes bibliographical references and index.
  1. Free trade – Developing countries. 2. Globalization – Economic
    aspects – Developing countries. 3. Poverty – Developing countries.
    4. Poor – Developing countries. I. Bussolo, Maurizio., 1964– II.
Round   Jeffery I. (Jeffery Ian), 1943– III. Series.
HF1413.G582 2005
339.4´6´091724–dc22   2005006194

ISBN10: 0–415–34360–7 (hbk)
ISBN10: 0–415–47967–3 (pbk)

ISBN13: 978–0–415–34360–2 (hbk)
ISBN13: 978–0–415–47967–7 (pbk)

Contents

Tables

Figures

Notes on contributors

François Bourguignon is Senior Vice President and Chief Economist at the World Bank. He has served as an advisor to many developing countries, the OECD, the United Nations, and the European Commission. He has been Professor of Economics at the École des Hautes Etudes en Sciences Sociales in Paris and has held academic positions with the University of Chile, Santiago, and the University of Toronto. François Bourguignon has authored and edited several books as well as numerous articles in leading international journals in economics.

Maurizio Bussolo is Senior Economist at the World Bank. His international journal publications and his research interests focus on quantitative analyses of economic policy and development, including studies on labour markets, environmental economics, and on the links between trade, growth and poverty. He has worked or has been a consultant for the OECD, the Inter-American Development Bank, IDRC, and has taught postgraduate economics courses in various universities in Italy, the UK, Switzerland, and Latin America. He has direct experience of working in developing countries, especially Latin America.

John Cockburn is Associate Professor of Economics at Université Laval (Québec) and co-director of the Poverty and Economic Policy (PEP) research network. He has been a consultant for the World Bank, IDRC, UNDP and other international organisations. His research is shared between CGE modelling, child welfare, manufacturing competitiveness and empirical trade policy analysis. His focus countries are Vietnam, Nepal, Ethiopia and francophone Africa.

Bazlul H. Khondker is currently Associate Professor in Economics at the University of Dhaka, Bangladesh. He obtained a PhD degree in Economics from Warwick University, UK. He has been a consultant for UNDP, the World Bank, IDRC, Canada, and other international agencies. His main research interests include computable general equilibrium modelling of trade and tax policies, poverty and income distribution and modelling cost and resource implications of key Millennium Development Goals. He was involved in the preparation of the first Poverty Reduction Strategy of Bangladesh and the first MDG progress report for Bangladesh.

Jann Lay is with the Kiel Institute for World Economics and the University of Göttingen, Germany, and is currently completing a PhD in economics. He has worked as a consultant for the World Bank and the German Technical Cooperation. His research interests include pro-poor growth, trade issues, and the resource curse. Methodologically, he focuses on CGE modelling, microsimulations, and ways of combining these approaches.

Neil McCulloch is currently Senior Economist in the World Bank Resident Mission Jakarta, Indonesia, and Fellow at the Institute of Development Studies, Sussex. His main publication fields and research interests include the linkages between trade liberalisation and poverty, domestic trade and the rural investment climate, and the determinants of movements in and out of poverty. He has an in-depth country interest in Indonesia and has also worked on China, Pakistan, Kenya and Zambia.

Mustafa K. Mujeri is currently working as the Poverty Monitoring and Analysis Advisor for UNDP in Cambodia. He has worked in various international and national organisations including the Centre on Integrated Rural Development for Asia and the Pacific, Bangladesh Institute of Development Studies, Bangladesh Planning Commission and was Associate Professor in the University of Rajshahi and Visiting Lecturer in the University of Queensland, Australia. His publications and research interests include poverty and development policy analysis, modelling and quantitative analysis, gender and social development, and poverty reduction strategy and programme development in South and South East Asia.

Yoko Niimi is a researcher at the Poverty Research Unit at the University of Sussex, UK. Her area of specialisation is in quantitative development economics. The main theme of her research is the impact of trade liberalisation on poverty with particular focus on Vietnam. She has also worked on non-monetary dimensions of inequality measurement in Brazil. She is currently pursuing her DPhil research at the University of Sussex, which examines households' behavioural response to liberalisation-induced food price shocks in Vietnam.

Jeffery I. Round is currently Reader in the Department of Economics at the University of Warwick, UK. He has been Visiting Associate Professor at the Woodrow Wilson School, Princeton, a Harkness Fellow at Harvard, and a consultant for the World Bank, DFID, and other international organisations. His main publication fields and research interests include the design and use of social accounting matrices (SAMs) for development policy analysis, poverty and inequality, measuring informal activity, and CGE modelling and regional modelling. He has several country interests, especially and most recently in Ghana.

Puja Vasudeva-Dutta is a researcher at the Poverty Research Unit at the University of Sussex. Her area of specialisation is quantitative development economics and she has worked on the analysis of the links between trade liberalisation and household poverty dynamics in developing countries such as China, Vietnam and Zambia. She is also currently pursuing DPhil research at the University of Sussex that investigates the links between trade liberalisation and the distribution of wages in India.

John Whalley is Professor of Economics at both the Universities of Warwick and Western Ontario, Canada. At Western Ontario he is a co-director of the Centre for the Study of International Economic Relations. He is a Fellow of the Royal Society of Canada, a Fellow of the Econometric Society, a research associate of the National Bureau of Economic Research (NBER), and is the Joint Managing Editor of the journal *The World Economy*. He has published extensively and widely, and is best known for his contributions to applied general equilibrium analysis, and trade and tax policy. In recent years he has worked on environmental issues, producing one of the early and most widely cited studies (jointly with Randy Wigle) on carbon taxes. He has served on a Canada–US trade dispute panel, and been a research director for the MacDonald Royal Commissions in Canada. He continues to work on WTO and global trade policy issues, and has a special interest in China.

L. Alan Winters is Director of the Development Research Group of the World Bank. He is on leave from the University of Sussex where he is Professor of Economics. He is a Research Fellow and former Programme Director of the Centre for Economic Policy Research (CEPR, London) and has previously worked in the Universities of Cambridge, Bristol, Wales and Birmingham, and as Economist, Division Chief and Research Manager in the World Bank. He has been Editor of the World Bank Economic Review and Associate Editor of the Economic Journal. In addition he has advised, *inter alia*, the World Bank, OECD, DFID, the Commonwealth Secretariat, the European Commission, the European Parliament, UNCTAD, the WTO, and the Inter-American Development Bank.

Acknowledgements

This volume comprises papers originally presented at a two-day workshop held at the OECD Development Centre in December 2002, on the theme: 'How do globalisation and poverty interact and what can governments do about it?', organised by Maurizio Bussolo. Some of the papers presented at that workshop were the outcome of a project undertaken in the Centre for Globalisation and Regionalisation (CSGR) at the University of Warwick, entitled, 'Globalisation and Poverty: Implications of the South Asian Experience for the Wider Debate', co-directed by John Whalley and Jeffery I. Round, and funded by the Department for International Development (DFID) under their Globalisation and Poverty Research Programme. As editors of this volume we therefore have several acknowledgements and notes of debt and gratitude to make.

The OECD Development Centre was instrumental in promoting and funding the workshop, and encouraging us to produce this volume. Our thanks are due to Ulrich Hiemenz and Catherine Duport and all the workshop participants for their various contributions. The comments and the discussion helped to improve, quite substantially, the papers included in this volume. Professors Richard Higgott and Jan Aart Scholte, co-directors of the CSGR, have also given us their unstinting support and encouragement in many ways, both at the initial project stage and in the production of this volume. We wish to express our sincere gratitude to both of them.

We thank Heidi Bagtazo and Harriet Brinton at Routledge for their patience and forbearance, and for giving us the necessary encouragement. The volume has been in the gestation stage for far too long, and we are glad and grateful to them for keeping faith in us. Finally, Giancarlo Ianulardo assisted in some of the editorial work which we would like to acknowledge accordingly.

The chapter by Jeffery I. Round and John Whalley was first published in *IDS Bulletin* Volume 35 No 1 (2004), pp 11–19, and is reprinted with permission from the Institute of Development Studies, Sussex.

Maurizio Bussolo
Jeffery I. Round

Foreword

François Bourguignon

The urgent need to eradicate global poverty has repeatedly been underlined by the international development community, as witnessed by the United Nations Millennium Declaration and the setting of the Millennium Development Goals. In order to address poverty reduction seriously it is necessary to develop a range of policies for action, both at global and country levels. But establishing what policies are appropriate – how they should be chosen amongst alternatives and what their likely consequences are for the poor, taking into account both direct and indirect effects – is both non-trivial and problematic. This volume focuses on those poverty-reduction policies which are linked to the globalisation process that characterises the evolution of the world economy.

Globalisation undoubtedly is a dominant fact of our times. Through facilitated transportation of merchandise, capital, labour, technology or information, the recent acceleration of globalisation is thought to have had a major impact on the distribution of standards of living both within the world and within countries. There is an increasing tendency to attribute the most salient features in the changes of the global economy to this phenomenon. This is the case, for instance, of the convergence of successful East-Asian countries towards rich countries' standards as well as of the increasing gap between the richest and the poorest countries, particularly sub-Saharan African countries. The same kind of explanation is used for the increase in disparities observed in several countries over the last 20 years. According to some, globalisation is making the poor poorer, whereas others believe it has been the most effective factor of global poverty reduction.

The linkages between globalisation, the policies supposed to exploit the opportunities it creates – and possibly to protect against its negative effects – and poverty are complex and depend on a wide range of factors. To simplify, globalisation may be seen as having two types of effects on poverty in a country. The first goes through modifying the rate of growth whereas the second goes through changes in the distribution of standards of living. Very much of the debate about the effects of globalisation on poverty has been about ascertaining the relationship between globalisation, growth and distribution, on the one hand, and the effects of growth and distribution on poverty, on the other.

As regards the first link, there is a large literature based on cross-country evidence suggesting that trade openness is conducive to growth – see for instance Sachs and Warner (1995), Edwards (1998) and Dollar and Kraay (2004). Although this evidence, or the way it should be interpreted, is contested (Rodriguez and Rodrik, 2000), there is little doubt that trade openness may have some positive effect on growth, presumably depending on the policy instruments being used to promote trade and the way they bear on the export or the import side of trade. Freeing trade in some specific way rather than constraining it is generally perceived as one of the most effective factors of growth (McCulloch, McKay and Winters, 2004). The issue is then to find the right policy mix that will indeed permit a country to integrate the globalisation process and to transform it into faster growth.

The relationship between globalisation and inequality has also received very much attention, mainly in terms of the linkage between trade and wage inequality in both developed and developing countries (Wood, 1994; Krueger, 1997). Evidence appears mixed, and very much country-specific. Wage and income inequality increased in some countries at the same time as the recent wave in globalisation but it did not do so in other countries with more or less the same characteristics with respect to trade and international markets. Moreover, in countries where inequality and relative poverty did increase, the channels through which trade would have been responsible for that evolution are not clear – see Katz and Murphy (1992) and Katz and Autor (1999) for developed countries and Wood (1998, 1999) for developing countries.

As regards the second link between globalisation and poverty it can be noted that poverty reduction is generally seen as merely synonymous of growth. To the extent that globalisation and associated policies may trigger growth, they thus should automatically reduce poverty. But this is only true under certain conditions. First, poverty must be defined in absolute terms, that is, with reference to a poverty line with some monetary equivalent, as with the $1-a-day poverty line used by international organisations for instance. Things are clearly very different if poverty is defined in relative terms, with a poverty line indexed on the mean income of a population. Second, the distribution of relative welfare within the population must not deteriorate at the expense of the poorest at the same time the economy grows. Thus, the ultimate poverty outcome of trade expansion and globalisation in a particular country depends not just on whether trade may enhance growth but also on whether an adverse effect in the distribution does not offset the effect of growth on poverty. It is true that, on average across countries, neither growth nor trade seems to be affecting in a significant way the distribution of relative incomes – see Dollar and Kraay (2002). But this does not mean that this conclusion also holds when particular country experiences are being analyzed.

Much of the two-stage empirical literature on the relationship between globalisation and poverty alluded to earlier has technical limitations which make it less than fully appropriate for country-specific policy recommendation. It relies heavily on cross-country data with limited possibilities for correcting estimates for country fixed effects and endogeneity biases. More importantly, this approach is essentially that of a reduced-form model. At best it permits testing for correlation and causality but it does not allow ascertaining the channels through which trade and globalisation affect growth and poverty. This is particularly worrisome when the objective of the analysis is to identify the total effect on poverty of policy interventions meant to enhance or, on the contrary, to compensate the impact of globalisation.

Case studies are not necessarily more useful if they are not carried out on the basis of some *counterfactual analysis* indicating what would have been the evolution of the economy in the absence of globalisation influences or with different trade-related policies. Such an analysis requires, implicitly or explicitly, the availability of economy-wide models showing the likely effects of some particular instruments or changes in the set of exogenous parameters that govern the evolution of an economy upon the variables of interest: growth, distribution, poverty. The model may be very simple, consisting for instance of extrapolating historical trends. It may also be more sophisticated, consisting of a set of accounting and behavioural equations, which may be econometrically estimated or possibly 'calibrated' on the basis of some priors on the value of some key parameters. At the heart of this approach to the effects of trade and globalisation on poverty is the use of economy-wide, general equilibrium type models and micro-simulation models.

The current state of the art (or science, depending on one's predilection) in the field of trade, growth and distribution offers a wide range of modelling approaches. They range from models that rely on representative household groups, through to economy-wide models that are fully articulated with a micro-data base and some representation of household micro-economic responses to changes in their macro environment. The increasing availability of micro databases, and household surveys in particular, indeed makes the idea of 'micro-simulating' the effects of macro policies and global shocks on actual individuals and households now within the realm of technical feasibility for many countries.

The papers in this volume provide a unique set of examples of the various modelling approaches to the issue of trade, globalisation and poverty in developing countries. At the same time, they offer a rather broad and complete view at the actual poverty effects of globalisation and trade by focusing on a diversified sample of countries. They perfectly illustrate all the gains that may be obtained in the field of policy analysis from rigorous counterfactual modelling work undertaken in an explicitly country-specific framework. It is to be hoped that the example they provide for policy analysis will be extensively followed by policy makers and analysts in developing countries and in the international development community, and the methods they propose will be perfected over time.

Although this volume exemplifies the progress made in accounting for poverty outcomes in quantitative policy analysis, it should be kept in mind that it does so with a definition of poverty that some may find restrictive. Throughout the various chapters, only the monetary or 'income' dimension of poverty is being considered. Yet, the multi-dimensionality of poverty is now at the core of the reflection on development, and at the forefront of development objectives as shown by the Millennium Development Goals. In that perspective, it is to be hoped that this volume will actually open the way to a more comprehensive quantitative treatment of poverty in both the modelling of policies and in the reflection on the effects of globalisation.

References

Dollar, David, and Aart Kraay (2002) 'Growth is Good for the Poor', *Journal of Economic Growth*, 7; 195–225.

Dollar, David, and Aart Kraay (2004) 'Trade, Growth, and Poverty', *Economic Journal*, 114 (493); F22–49.

Edwards, Sebastian (1998) 'Openness, Productivity and Growth: What Do We Really Know?', *Economic Journal*, 108(447); 383–98.

Frankel, Jeffrey, and David Romer (1999), 'Does Trade Cause Growth?', *American Economic Review*, 89(3); 379–99.

Katz, Lawrence F. and D. Autor (1999) 'Changes in the Wage Structure and Earnings Inequality', in O. Ashenfelter and D. Card (eds) *Handbook of Labour Economics*, vol.3A, North-Holland; 1463–1555.

Katz, Lawrence F. and K. M. Murphy (1992) 'Changes in Relative Wages, 1963–1987: Supply and Demand Factors', *Quarterly Journal of Economics*, 107(1); 35–78.

Krueger, Alan B. (1997) 'Labor Market Shifts and the Price Puzzle Revisited,' NBER Working Papers 5924, National Bureau of Economic Research.

McCulloch, Neil, Andrew McKay, and L. Alan Winters (2004) 'Trade Liberalisation and Poverty: The Evidence So Far', *Journal of Economic Literature*, 42(1); 72–115.

Rodriguez, Francisco, and Dani Rodrik (2000) 'Trade Policy and Economic Growth: A Skeptic's Guide to the Cross-section Evidence', in B. Bernanke and K. Rogoff (eds) *NBER Macroeconomics Annual 2000*, Cambridge, MA: MIT Press.

Sachs, Jeffrey, and Andrew Warner (1995) 'Economic Reforms and the Process of Global Integration', Brookings Papers on Economic Integration, 1; 1–118.

Wood, Adrian (1994) *North–South Trade, Employment and Inequality: Changing Fortunes in a Skill-driven World*, Oxford: Clarendon Press.

Wood, Adrian (1998) 'Globalisation and the Rise in Labour Market Inequalities', *The Economic Journal*, 108 (450); 1463–82.

Wood, Adrian (1999) 'Openness and Wage Inequality in Developing Countries: The Latin American Challenge to East Asian Conventional Wisdom', in R. E. Baldwin, D. Cohen, A. Sapir and A. Venables, (eds) *Market Integration, Regionalism and the Global Economy*, Cambridge: Cambridge University Press.

Introduction

Maurizio Bussolo and Jeffery I. Round

During the last two decades, policy advice from bilateral and multilateral donors to developing countries has been conditioned by increasing market openness and more integration into the global economy – a process that characterises globalisation. Some of this advice is predicated on two major assumptions. The first is that outward-oriented economies are not only more efficient and less prone to resource waste, but also appear to have performed well in terms of overall development. Second, that raising average incomes generally benefits all groups in countries, though not necessarily to the same extent. Thus, it subscribes to the notion that as long as inequality is not increasing too much, economic progress through growth will reduce poverty. However, the validity of these assumptions is being challenged in some quarters (especially by the anti-globalisation movement) and there are doubts and uncertainties about the effects some liberalisation policies might have on poverty in a globalising world. Despite these doubts, the relationship between globalisation and poverty remains inadequately researched and poorly understood. Clearly, if the effects are ambiguous, and the relationships are obscure, then the appropriate policy directions in the current environment are even more uncertain.

The meaning of globalisation has been a matter of considerable debate. In this book globalisation is viewed as a process of increased *integration* between and within countries – especially in relation to the movement of commodities, people, capital and/or technology. Clearly it is not a new or recent phenomenon. There is evidence that over a long sweep of time globalisation has occurred in phases, in different ways and degrees, and for quite different reasons (O'Rourke and Williamson, 1999; Dollar, 2004). Dollar (2004) identifies three broad phases of globalisation since 1870, and from that perspective the evidence suggests that since 1980 global integration has been unprecedented and, furthermore, that it has impacted on developing countries as never before.

Although globalisation is generally acknowledged to be multi-faceted, a good deal of the debate, and much of this book, is centred on trade liberalisation, its effect on growth, and on the impact on the poor – the so-called 'Trade–Growth–Poverty' linkage (Dollar and Kraay, 2002). However, even this more restricted perspective does not lead to a consensus view. In a way the discussion of trade policy is part of the bigger debate on the role of markets and government in development.

Indeed as Kanbur (2001) recently put it: "trade and openness is the archetypal, emblematic, area around which there are deep divisions, and where certainly the rhetoric is fiercest." He identifies three broad areas of disagreement in the current discourse on economic policy, distribution and poverty. The first disagreement is on the *level of aggregation*. Poverty experts, as well as NGO activists focus on high levels of disaggregation, and emphasise the heterogeneity of the causes of poverty. They consider the welfare of individuals within households, or, at least, of groups of households differentiated by socioeconomic group, geographic region, ethnic group, or by some other characteristic. Conversely, macro or trade economists focus more on average levels of income or aggregate poverty indicators.

The second disagreement is on the *time horizon* of the analysis. Most economists probably assess the consequences of trade reform having a medium term time horizon in mind. According to Kanbur: "[a] five to ten year time horizon [...] is implicit in the equilibrium theory which underlies much of the reasoning behind the impact of policy on growth and distribution". In contrast, others emphasise the shorter or the long run time horizon in their analyses. Some focus on the effects of withdrawing children from school, or selling assets at uneconomic prices, or falling into starvation in the immediate aftermath of an adverse shock. Others worry, as environmental analysts do, about developments in the far future, fifty or a hundred years from now. Although not always explicitly stated, different methodologies have different time frames and may not be suitable to analyse concurrently short term adjustment problems, with their associated rationing and regime-switching issues, and medium or longer term problems.

Finally, a third area of disagreement is on *market structure and power*. A standard conclusion, derived from the Stolper–Samuelson model of international trade, that trade openness is good for the poor is based not only on the fact that unskilled labour is often abundant in developing countries but also on the more controversial assumption that goods and factors markets are competitive. Many claim, and provide empirical evidence in support, that distributive channels, capital ownership, institutional settings, foreign interventions, and other public or private practices may dramatically affect how markets operate. However, analysts do not always take these features into account.

These areas of disagreement, namely the *level of aggregation, time horizon*, and *market structure and power* are particularly relevant to the debate about globalisation and its effect on poverty, and are clear and manifest in the chapters of this book. The authors examine a variety of evidence-based analytical approaches in assessing globalisation 'shocks' on the poor. Thus, rather than demonstrating that theory alone can provide a set of conclusive results as to whether (or not) globalisation leads to a reduction in poverty, the most important collective contribution of the authors consists of looking carefully at empirical evidence and trying to establish directions and magnitudes of effect. It is through the cumulative experience gleaned from these disparate exercises that a deeper knowledge of these complex phenomena can be acquired. The book builds on a strong argument suggesting that globalisation may be more of an opportunity than a threat to poor people, providing – and this is a key qualification – that circumstances and timing are taken into account.

Before presenting an outline of the volume, we now set out the main ingredients of a general reference framework that subsequent chapters will address with more specificity and detail. It provides an overall picture and, although neither exhaustive nor formal, we believe it helps in highlighting the main factors and linkages in the globalisation and poverty nexus.

Globalisation and poverty: determining the key impacts[1]

McCulloch, Winters and Cirera (2001) have already set out and discussed in detail a set of channels and pathways through which trade liberalisation impacts on the poor. Trade liberalisation is a major, policy-induced, ingredient in the recent surge of globalisation processes. A more general set of channels pertaining to globalisation shocks can be portrayed in a similar fashion. But in doing so, we continue to restrict our focus on the income or expenditure based outcomes, though not denying the fact that other facets of poverty (health, education, environment, and human rights and freedom) may only loosely correlate with these economic outcomes.

With changing international and domestic prices and by varying the availability of factors of production, globalisation affects the poor through its influence on a country's economic growth and income distribution. Of course, these are by no means the only channels of influence. For example, by affecting government revenue-raising and spending capacities, globalisation can also increase the exposure of individuals to risk and volatility. But given that a key ingredient to long run eradication of absolute poverty is economic growth, understanding how globalisation-induced growth (or even growth in general) affects poverty is a prime consideration.

Many recent studies (Ravallion and Chen, 1997; Dollar and Kraay, 2002) focus on the statistical relationship between growth and poverty across countries and between time periods. And this is referred to by Francois Bourguignon in the Foreword to this volume. The main conclusion from these studies is that growth strongly reduces poverty: Ravallion and Chen (1997) find an elasticity close to three, which means that a one per cent increase in the mean income or consumption expenditure reduces the proportion of people living below a $1-a-day poverty line by three per cent. Taken at face value, these estimates suggest a rather strong policy implication, namely that poverty reduction strategies should be based on growth. However, this may be problematic if such strategies are validated only by cross-country evidence. As pointed out by Bourguignon (2003), the heterogeneity across countries of the poverty change due to income growth is very high, and it is possible to find cases of fast-growing countries that record virtually no poverty reduction alongside countries with low growth rates that show considerable improvement in poverty. In other words, only a small proportion (26 per cent in Bourguignon's calculations) of the total variance of poverty effects is explained by differences in growth rates. Intuitively, accounting for the large unexplained share of this variance means that a growth rate may, in one country, benefit the urban, more affluent population, whereas in another country with the same growth rate poorer rural farmers benefit more than proportionately. Bourguignon (and others) formalises this intuition by linking poverty reductions to both the growth of the mean income and changes in the distribution of relative incomes (that is, inequality).

The formal link between changes in poverty, growth and inequality can be used to re-estimate the growth elasticity of poverty. In doing so Bourguignon (2003) obtains the following key results: (a) the introduction of inequality in the relationship explaining poverty change doubles its explanatory power, which means that growth and inequality have the same weight in explaining the variance of poverty changes across countries; (b) by adding the initial level of development, initial inequality, and interaction terms of growth with these variables, the estimate of the growth elasticity of poverty is more precise and depends, as expected, positively on the level of development and negatively on the initial degree of inequality. So although redistribution can be very effective, in fact just as effective as growth in reducing poverty in the short term, a long run strategy based on redistribution alone is not sustainable, and growth is the only viable primary option. However, Bourguignon's results suggest more than this. Redistribution seems to have a double effect: it immediately reduces poverty, the direct effect, but it also permanently increases the growth elasticity of poverty, thereby making a given growth rate more effective in achieving poverty reductions.

The statistical relationships outlined above tell us a good deal about the relationships between growth, inequality and poverty in terms of outcomes. But they do not tell us much about the mechanisms and the channels through which globalisation and liberalisation influence growth, inequality and poverty. We first examine what theory tells us. The theory explaining how trade liberalisation affects goods and factor prices and hence the level and the distribution of income was crystallised in the well-known Heckscher–Ohlin model of international trade. The main conclusions of the model are that (a) trading economies specialise in the production of those goods or services that use more intensively the most abundant factor, and (b) changes in the relative price of goods have direct effects on the relative prices of factors. So, for example, in the case of a poor African country such as Mali – which has a comparative advantage in cotton because of its intensive use of the relatively abundant unskilled farmers' labour – a rise in the *relative* price of cotton would be translated into increased profitability in this sector, leading to an increased demand for farmers' work and higher wages, and, consequently, a reduction in the number of poor. The rise in the *relative* price of cotton may be induced by a reduction in tariffs protecting the (presumably capital-intensive) manufacturing sectors, thereby reducing the cost of the cotton sector's inputs.

Interestingly, one of the central findings of the Heckscher–Ohlin model is that by altering factor returns, trade liberalisation has strong redistributive implications. Given the importance of distributional changes in affecting poverty, one could reasonably conclude that trade reform might be a powerful instrument in the fight against poverty. But some caution towards such a generalisation is necessary. The price changes and poverty consequences, so described, result from the basic version of the Heckscher–Ohlin model. However, many modifications to the model have been proposed, aimed at making it more realistic, and their introduction can radically alter the conclusions of the basic version. Besides numerous additional variables, especially to accommodate domestic public policies – including institutional and regulatory reform, or policies aiming at increasing efficiency of customs and ports, the so-called trade-facilitation domestic policies – influence the effectiveness of trade reforms and the broad-reaching contributions that trade and, more generally, globalisation can make to social welfare and development. Because of these factors, similar trade- or globalisation-friendly policies are likely to produce different outcomes in different countries, and in-depth country-specific investigations are needed to estimate the potential poverty consequences of particular interventions.

These theoretical arguments and the statistical enquiries outlined earlier provide an essentially macro perspective on the links between globalisation and poverty, and a more detailed micro analysis of these links is needed to assess fully the final outcome of the effects of globalisation on the poor. In fact, even for the same country, when the effects of globalisation reach households, their poverty impacts depend on the micro characteristics of the households concerned. In particular, we refer to consumption and production baskets, human capital, physical assets, access to credit, and the capacity to bear risks. These are all factors determining how a global shock will influence each household. As Winters *et al.* (2004) put it, poverty is heterogeneous: 'there are many reasons why people are poor; and even within broadly-defined groups there are huge differences in the circumstances of individual households'. Beyond this households' heterogeneity, the potential reasons for either reductions or even reversals of the macro effects described above can be highlighted for each of the following transmission channels: (i) goods markets channel, (ii) factor markets channel, (iii) government taxes and spending, (iv) investment/productivity channel, (v) other channels (e.g. adjustment/transaction costs). Some illustrative arguments now follow.

(i) Goods markets channel

Before being transmitted to households, price changes induced by globalisation shocks are influenced by internal factors such as trade costs, institutions and local competition. Those factors soften (or maybe even amplify) the effect on households.

In pure accounting terms, policies affecting trade or other international transactions provide a filter between the world price and the border prices of imported goods and factors. Once inside a country, the goods still face taxes, transportation costs, regulatory measures, and competition from substitutes, all of which influence the final price faced by the households. The particular effects of these policies on a local market depend on a series of factors that affect the price transmission from the world markets. For example, the existence of an administrative price for a particular product is likely to isolate the product from any external shock. Similarly, if infrastructure is weak (which implies high transportation costs) the transmission mechanism might be restricted or even blocked in some areas of the country. Also, the presence of import-competing products and home-bias toward domestically produced products might inhibit the price transmissions reaching households. Finally, in the case of weakly competitive markets, movements in the prices of goods at the border are likely to be absorbed by traders instead of being directly transmitted to households.

The above considerations for imported goods can also be made in the case of exportable goods. In this case, the price paid to households (the farm gate price) is simply a function of the world price filtered by a series of factors such as transfer margins (from the farm to the border) and mark-ups applied by the various agents involved. The empirical literature[2] has found that 'pass-through' elasticities are different across countries and across products; although on average, these elasticities have been found to be around 0.5.

(ii) Factor markets channel

The second link is provided by the globalisation-induced changes in the returns to factors of production, and in particular to the returns to labour. For example, standard trade theory suggests that an increase in the price of a particular good will increase the returns to the factor used intensively in the production of that good. This conclusion crucially depends on some strong assumptions, such as full employment and perfect competition in the factor markets (as well as a two-factor, two-good economy), and may therefore not always be confirmed in practice. In developing countries, with high unemployment (or underemployment) and a large informal sector, the upward pressure on wages (especially of unskilled workers) due to trade reforms is likely to be muted. In the Mali cotton example, the effect of the trade policy on the labour market will probably show up as an increase in employment, rather than as an increase in wages.

This functioning of the labour market can be summarised according to two different analytical approaches: the trade approach, based on Heckscher–Ohlin theory, for which growth in a specific industry will produce an increase in the remuneration of the factor that is used more intensively by that industry; and the development approach, for which the growth in the industry is fuelled by an increase in the employment at a more or less constant wage. These approaches effectively represent two extremes in modelling the labour market: a very tight market and a wholly flexible market. In most cases, reality will be somewhere in between. Furthermore, especially in developing countries, labour markets are often segmented by skill, gender, and location, and wage and employment responses to trade shocks may differ across segments. For example, given that in most developing countries skilled labour is in limited supply whilst unskilled labour is relatively abundant, the trade-induced expansion of a sector employing a mix of skilled and unskilled labour, will be fuelled by increases in skilled wages and in unskilled employment.

The extent to which globalisation-induced (especially trade-related) changes in prices influence factor returns (especially wages) has been at the centre of a large literature and more sophisticated analyses than these two extreme approaches have been developed. For instance, many studies explain wage responses that are not in line with the predictions of the Heckscher–Ohlin model[3] in terms of skill-biased technological change. Early literature, based on the measurement of the factor content of trade, finds that trade-induced changes in labour demand (by skill) are not sufficient to account for the actual changes in relative wages.[4] More recent studies, by comparing relative product price changes with relative wage changes, conclude similarly that the trade contribution is negligible and that technological progress explains most of the premium paid to skilled labour.

Another approach has been to estimate price–wage elasticities using earnings equations with prices of goods among the explanatory variables.[5] In some cases, the necessary time series data on prices and wages can be obtained by the analysis of a series of compatible household surveys using pseudo-panel methods. Whenever the quality or availability of data is not sufficient to estimate price–wage elasticities, the relationship between prices and wages can be also extrapolated by linking national statistics on prices with wage data from surveys of firms or labour force surveys.

Other studies challenge the assumption of perfectly competitive labour markets,[6] and examine the consequences of state regulation, unions, collective bargaining, as well as other institutional rigidities. Labour market adjustments induced by changes in trade policies might be quite different when some of these labour market characteristics are present. Bussolo, *et al.* (2002) show, in an empirical study for Chile, how the introduction of labour market imperfections in an otherwise standard trade model is enough to break down the expected Heckscher–Ohlin outcome and generates the observed increase in the wage gap between skilled and unskilled workers.

As in the case of prices of goods, the aggregate wage and employment changes need to be translated into micro effects at the household and even individual levels, and their ultimate impact on poverty depends on household factor endowments and labour force participation decisions. Some households may experience an increase in real wages, while others may increase their income through new employment if the individuals in such households choose to participate in the market.

(iii) Government taxes and spending

A third channel through which globalisation may affect the well-being of the poor is via changes in government revenues and spending, and in government policies more generally. For example a change in trade policy can be quite important for countries where a large part of government revenue is collected in the form of trade taxes (up to 50 per cent in some cases). If trade taxes fall then either compensatory taxes have to be levied, or government expenditure on publicly-provided goods and services (or public transfers) should be reduced. However, this simple relation has to be qualified. Trade tax revenues may increase with falling tariffs if, initially, tariffs exceed their revenue-maximising levels,[7] or if quantitative restrictions are replaced by tariffs and the initial rents were not appropriated by the government. Besides, reforms that simplify tariff collection (by establishing fewer rates and exceptions) and streamline custom procedures may be revenue-increasing.

More generally, some stylised, empirically-based facts linking development, trade and the size of governments have been highlighted in the literature. On average, richer economies tend to have larger governments, suggesting some support for 'Wagner's Law'.[8]Additionally countries that trade more intensively tend to have larger governments.[9] Thus, compensating for the loss of trade tax revenues might not be a problem at all for some countries, and it may be just a temporary problem for others.

To a first approximation, changes in revenues due to tariff reductions can be estimated econometrically using import demand functions or via numerical simulation. In the next step, the losses or gains due to variations in government expenditure and/or compensatory tax payments need to be assessed on a household-by-household basis. Detailed data on government spending or tax incidence by household are not often available. However some existing evidence suggests the following: (a) poverty impacts are strongly dependent on the type of replacement tax (Rodrik, 1998); (b) budget balancing does not necessarily imply expenditure reductions in sectors that directly benefit the poor (McCulloch *et al.*, 2001 and references therein).

(iv) Other channels

Empirical studies have also found that the factor market channel (both factor price and income/employment) is usually the most important of all the links between globalisation and poverty. Nevertheless, since markets and institutions function differently in each country it would be difficult, *a priori*, to judge the relative importance of these channels. Therefore analyses of household surveys help in identifying which are most relevant in each case. Household data provide insights on the functioning of labour markets, the relative abundance of skilled or unskilled labour, and the receipt of government transfers. For example, in the case of a rural agricultural economy where households obtain their income from the sale of agricultural products, the impact of trade policy on household welfare would occur through the movement in prices of goods while the wage effect would probably be negligible. On the other hand, in urban areas, household welfare will be mostly affected by labour market outcomes and government spending.

Beyond the three channels identified and discussed above, other channels may assume significance in a long term, dynamic context. This includes an investment and productivity channel, whose ultimate positive or negative effects on poverty are again an empirical matter. There is little doubt, for instance, that significant poverty reductions in South Asia were connected with international technological transfers that allowed the green revolution in agriculture. But it is also true that increased productivity may initially translate into lower input demand and this may hurt the poor. Furthermore, international movements of factors, both capital and labour, may affect and even alter some of the static responses outlined above. Equally, the transmissions of global shocks and their effects on particular households and individuals may be affected by a host of economic realities, potentially the most significant of which are as follows.

(a) Market failures, transaction costs

Various market imperfections that may hinder price signals have already been mentioned, however an extreme case is that in many developing countries some rural markets may be absent. Remoteness, and its associated (at times, prohibitive) transaction costs, may be the greatest obstacle to creating interconnected domestic markets, thereby leaving a large proportion of the population isolated from policy effects and globalisation opportunities.

(b) Subsistence households

Another issue in analysing the effect of any global shock on household welfare is that in poor countries many rural households live in a self-sustaining environment. That is, a large part of household income and expenditure is own production. This has the effect of essentially isolating many households from the price system. When a household's production and consumption are not purchased or sold in the market, the movement in the market prices of the goods it produces or consumes has no direct effect on its income. But given incomplete markets (for capital and insurance, as well as for goods and factors), subsistence farming can lead to sub-optimal outcomes and is often associated with high poverty incidence.

(c) Private transfers

Since trade and other globalisation-related policies are redistributive in income they are likely to produce an effect on private transfers across households. Also, these policies may create movements in the labour force (involving national and international migration) which may in turn have an effect on remittances and therefore on household income and social welfare. In quantitative analysis, private transfers are often modelled as a function of earnings. However, in some cases the data available in household surveys can help identify a better approach.

(d) Distribution within the household

Globalisation may also have an effect on the distribution of resources across individuals within households. When several members of a household sell labour (or goods), it is possible that each individual's share of total household income may change, altering the relative power of the different members of the household. There is evidence that the income earned by women is spent more altruistically than income earned by men (thereby affecting more the welfare of other members of the household). This implies that policy intervention may have a stronger welfare effect if it is targeted towards the employment, and hence income, of women.

In conclusion, we see that theory can get us just so far in assessing the possible directions of effect of globalisation shocks on household poverty. The channels are many and complex, and the directions and size of impacts are far from clear, hence our ability to inform policy is necessarily limited. It is this reality that motivates the research agenda that, in turn, underpins the papers in this volume.

Outline of the volume

Background to the volume

This book is based on a selection of papers presented at a two-day seminar held at the OECD Development Centre in December 2002. An important objective of the seminar was to show why knowledge advancement in this area, although difficult to achieve, is necessary and to emphasise that without a sound knowledge base there is increased risk of adopting overly simplistic responses in devising poverty reduction policies. The seminar brought together researchers from institutions in both industrialised and developing countries, who contributed papers, all of which were empirically-based and country-focused. The seminar participants addressed the following core issues:

- What are the main channels through which globalisation affects poverty? Are these impacts negative or positive and what is the intensity of the impact? Do all channels have the same importance for most countries? How do these channels operate?
- What policy measures can governments adopt in order to alleviate negative poverty outcomes? Are the impacts of these policy measures country-specific or can some more general lessons be learned?
- How can governments increase their monitoring capacity in order to pursue a robust macro-micro strategy of growth in income aggregates and an equitable distribution of individuals' incomes?

The analytical techniques and approaches used in the papers are not identical. Indeed, the variety of analytical approaches is a central feature of the volume. Only in one or two cases is there an attempt to look at the evidence *ex post*; the reason for this is that cause and effect are often inextricably linked. Many of the papers represent *ex ante* analyses; indeed most are based in particular on computable general equilibrium (CGE) and numerical simulation methods. It is entirely debatable of course whether results derived from simulation methods constitute *empirical* evidence or whether this is more accurately described as *numerical* evidence, on the grounds that it is based on analytical structures and perceived representations of how these economies function. Nevertheless, in those cases where CGE models are used, a great strength is that they do provide the basis for laboratory experiments to be conducted. This is especially useful in considering alternative policy responses. Also, in all cases the studies rely on actual country-specific data – either to calibrate the models, to conduct counterfactual analyses, or to study econometrically the transmission mechanisms of policies on poverty.

Overview

The book is organised essentially along methodological lines. However the main messages that emerge from the volume are less to do with methodology and more to do with identifying the important channels of effect and the possible outcomes of globalisation shocks and policy responses. The first two papers rely only on observed evidence, and in quite different ways they trace through the effects of trade and price reforms on households of different types using partial equilibrium analysis. The next four papers employ general equilibrium models in a wide variety of contexts. By definition, the common feature of all these applications is to capture second and higher order effects transmitted through alternative channels, markets and equilibrating mechanisms. The final two papers extend the general equilibrium analysis to embrace microsimulation analysis of individual household behaviour. The papers are therefore representative of a range of simulation and counterfactual analyses.

The first two papers, by McCulloch and by Niimi, Vasudeva and Winters, approach the identification of channels of effect (of globalisation shocks on poverty) using essentially partial equilibrium and econometric approaches. McCulloch's paper is primarily methodological, with applications to data for Cambodia and Nepal, that trace out the impact of structural and price reforms (rice) on poverty of different households according to their relative positions as producers and consumers of rice. There is no modelling of markets *per se* but the paper embraces well-known features of the household economy, and agricultural household models, that are often missing in economy-wide empirical analysis. Niimi *et al.* set out and explore different channels of effect (price, wage and employment channels) of trade liberalisation and reform in Vietnam. They conduct an econometric analysis of trade liberalisation-induced household poverty dynamics, using panel data from a household survey. Various implications stem from the results detailing the effects of trade reforms on the movement into and out of poverty of individual households. Both papers are good examples of *ex post* analyses of the empirical evidence, though they are quite different in what they attempt to do.

Round and Whalley review the evidence from a series of studies that examined the impact of liberalisation, and globalisation more generally, on relative and absolute poverty in four South Asian countries (India, Sri Lanka, Bangladesh and Pakistan). The studies were undertaken as part of a project financed by the Department for International Development involving researchers from, and based in, the four countries in question. This paper demonstrates that dating globalisation is itself a hard exercise to undertake; that the countries, though geographically contiguous, differ in respect of the speed and extent of globalisation; and that there may be excluded variables and other global influences that hamper a simple analysis of cause and effect in terms of poverty outcomes. Overall the results give an early indication that there is unlikely to be a simple, direct and universal answer to the question of whether globalisation is good for the poor; the channels are multifarious and too complex for that. It further suggests that it may be difficult to generalise about policy responses, because of either the nature of the globalisation shocks or the specific character and structure of the economy.

Many empirical studies of globalisation concentrate on trade liberalisation. As outlined earlier there seems to be no clear analytical evidence on whether or not other facets of globalisation benefit the poor. So Bussolo and Whalley examine empirically the possible effects of reductions in transaction costs on relative poverty in India – considering transactions costs in different markets using various experimental structures. The experiments embrace both *ex ante* and *ex post* forms of analysis and rely on a small, stylised CGE model. Their first analysis is to see what effect a reduction in transaction costs alone might have on relative wages (used as a proxy for relative poverty) under simple model variants and configurations. This is an *ex ante* analysis as it starts from an actual base case but does not attempt to reproduce an actual final outcome. The second analysis, an *ex post* analysis, aims to see how much transactions costs would have to change in order to meet an observed change in relative wages during the reform period after allowing for observed changes due to tariff reduction, terms of trade, labour supply and technological progress. Several messages emerge from these analyses. The results of the *ex ante* simulations broadly confirm intuition; it matters whether transaction cost reductions apply in product or factor markets and whether there are differences in transaction cost mark-ups across sectors. The *ex post* analysis reveals that to be compatible with the observed recent spike in real incomes and in addition to the changes in tariffs, the terms of trade, labour supply and technology, transaction costs would have to have fallen by about 65 per cent. By providing some additional evidence listing a series of 'obstacles' in setting up formal business and employing labour that have recently been eliminated in India, the authors put in context this large 65 per cent reduction estimate and motivate further policy reforms towards fostering reductions in transactions costs in all quarters.[10]

Focusing on the poverty effects of trade liberalisation, Khondker and Mujeri examine two issues using a large-scale CGE model for Bangladesh. They employ both *ex ante* and *ex post* analysis. First, they consider the household income, welfare and poverty consequences of an across-the-board elimination of tariffs. Although the current tariff levels are low compared with other South Asian economies, they are still at around 20 per cent on average. Second, as private capital inflows have been a feature in Bangladesh in recent years, they assess the poverty impacts of such inflows concentrated mainly as investment in the gas and service sectors. Both simulations record welfare gains across all socio-economic groups of households, but more especially across the better-off groups. The poverty calculations confirm that an elimination of tariffs are pro-poor, though benefiting the better-off households most, whereas in the case of increased private capital inflows the poverty of rural households reduced against an increase in the poverty of urban households. These are *ex ante* analyses, simulating the effects of exogenous shocks applied to some base equilibrium. Khondker and Mujeri also carry out an *ex post* experiment, which attempts to apportion observed outcomes to different kinds of shocks. Between the mid 1980s and late 1990s wage inequality between skilled and unskilled workers widened, and they therefore assess the extent to which this increase can be attributed to trade and non-trade factors. Identifying non-trade factors as combinations of changes in factor endowments (labour and capital) or technical changes, Khondker and Mujeri's analysis suggests that trade factors are a relatively unimportant contributor to inequality. Overall, the policy implications from their simulation analyses are stark: trade reforms do not appear to have brought significant direct benefits to the poor in Bangladesh – relative, that is, to other events during the era of liberalisation.

The experimental framework of these analyses shows how important it is to distinguish the effects of globalisation shocks from concomitant policy-induced changes and responses. The analysis carried out by Khondker and Mujeri raises a number of important questions about the experimental design to do with, for example, the effects of raising replacement revenues to compensate for the loss in tariff revenue under trade liberalisation. Bussolo and Round consider these issues in a different, though closely related context. Based on a large-scale CGE model for Ghana they consider the poverty consequences of making redistributive (ostensibly, poverty-reducing) income transfers between household groups under alternative revenue-neutral financing schemes. The results for Ghana show that the choice of financing scheme does matter. So too does the issue of whether one considers the effects in the short run, when there are rigidities in the movement of labour between sectors, or in the long run when labour moves between sectors more freely.

Up to this point all of the papers treat poverty measurement in a fairly pragmatic fashion. In small, stylised models changes in relative poverty can be assessed on the basis of relative wages or relative incomes of two or more groups (Bussolo and Whalley; Khondker and Mujeri). In larger, CGE models authors undertake poverty calculations under assumptions about the parametric distributions of incomes within household groups (Khondker and Mujeri; Bussolo and Round). The assumptions usually involve constant second and higher order effects (spread), so that poverty measures are only affected by shifts in the group means. The final two papers (Cockburn; Bussolo and Lay) combine micro-simulation models with CGE models and, in consequence, the results of the experiments are far more sensitive in their assessment of the effects of external shocks on individual households. The applications of the methodology enable the authors to explore additional mechanisms, especially income distribution (Cockburn) and the labour market (Bussolo and Lay). In consequence the models are dimensionally larger and a great deal more complex.

A common method of adapting CGE models to the study of income distribution and poverty is the so-called 'representative household' approach (e.g. the papers by Bussolo and Whalley, Khondker and Mujeri, and Bussolo and Round). The equilibrium effects of exogenous shocks are first assessed on the basis of the changes in average incomes of representative groups of households, usually defined according to appropriate socio-economic categories. Then, poverty effects are calculated on the basis of the shifts in mean income, while holding the variance of income in each group constant, assuming alternative parametric forms for describing income distribution. Cockburn adopts an alternative approach in a study for Nepal. He potentially models each household differently, constructing a model with as many household categories as there are households in the base data (household survey). This avoids the restrictive assumptions of the representative household group (RHG) approach. The results of an experiment based on eliminating tariffs and replacing them by a uniform consumption tax suggest a wide variation of effects across households, although overall urban poverty falls and rural poverty increases. But beyond this Cockburn suggests the approach might be useful to policymakers in tailoring policies towards a pro-poor outcome.

Bussolo and Lay undertake an analysis for Colombia to try to understand more about the effects of the substantial trade liberalisation in the early 1990s in the context of other substantive changes in the economy that took place between 1988 and 1994. The changes include major shifts in the composition of the labour force (male/female participation, skilled/unskilled proportions). Leaving aside the many differences in the modelling approach, unlike the studies for Bangladesh (Khondker and Mujeri) and Nepal (Cockburn) the analysis by Bussolo and Lay suggests that trade liberalisation in Colombia results in a general and significant reduction in poverty across all societal groups. This is a strong result but the historical evidence suggests that actual levels of poverty fell by substantially greater amounts than is due to tariff reductions alone. Additional modelling features are also important. These include a more sensitive treatment of the labour market and, partly as a result of incorporating the micro-simulation model, a means of basing the poverty calculations on the full sample of households rather than representative household groups (RHG). The latter avoids relying on an assumption about the nature of the income distribution within household groups and, more importantly, on an assumption that the variance (or inequality) within groups is constant. The data for Colombia suggests that inequality rose between 1988 and 1994 and this means that the model results based on 'full sample' (microsimulation) methods are closer to the actual change than those based on RHG methods. Another major feature of the Bussolo and Lay analysis is that, in addition, they simulate the effects inclusive of the historic changes, introduced as additional shocks. The poverty calculations based on the combined trade and historic shocks are closer to the actual changes, though not equal to them. Like Khondker and Mujeri, the analysis is *ex ante* and does not therefore exhaust the components of change.

The labour market is a direct and important channel of impact of globalisation on the poor. In money-metric based poverty analysis, households are either affected by price changes (in terms of the goods and services they can buy) or by changes in their incomes. Incomes, in turn, are determined mainly (or at least in part) by changes in factor market outcomes, including changes in wage rates, the decisions to participate in various labour markets or to engage in self-employment or own-account activity. Bussolo and Lay highlight the importance of the labour market; formal versus informal labour markets, occupational choices of different household members; and to some extent, gender differences.

Policy insights

The papers in this volume confirm our intuition that the poverty responses to globalisation may not be a one-way bet. It is hard to predict that there will be an unequivocal positive (or indeed a negative) outcome for all types of households in all kinds of circumstances. As suggested by McCulloch *et al.* (2001) there are many channels of effect in translating the macro-level initial shock to the micro-level impact on households and individuals. The more easily identifiable (and quantifiable) channels will include price responses and labour market responses – both on the demand and supply sides, including changes in wage rates in different market segments. Other channels, such as changes in infrastructure, may also affect social well-being although these are often much harder to quantify. Nevertheless the variety of price and factor market responses in the country studies portrayed in this volume suggests a few insights.

First, the studies confirm our intuition that globalisation 'shocks' may not benefit all segments of society uniformly – or, indeed, positively. There are many reasons for this, but the studies examine a number of channels of effect on individual households, and they demonstrate that the direction and level of effects crucially depend on household endowments; differential price responses in markets (e.g. prices of goods and factors); rigidities (e.g. supply constraints); and, of course, heterogeneity in individual responses. To these we might add other factors, not explicitly examined in these studies, such as the importance of good institutions (e.g. financial institutions, governing the availability of credit; agricultural and industrial extension services; etc), and referred to in the papers by McCulloch, and Khondker and Mujeri.

Second, the studies highlight the role and importance of household poverty dynamics – more specifically, whether trade reform affects the chances of households of different types escaping poverty. The principal reasons for households to fall into or exit from poverty have been examined in terms of household demographics and characteristics in earlier studies. Niimi, Vasudeva and Winters report that location, the level of education and occupation of the household head, and infrastructure had previously been found to be among the main factors that increased the chance of households escaping from poverty. In their study, Niimi *et al.* consider additional 'trade' factors, such as engaging in the production of specific agricultural export crops, and the proportion of household members engaged in export sectors. Both are found to be significant. Bussolo and Lay also consider poverty dynamics and suggest that trade and occupational choice matter for the poor. These results provide clear insights for policy intervention.

Third, outcomes might well differ (and substantially) between the long run and the short run, as highlighted in the paper by Bussolo and Round. None of the papers examine full dynamic effects so this can only be indicative. It suggests that policy ought to be directed to improving the supply response of households to changes in their external environment induced by globalisation – for example, enabling households to cope with risk and uncertainty, and improving their skills, health, and other factor endowments.

Fourth, policy responses to external shocks might have to be explicitly 'pro-poor'. Cockburn suggests there might be scope to choose between alternative replacement taxes to compensate for the initial loss in government revenue through trade liberalisation, tailoring the choice explicitly towards poverty reduction. Bussolo and Round do precisely this in their experiments for Ghana, though with a less-disaggregated (and static) model, and demonstrate that there may be quite different poverty outcomes from different replacement taxes. Clearly the nature and degree of policy intervention matters greatly alongside the primary consequences of natural-, technological- or policy-induced globalisation. It is our hope that these quantitatively-based studies lead to a better understanding of their consequences.

Notes

1 Parts of this section are further elaborated in Bussolo and Nicita (2004).
2 See Goldberg and Knetter (1997) for a review, and Nicita (2003) for an application to trade liberalisation.
3 For instance, increased relative wages for skilled labour are observed in many developing countries abundantly endowed with unskilled labour: Slaughter and Swagel (1997) cite evidence for Mexico, Meller and Tokman (1996) study the Chilean case, and Sanchez and Nuñez (1998) examine the Colombian case.
4 Although, as reported by Abrego and Whalley (2003): 'These estimates, based on factor content of trade calculations, were later criticised by Wood (1994) who argued that trade is a considerably more important factor than these analyses show. He argued that for many products, especially those from developing countries, there is no comparable domestic product, and so factor substitution effects attributed to trade using conventional elasticities are understated. He also argues that technological response to trade will occur in expectation of future trade surges, and so some of what is attributed to technology in factor content analyses should in reality be attributed to trade.'
5 See for example Porto (2003), and Nicita (2004).
6 One interesting exception is Devarajan, Ghanem, and Thierfelder (1997).
7 Ebrill, Stotsky and Gropp (1999), cited in Winters *et al.* (2004).
8 The validity of Wagner's Law has survived recurrent scrutiny; for an interesting look at it see Easterly and Rebelo (1993).
9 See Rodrik (1998).
10 This is also one of the key messages of the 2004 World Bank report on the investment climate.

References

Abrego, L. and J. Whalley (2003) 'Decomposing Wage Inequality Using General Equilibrium Models', in J. Whalley, T. N. Srinivasan and T. Kehoe (eds) *Frontiers in Applied General Equilibrium Modelling*, Cambridge: Cambridge University Press.

Bourguignon, F. (2003) 'The Growth Elasticity of Poverty Reduction' in T. Eicher and S. Turnovsky (eds) *Inequality of Growth*, Cambridge, MA: MIT Press.

Bussolo, M. and A. Nicita (2004) 'Key Issues in Trade Policy Reform, Poverty and Social Impact Analysis', informal paper, Washington DC:World Bank

Bussolo, M., A. Mizala and P. Romaguera (2002) 'Beyond Heckscher–Ohlin: trade and labour market interactions in a case study for Chile', *Journal of Policy Modelling*, 24(7–8): 639–666.

Devarajan, S., Ghanem and K. Thierfelder (1997) 'Economic Reforms and Labour Unions: A General Equilibrium Analysis Applied to Bangladesh and Indonesia', *World Bank Economic Review*, 11(1): 145–170.

Dollar, D. (2004) 'Globalization, poverty, and inequality since 1980', Policy Research Working Paper No WPS 3333, World Bank: Washington D.C. http://wdsbeta.worldbank.org/external/default/WDSContentServer/IW3P/IB/2004/09/28/000112742-20040928090739/Rendered/PDF/wps3333.pdf (accessed: 08 June 2005).

Dollar, D. and A. Kraay (2002) 'Growth Is Good for the Poor', *Journal of Economic Growth*, 7(3): 195–225.

Easterly W. and S. Rebelo (1993) 'Fiscal Policy and Economic Growth: an Empirical Investigation', *Journal of Monetary Economics*, 32(3): 417–458.

Ebrill L., J. Stotsky and R. Gropp (1999) 'Revenue Implications of Trade Liberalization', Occasional Paper 42, IMF, Washington DC.

Goldberg, P. K. and M. M. Knetter (1997) 'Goods Prices and Exchange Rates: What Have We Learned?', *Journal of Economic Literature* 35(3): 1243–1272.

Kanbur, R. (2001) 'Inequality, Distribution and Policy: the Nature of Disagreements', *World Development*, 29(6): 1083–1094.

McCulloch N., L. A. Winters and X. Cirera (2001) *Trade Liberalization and Poverty: A Handbook*, Department for International Development.

Meller, P. and A. Tokman (1996) 'Apertura Comercial y Diferencial Salarial en Chile', in P. Meller (ed.) *El Modelo Exportador Chileno,* Economic Research Corporation for Latin America, Santiago, Chile.

Nicita, A. (2003) 'The Effects of Mexican Trade Liberalization on Household Welfare', World Bank, Development Economics Research Group, Trade, Washington DC Processed.

O'Rourke, K. and J. G. Williamson (1999) *Globalisation and History: The Evolution of a 19th Century Atlantic Economy*, Cambridge: MIT Press.

Porto, G. G. (2003) 'Trade Reforms, Market Access, and Poverty in Argentina', Policy Research Working Paper 3135, World Bank, Development Economics Research Group, Trade, Washington DC.

Ravallion, M. and S. Chen (1997) 'What Can New Survey Data Tell Us about Recent Changes in Distribution and Poverty?', *World Bank Economic Review*, 11(2): 357–382.

Rodrik, D. (1998) 'Trade Policy and Economic Performance in Sub-Saharan Africa', EGDI Discussion Paper, Ministry of Foreign Affairs, Department for International Development Cooperation, Expert Group on Development Issues, Stockholm.

Sanchez, F. and J. Nuñez (1998) 'Educación y Salarios Relativos en Colombia, 1976–1995: Determinantes, Evolución e Implicaciones para la Distribución del Ingreso', *Archivo de Macroeconomia* 74, National Planning Department, Bogota.

Slaughter, M. J. and P. Swagel (1997) 'The Effects of Globalisation on Wages in Advanced Economies', Working Paper 97/43, International Monetary Fund, Research Department, Washington DC.

Winters L. A., N. McCulloch and A McKay (2004) 'Trade Liberalization and Poverty: The Evidence so Far', *Journal of Economic Literature*, XLII (March): 72–115.

Wood, A. (1994) *North–South Trade, Employment and Inequality*, Oxford: Oxford University Press.

1 The impact of structural reforms on poverty

A simple methodology with extensions

Neil McCulloch

Introduction

For many years there has been considerable interest in the impact of economic reforms upon poverty and more generally on the distribution of welfare within society. This interest has arisen from a number of different sources. A large number of NGO and civil society organizations, along with many developing country governments have expressed concern about the potential negative distributional impact of structural reforms. At the same time much academic work has pointed to the wide variety of outcomes resulting from reforms in different countries.[1]

Economic reforms are typically split into two categories: macroeconomic reforms, often pursued under the auspices of the IMF; and structural or price reforms designed to improve resource allocation and increase efficiency. Although the maintenance of macroeconomic stability remains the cornerstone of effective economic development, there has been a stronger emphasis in recent years on structural reforms since these are key to achieving pro-poor growth.

Understanding the impact of structural or price reforms on poverty is key in several different areas of reform. For example, the imposition or removal of a tariff on the staple food can have a major impact upon the incomes of the poor. The same is true of a reduction in the transaction costs faced by the poor in reaching markets through, for example, investments in rural feeder roads, policies to enhance competition in the transportation sector, or marketing reforms. Similarly the reform and privatization of utilities often have a dramatic impact upon the prices for such services and for poverty if the purchase of such services is important for the poor. And the same is true of changes in the wide variety of taxes and subsidies which may be imposed by the government.[2] The central characteristic of all these reforms is that they are designed to change prices and thereby influence resource allocation to different activities. Therefore, for the purpose of understanding the impact of structural reforms upon the poor, it is essential to have a good methodology for linking price changes to changes in poverty.

The theoretical framework for linking such reforms to poverty is probably best developed in the area of trade (see Winters, 2002a; McCulloch, Winters and Cirera, 2001), although the approach is generally applicable to a wide range of price reforms. The analysis of the linkages between price reforms, including trade reform, and poverty is complex and there are a large variety of different methods available (Reimer, 2002, and McCulloch, Winters and Cirera, 2001, provide reviews of methodologies and papers).[3] In an ideal world the relationship between price reform and poverty could be accurately predicted using a general equilibrium model with a suitably disaggregated household sector. If the macroeconomic and microeconomic data required for such an approach are available and reasonably accurate and the parameters of the model are empirically estimated from the available data and the functional forms of the behavioural relationships in the model are broadly correct, then such models can provide useful *ex ante* predictions of the impact of price shocks upon different types of households and thereby upon poverty. Furthermore, even where these conditions are not completely satisfied, CGE models can provide a valuable indication of the sorts of effects which we might expect given any set of assumptions about data, parameters and behavioural relationships and thereby give an indication of how sensitive the results are to particular sets of assumptions.

CGE models have now been used to examine the impact of a variety of price reforms (including trade, marketing and shifts in agricultural technology) in a large number of different countries.[4] However, the data requirements for such models can be considerable. Unless a recent Social Accounting Matrix (SAM) is already available, the construction of a useable SAM can take substantial time and expertise. Furthermore, the econometric estimation of behavioural parameters (as opposed to merely calibrating such parameters from the original SAM) can be complex and time-consuming and the choice of functional form for the behavioural relationships, although based upon plausible arguments, is essentially arbitrary (Deaton, 1997).

To reduce the data and resource requirements, many analysts have used simpler partial equilibrium techniques which can be implemented more quickly on readily available data. Such analysis has typically involved detailed microeconometric work on household survey datasets. This can yield information about the pattern of consumption and how it varies across different household groups (e.g. deciles, gender of household head, type of main activity, region, etc). In addition, surveys sometimes have income information which can tell us the relative importance of different sources of income again disaggregated by different groups. Such work can provide a rich picture of the poverty profile of any given country and an initial indication of the likely impact of reforms.

This chapter describes a simple practical methodology for estimating the poverty impact of price reforms which can be implemented in a reasonably short period of time using almost universally available household survey data. This methodology is not new, but by providing a comprehensive description of the methodology in one chapter, we hope that it will become a standard 'minimum' analysis of the potential impact of such reforms upon the poor. We provide some examples of the application of the methodology from the World Bank's Diagnostic Trade Integration Studies conducted as part of the Integrated Framework programme[5] to assist least developed countries with integration into the world economy. In addition, since the reforms which are likely to have the greatest impact upon the poor will vary from country to country, we provide some pointers to how the analysis can be made more sophisticated in the areas of most importance to a particular country. We conclude with a discussion of areas for future research.

A basic methodology[6]

The basic methodology draws on the approach of Nicita, Olarreaga and Soloaga (2002) in their study of the impact of trade reform in Cambodia. They express the income of a household as the sum of three components: own production, wage employment and net transfers. Own production includes both the value-added from farming as well as the value-added from any other enterprises owned by the households (e.g. small enterprises engaged in trading or the provision of services). Wage employment includes all payments made by those outside the household for the labour services of members of the household, e.g. payments for working on someone else's farm, or the payment resulting from a job. Net transfers refers to the net payments from the government (pensions, grants and other transfers minus any fees or taxes) as well as net transfers from other households, i.e. net remittances.

The idea behind the methodology is that in the short run households cannot change their activities in response to a change in prices (in the long run households may well change their activities as a result of the price change – indeed this may be the intention of the reforms). In this case income from own production and wage employment can be written as the product of a set of prices and a set of quantities. For example, income from own production is equal to the prices of the outputs produced times the quantity of output produced minus the prices of the inputs used times the quantities of inputs used. Similarly income from wage employment can be written as wages times the (net) quantity of labour sold.[7] If households are unable to change their activities immediately when prices change, then a first approximation to the change in their income resulting from a price shock can be given by the sum of the price changes times the original quantities produced. Thus if the rice price increases, a first approximation to the increase in income for rice farmers is given simply by the change in the rice price times the quantity of rice produced. Similarly if the wage increases, a first approximation of the benefit is given by the change in the wage times the quantity of labour sold.

However, households consume as well as produce and price changes affect consumption too. Just as with production, price changes will change the long run consumption pattern of households, causing them to consume relatively more of cheaper goods and relatively less of goods which have become more expensive. Also price changes will affect real incomes making households consume more or less of all goods. But, in the short run we can make the same assumption as for production – that the quantities of goods consumed by the household do not change. If this is the case then a first approximation of the increase in the cost associated with a price increase can be given simply by the change in the price times the quantity of the good originally consumed.

Putting the production and consumption effects together, it is possible to show that the change in welfare[8] can be approximated as the change in income minus the change in consumption. This makes intuitive sense: an increase in the price of a good which is both produced and consumed will increase income and also increase the cost of achieving the original level of consumption – the difference between these is therefore an approximation to the welfare change.

Note that the basic methodology is a 'worst case' analysis because it assumes no quantity response at all – if households are able to substitute away from the consumption of goods whose price has risen or to substitute towards the production of such goods then it must be better off than the situation in which it could not do so. In some respects this makes the simple model more attractive because if the model points to a relatively small negative or positive impact then the incorporation of substitution effects is likely to make the situation better.

Finally, if one wishes to express the change in welfare as a percentage then one can divide it by the original level of welfare (given by the initial level of income). If we do this we can write:[9]

$$
\frac{\Delta W}{W} = \left[\sum_j IS_j^O \left(\frac{\Delta p_j^O}{p_j^O} \right) - \sum_k BS_k^I \left(\frac{\Delta p_k^I}{p_k^I} \right) \right] + \sum_f IS_f^w \left(\frac{\Delta w_f}{w_f} \right)
$$
$$
- \sum_i BS_j^C \left(\frac{\Delta p_j^C}{p_j^C} \right) \tag{1.1}
$$

where W is the measure of welfare, IS_j^O indicates the value of output j as a share of household income, $(\Delta p_j^O / p_j^O)$ is the percentage change in the price of output j, BS_k^I is the budget share of input costs, IS_j^w is the income share of net factor income from factor f (in most cases equal to the income share of wages), and BS_j^C is the budget share of good j in consumption.[10]

Equation (1.1) is the core of the basic methodology. The key thing to note is that the first-order percentage change in welfare can be calculated using only information on the income shares of different income sources, the budget shares of different items of expenditure, and the percentage changes in prices experienced. Such information is readily available from many household surveys making the application of this methodology relatively straightforward in a large number of countries.

Application of the basic methodology

Given the above methodology, the impact of a price change upon a household will clearly depend on two things: which prices change (and by how much); and the nature of the household. We consider each issue in turn.

Determining price changes

The easiest way to 'determine' price changes is to assume them. That is, the methodology can be used to explore the potential impact upon different groups of households of a set of possible price changes. This is particularly valuable where the price changes likely to result from the implementation of a reform are not known with any degree of accuracy (or where the analysis of how the policy reforms might change prices is complex, costly or simply has not yet been undertaken). Even where price changes have been predicted by some other model, assuming a set of exogenous price changes allows policymakers to conduct sensitivity analysis on the poverty impact of the model's predictions.

Rather than assuming exogenous changes in the prices faced by households, one might instead wish to assume exogenous changes in a policy-related price and some transmission mechanism between the policy-related price and the price faced by the household. For example, if one is interested in the poverty impact of a 10 per cent increase in the rice tariff we could write down the price of tradable goods as a function of the various taxes and costs which incur between the border and the household, i.e.

$$p^h = p^w(1-t) \text{ for output prices and} \tag{1.2}$$

$$p^h = p^w(1+t) \text{ for the price of tradable inputs and consumption goods}$$

where p^h is the price experienced by the household, p^w is the world price and t is the tariff, tax or unit cost between the border and the household. If we know the world price and the tax then we can calculate the percentage change in the household price for any change in the tax.[11] Alternatively, one could treat the tax as endogenous and use the unit price experienced by the household to calculate the total unit transaction cost between the border and the household and then simulate a percentage reduction in this cost.

The more detail one has regarding the transmission of prices from the policy price to the price faced by the household, the more accurately one can predict the likely percentage change in price faced by the household. For example, if information on transport costs is available between different regions and one wishes to simulate the impact of a particular infrastructure development on the price of a tradable good which is not produced domestically then we can write:

$$p_r^h = p^w(1+t)(1+t_r) \tag{1.3}$$

where p_r^h is the price faced by household h in region r, t is the tax at the border and t_r is the transport cost from the border to region r. One may then use the information about the different effects which the infrastructure development may have on transport costs between the border and each region to determine the likely impact of the infrastructure development on the prices faced by households in each region.

One may also simulate technological shifts in the same way. For example, Nicita, Olarreaga and Soloaga (2002) write the value of rice output as:

$$\text{Value of rice output} = q^{\text{paddy}}(1 - phl^{\text{paddy}})\lambda(1-\alpha)(1-t^{\text{rice}})p^{\text{rice}} \tag{1.4}$$

where q^{paddy} is the quantity of paddy produced, phl^{paddy} is the post harvest losses, λ is the milling yield of paddy-to-rice, $(1-\alpha)$ is the milling unit transformation costs, t^{rice} is the tax on rice and p^{rice} is the world price of rice. They then simulate changes in technological parameters, e.g. improved storage lowering post-harvest losses, improved efficiency raising milling transformation or lowering transformation costs, as well as changes in the tax rate.

Similarly, if the price change is the result of changing a tax or subsidy applied by the government on a particular good or service, then the simplest possible approach is to assume that there is a proportional increase in the consumer price, while the producer price remains fixed. If estimates of the own price elasticity of demand and supply are available, then a better approximation to the effect upon consumer and producer prices can be found by calculating the price at which the market clears when a wedge equal to the tax is placed between the consumer and producer prices.[12]

Thus there are a large number of ways in which one can derive plausible price changes resulting from policy reforms. However, the impact of these price changes upon the poor depends on the nature of the household, to which we now turn.

The nature of the household

The impact of a price change upon a household will clearly depend on the relative importance of different sources of income and of different goods in the consumption basket. For example, if the price of a staple food rises sharply then net producers will benefit, whereas net consumers will lose, but the extent of the gain or loss depends upon how much income depends upon the production of this good and how important this good is in the household's consumption basket. Consequently, the best place to start in determining the impact of a price shock is to obtain, for different groups in society, information about the relative importance of different sources of income and the relative importance of different goods in household consumption. Table 1.1 shows a typical table, from Cambodia, of sources of income for different deciles of the consumption distribution; Table 1.2 shows the expenditure shares, by decile of per capita consumption.

Table 1.1 shows that income from self-employment is the most important source of income for the vast majority of the population, only falling substantially below 70 per cent of income for the top two deciles. Most of this income comes from cultivation, particularly rice cultivation, but livestock and forestry products are also of importance to the poor. The poorest decile obtain a higher share of their income from wages than all except the two highest deciles, probably reflecting landlessness among the poorest households in Cambodia. The most striking thing to note from Table 1.1 is the dramatic differences between the top two deciles and the rest of the population. The rich in Cambodia (and in many other countries) really are different, typically earning a far higher share of their income from non-farming activities, wages, and rental income than the rest of the population. Given that the top two deciles of most populations tend to live in the major urban centres and are much more closely connected to the policy process than most other groups, it is important to analyse policies to see if they are really serving the interests of the majority of the population (and in particular the poor) rather than those of the (rather different) top two deciles.

Table 1.1 Contributions to income in Cambodia from different sources (per cent)

| Source of Income: | Deciles of per capita consumption | | | | | | | | | | |
	Poor 1	2	3	4	5	6	7	8	9	Rich 10	avg
Self-employment	67.8	71.4	71.7	70.3	73.6	68.5	71.2	70.7	63.3	36.3	60.9
Cultivation	27.8	29.7	31.1	30.3	31.9	32.1	30.6	32.3	19.8	3.2	22.4
Rice cultivation	21.4	24.3	25.3	23.6	25.7	25.0	22.7	20.4	9.7	2.1	16.3
Other crops	6.4	5.4	5.8	6.7	6.2	7.1	7.9	11.9	10.1	1.1	6.1
Livestock	16.6	14.3	14.2	13.0	12.4	11.9	11.6	12.0	8.3	1.5	9.4
Fish growing, etc	6.1	7.1	5.5	8.7	6.9	6.8	8.7	7.1	5.2	2.1	5.6
Forestry and hunting	8.3	10.2	9.7	7.3	7.7	7.9	8.1	6.1	4.9	0.6	5.7
Non-farming activities	8.9	10.0	11.2	10.9	14.7	9.8	12.2	13.2	25.1	29.0	17.7
Other sources	32.2	28.6	28.3	29.7	26.4	31.5	28.8	29.3	36.8	63.9	39.1
Wages	19.0	15.0	15.9	14.5	14.3	18.5	17.6	16.5	21.0	30.2	20.5
Remittances	1.2	1.9	1.6	2.8	1.3	2.4	1.6	1.7	2.3	2.6	2.1
Other (rents, dividends)	12.1	11.7	10.9	12.4	10.8	10.6	9.6	11.1	13.4	31.0	16.5
Total	100.0	100.0	100.0	100.0	100.0	100.0	100.0	100.0	100.0	100.0	100.0

Source: CSES Survey 2001.

Table 1.2 Expenditure shares in Cambodia (per cent)

| Consumption item | Deciles of per capita consumption | | | | | | | | | | |
	Poor 1	2	3	4	5	6	7	8	9	Rich 10	avg
Food total	75.7	76.3	76.0	73.7	73.7	72.6	72.0	70.3	64.4	38.6	63.5
Rice, all varieties	28.4	23.3	22.7	20.7	20.6	18.9	17.5	15.1	12.5	5.8	15.6
Fish and fish products	9.9	11.1	10.6	10.5	10.9	10.8	10.0	10.0	9.2	5.0	8.9
All other consumption items	37.4	41.9	42.7	42.5	42.2	43.0	44.5	45.2	42.7	27.8	39.0
Non-food total	24.4	23.8	24.1	26.4	26.3	27.5	28.0	29.7	35.6	61.4	36.5
Housing, fuel and transportation[a]	15.7	15.5	15.2	17.1	17.3	17.4	17.5	19.4	24.1	46.7	25.5
Clothing[b]	2.9	2.8	3.0	3.0	2.8	3.4	3.4	3.2	2.9	2.3	2.9
Other expenditures[c]	5.8	5.4	5.9	6.2	6.1	6.6	7.1	7.1	8.6	12.4	8.2

Notes
a Includes house rent (rental value of subsidized housing, rental value of owner-occupied housing, hotel charges), house maintenance and repair, water and fuel, medical care, transportation and communication, and personal care.
b Clothing and footwear (tailored clothes, ready-made clothes, shoes, etc).
c Includes furniture and household equipment and operation, expenditures in recreation, education, personal effects and miscellaneous items.

Source: CSES Survey 2001.

Table 1.2 shows the expenditure shares on different commodity groups broken down by the same per capita consumption decile groups as above. Again we see a remarkable homogeneity across the bottom eight deciles and dramatic differences for the top two deciles. Food expenditure accounts for over 70 per cent of total expenditure for the bottom 80 per cent of the population, but rice consumption increases in importance for poorer households, whilst the share of all other consumption items (except fish and fish products) declines. Similarly non-food shares are quite similar for the bottom eight deciles, with the share of housing, fuel and transportation rising dramatically for the top two deciles.

Taken together Tables 1.1 and 1.2 give us a good indication of the likely initial impact of a given price shock. Clearly changes in rice prices will have the largest impact given their large share in both income and consumption. Of course what matters is the households' *net* consumption position; the tables suggest that the poorest decile will be net consumers on average (28.4 per cent of their consumption is on rice, 21.4 per cent of their income is from rice) as are the top two deciles, whilst all other deciles are net producers. Thus a sharp increase in the rice price may hurt the poorest, but help the not quite so poor at the same time. The tables also give us insight into issues which might not otherwise be apparent. For example, decreases in livestock prices could hurt the poor to a significant extent, but would be of much less significance for the upper deciles of the population. Similarly, shifts in wage income will matter more to the poorest decile than to slightly less poor households in deciles 2 to 5. And increases in housing, fuel and transportation costs will hit the richest hard, but will have a much smaller effect upon the poorest 80 per cent of the population. Thus a careful examination of the income sources and expenditure shares of the population can provide much of the 'story' about the potential impact of price shocks upon the poor.

The ability to tell a relevant story about who is affected by various reforms also depends upon the ways in which households are grouped. Tables 1.1 and 1.2 grouped households into deciles of per capita consumption expenditure, which is a natural grouping if one is interested in determining the impact upon the poor. However, deciles of consumption expenditure are rarely a relevant classification for policy purposes. Policymakers tend to be interested in what the effects of a reform are in relation to functional or geographical groupings, e.g. rice farmers versus informal urban workers or Western province versus Eastern Province. Indeed there is an infinite variety of possible groupings, e.g. level of education, gender of household head, ethnicity, location, principal activity, land ownership, etc. The particular combinations of groups that are relevant will depend on the precise context, but if the analysis is conducted at the household level, then it is possible to put together any grouping for which the relevant variables are available from the survey data.

Furthermore, if one wishes to explore non-income 'dimensions' of poverty (e.g. educational attainment, remoteness, health, etc) and these variables are available in the dataset, then it is possible to present the above tables in terms of deciles of these variables. Table 1.3 for example, breaks down households' income sources in Nepal by deciles of time to get to the market. It shows for example that income

Table1.3 Household income sources by time to market in Nepal

Share of Income	Deciles of distance to market								
	Closest decile	2	3	5	6	7	8	9	Distant decile
Cash wages from working on other's farm	2.1	3.9	8.8	8.1	6.6	7.0	8.9	6.4	5.4
Other wages	18.0	13.8	13.7	15.9	11.2	8.5	8.2	11.6	16.1
Land rent	1.8	0.6	0.7	1.1	0.6	0.1	0.1	0.2	0.1
Net agricultural income from sales of crops	1.8	3.7	7.7	10.7	10.2	3.7	6.8	4.4	1.5
Net livestock income	1.5	2.0	3.6	3.8	3.9	3.3	3.6	4.1	5.8
Net income from own enterprises	48.2	29.7	13.1	7.0	8.2	15.4	5.6	10.1	5.1
Total net remittances	7.1	20.3	9.4	5.8	12.7	8.4	14.3	8.6	8.3
Other income	8.1	6.0	3.2	1.4	2.9	4.6	2.2	2.6	2.6
Consumption of own production	11.4	20.0	39.7	46.2	43.7	49.1	50.4	51.9	55.0
Total income	100.0	100.0	100.0	100.0	100.0	100.0	100.0	100.0	100.0

Source: Baris Sivri – personal communication.

from own enterprises is only of real importance to households who are relatively close to markets, whilst consumption of own production increases as a proportion of total income the further away one is from markets, rising to over half of total income for the most remote three deciles.

There are many different dimensions across which such tables may be constructed. For example, Table 1.4 shows household income share for each of the 10 geological and economic regions of Nepal along with summary poverty and illiteracy figures for each region. It shows large differences in sources of livelihood between different regions. Income from own enterprises and non-agricultural wages are key in Kathmandu and other urban areas, whereas in Terai and the hills and mountains, own production is the most important source of income. Even within broad geographical regions there are substantial differences: in rural eastern and central Terai almost a fifth of income comes from own enterprises, whereas in mid- and far-west Terai only 4 per cent of income comes from this source. Similarly remittances are key to those living in the rural western hills, but mostly irrelevant to those in the eastern hills.

Constructing such tables can thus give a good indication of how groups of households differentiated by dimensions other than income will be affected by reforms.

Once such tables have been constructed the basic methodology outlined above can be applied to calculate the impact on each household. This has been done using data from several different countries and a wide variety of policy experiments.[13] Table 1.5 provides an example of a typical set of results based on the simulation of a 10 per cent increase in the price of rice in Cambodia.

The results show that the main losers from a rice price increase would be the poorest net buyers in urban areas (because they spend a large proportion of their income on rice), whilst the largest gainers would be the net sellers in the top decile of the urban areas. In rural areas the gains among net sellers are more evenly distributed, but the losses are still concentrated among the poor due to their large expenditure share on rice.

As noted above, there are a large number of different simulations which can be done with the above framework. For example, Ajwad, Duygan and Sivri (2002) simulate the impact of a 25 per cent reduction in transportation costs for farmer households on household consumption in Armenia. They estimate that rural households gain on average 0.95 per cent of total per capita expenditure, compared with 0.1 per cent for urban households, but the gains are reasonably evenly spread among the poor and the non-poor. They also simulate the impact of a 10 per cent increase in irrigation charges; this hurts both urban and rural households by roughly the same extent on average, but poorer rural households are hit much harder than well-off rural households because a much higher share of their expenditure is on irrigation. Similarly Ajwad, Aksoy and Sivri (2002) simulate the poverty impact of a 30 per cent increase in tobacco and maize yields in Malawi. The simulated increase in tobacco yields raises incomes of the poorest quintile by 1.5 per cent compared with 0.99 per cent for the top quintile; but raising maize yields has a dramatic impact upon the poor, raising their incomes by 5.66 per cent compared with just 0.5 per cent for the best off.

Table 1.4 Household income sources and poverty by region in Nepal

Share of income	Urban Kathmandu Valley	Other urban	Rural eastern Terai	Rural central Terai	Rural western Terai	Rural mid and far-west Terai	Rural eastern hills, mtns	Rural central hills, mtns	Rural western hills, mtns	Rural mid and far-west hills, mtns
Cash wages from working on other's farm	2.4	1.8	10.6	10.1	8.0	10.2	3.6	4.5	6.3	5.9
Other wages	12.6	20.1	12.3	12.3	8.3	9.2	12.4	12.6	9.0	15.0
Land rent	0.0	1.7	0.9	1.5	0.1	0.6	0.2	0.0	0.1	1.1
Net agricultural income from sales of crops (sales − expenditures)	5.6	1.2	17.4	7.9	6.0	15.8	5.1	1.3	2.0	3.6
Net livestock income	10.3	2.0	2.4	3.9	3.7	0.5	6.1	3.8	1.9	4.6
Net income from own enterprises	40.4	44.5	19.3	17.2	10.9	4.0	5.9	31.2	10.7	9.7
Total net remittances (received − sent)	4.3	10.0	6.1	9.8	7.8	4.4	1.1	9.5	22.0	7.7
Other income	7.4	7.9	2.0	0.9	2.6	0.6	3.6	1.4	8.3	1.4
Consumption of own production	17.0	10.7	29.0	36.4	52.6	54.7	62.0	35.7	39.7	51.0
Total income	100.0	100.0	100.0	100.0	100.0	100.0	100.0	100.0	100.0	100.0
Poverty incidence (%)	4.0	34.0	42.0	38.0	40.0	53.0	28.0	67.0	40.0	72.0
Poverty gap	0.00	0.11	0.10	0.08	0.09	0.13	0.07	0.11	0.13	0.28
Illiteracy (%)	24.0	45.0	62.0	77.0	69.0	72.0	59.0	66.0	54.0	73.0
Share in Nepal Population (%)	1.4	6.8	12.6	16.2	7.2	6.7	9.7	13.1	13.0	13.4

Source: Baris Sivri – personal communication.

Table 1.5 Effect of a 10 per cent increase in the price of rice, by decile, as percentage of total household expenditures, Cambodia

| | Deciles by per capita consumption | | | | | | | | | | |
	Poor 1	2	3	4	5	6	7	8	9	Rich 10	Total
Urban											
Net sellers	1.9	2.8	3.2	3.5	2.9	2.9	1.7	2.2	1.8	5.7	2.5
Net buyers	-2.2	-1.5	-1.7	-1.5	-1.5	-1.3	-1.2	-1.2	-1.0	-0.6	-1
Total urban	-1.3	0.5	-0.4	-0.3	-0.5	-0.1	-0.1	0.3	-0.2	-0.3	-0.2
Rural											
Net sellers	2.2	2.6	2.4	2.4	2.9	2.8	2.4	2.3	1.4	1.9	2.4
Net buyers	-1.9	-1.4	-1.1	-1.2	-1.2	-1.2	-1.2	-1.2	-1.0	-0.7	-1.3
Total rural	-0.4	0.5	0.7	0.8	1.1	1.0	0.9	1.0	-0.1	-0.5	0.6
All country											
Net sellers	2.2	2.6	2.4	2.5	2.9	2.8	2.4	2.3	1.5	3.8	2.5
Net buyers	-1.9	-1.4	-1.1	-1.2	-1.2	-1.2	-1.2	-1.2	-1.0	-0.7	-1.2
Total	-0.5	0.5	0.7	0.7	1.0	1.0	0.8	0.9	-0.1	-0.4	0.5

Source: Nicita, Olarreaga and Soloaga (2002).

Applying the basic methodology in this way thus provides a valuable first estimate of the potential effects of a reform. However, the results of such simulations are contentious because they do not take account of how producers or consumers may respond to price changes. Possibly more seriously they ignore the role of labour markets; the above simulation must, by construction, give the result that net consumers of a product whose price falls will gain. However, there is some evidence that households who are net consumers of a staple food do not necessarily gain when the price of that food falls if they obtain much of their income from working on farms producing that good, because the reduction in profits for the farm owners results in a downward pressure on wages or employment. The next section shows various ways in which the methodology can be extended to address these and other concerns.

Extensions of the basic methodology

The above approach to the analysis of the impact of structural reforms on the poor is attractive because its data requirements are relatively low; most reasonable income and production surveys will contain data on quantities produced, inputs used and income received from a variety of different sources.[14] However, it has a number of important weaknesses.

Firstly, the model does not allow for substitution in consumption or production. In reality quantities will adjust (indeed the reallocation of resources may be one of the objectives of the reforms). One might expect resources to shift into the production of goods whose prices have increased, and away from the use of inputs and the consumption of goods whose prices have gone up.

Secondly, the model does not include any markets. Prices are completely exogenous and, unless changed for the purpose of the simulation, they remain fixed. Yet in many cases prices will be determined by markets; in particular changes in the demand and supply of labour will determine the real wage of unskilled labour – a key variable for understanding the poverty impact of a reform.

Thirdly, the model does not allow for growth. Yet promoting growth – particularly growth which includes the poor – is often the central aim of such reforms. Allowing the model to incorporate assumptions about growth can be important for simulating medium- to long-run impacts. We consider each of these areas below.

Substitution in consumption and production

To allow for substitution in consumption one needs to obtain at least income and own-price (and preferably also cross-price) elasticities of demand. The easiest way to obtain these is to draw them from existing studies of the country of interest. Alternatively, one could attempt to estimate commodity demand equations using one of the standard demand systems (LES, AIDS, AIDADS, etc). Ideally time series data on demands for various goods, prices and incomes is needed to ensure a reasonable amount of variation in prices. Alternatively, one may use Deaton's method of exploiting spatial variation in unit prices to estimate own and cross-price elasticities (see Deaton and Grimard, 1992; Deaton, 1997). Nicita (2004) provides an example of the application of this approach to Mexico.

Estimating these elasticities provides a partial equilibrium way of assessing the magnitude of 'second round' consumption effects of price reforms. However, estimating such elasticities is not a trivial matter, especially if only cross-sectional data are available. Moreover, it is not clear that incorporating the ability to substitute in consumption is that important. When prices change simultaneously for a large number of commodities, incorporating the ability to substitute in consumption appears in many practical circumstances to make little difference to the overall welfare effects. This suggests that it may only be worth the additional effort of estimating such elasticities if one has a particular reason for believing that consumption substitution effects are likely to be important. On the other hand, if reasonable consumption elasticities are already readily available from other studies, their incorporation within the above framework is straightforward (see below) and there is no reason for not doing so.

To allow for substitution in production one could attempt to estimate output supply or factor demand equations. As with estimating consumption demand systems, this requires one to make assumptions about the functional form of the output supply/factor demand functions, and there must be a reasonable amount of variation in prices in the data. Again the easiest approach is to draw supply elasticities from existing studies. If these are not available then time series data is needed on outputs, prices and factor demands. Alternatively, one may attempt to estimate elasticities by combining cross-sectional and time-series data (see Mundlak, 1963), but estimating such elasticities solely from cross-sectional data is particularly difficult for agricultural production because natural conditions also cause large variations in supply. Furthermore, estimates of supply functions tend to assume smooth substitutability between the production of different commodities whereas in fact the major welfare changes may occur when markets are created or destroyed as a result of reforms. Such discontinuities are not generally captured in traditional supply systems.

Does the incorporation of such supply elasticities matter? In the short run it may be reasonable to suppose that changes in the activities undertaken by households may be relatively slow (certainly compared with changes in consumption), so that the short-run poverty impact may justifiably assume fixed quantities of production. However, data from numerous countries suggest that households tend to be much less diversified in production than in consumption, so that reforms which change the returns to different activities are likely to have much larger welfare effects than reforms which change the prices of goods which households consume. Certainly, long-run supply response is critical to long-run poverty alleviation, so the incorporation of long-run supply elasticities in calculations of the poverty impact is probably more important in most cases than the incorporation of consumption elasticities.

Even if it is not possible to estimate a full supply or demand system, it may still be worth incorporating reasonable estimates of the own-price demand and supply elasticities for the goods which are subject to price changes since a range of plausible values is more likely to reflect reality than assuming that all elasticities are zero. These elasticities may be easily incorporated within our simple framework by amending equation (1.1). Each element of equation (1.1) consists of an income or budget share (IS_j or BS_j) multiplied by a percentage price change ($\Delta p_j/p_j$). Incorporating price elasticities into this equation simply involves replacing each $BS_j.(\Delta p_j/p_j)$ term with

$$BS_j \frac{\Delta p_j}{p_j} + \frac{1}{2} BS_j \left(\frac{\Delta p_j}{p_j} \right)^2 \varepsilon_j \tag{1.5}$$

where ε_j is the relevant own-price demand elasticity for good j (and similarly for the income share terms and the own-price elasticity of supply).[15]

Modelling the labour market

Assuming that quantities remain fixed (and therefore that only wages adjust) is especially problematic for the labour market since it is equivalent to assuming a labour supply elasticity of zero. In reality, the price and cost changes induced by reforms will make some activities more profitable and others less so; demand for labour in the benefiting sectors will rise increasing both employment and wages, whilst demand in the losing sectors will fall reducing employment and wages. If adjustment is smooth and instantaneous then there will be no net effects upon employment and the effect on wages of different types of labour will depend on the relative intensity with which they are used in the gaining and losing sectors. However, in many circumstances adjustment is far from smooth or instantaneous. Companies that lose from reforms may simply be unprofitable and close, shedding large numbers of jobs; if employment in the affected sector dominates the local economy then this can have large negative externalities on other businesses. Enterprises in the sectors gaining from reforms may be located in different places and draw upon a different pool of labour. Thus although the national aggregate of employment may be little affected by reforms, local effects can be considerable and longer lasting.

The opposite extreme from assuming a zero wage elasticity of labour is to assume that it is infinitely elastic implying that, if a sector expands, employment rather than wages tends to rise. In some sectors and countries this may be nearer the truth than assuming a zero elasticity (the empirical evidence is mixed – see the survey by Matusz and Tarr, 1999; Winters, 2002b presents evidence that employment adjusted more than wages in India during the 1990s). In practical terms it may be sensible to take into account the segmented nature of many labour markets in developing countries, since the simplest assumption of an infinitely elastic labour supply suggests somewhat unrealistically that the 'wage' when out of work is exactly the same as the wage in employment. It may be better to assume that employment expands in the gaining sectors at the existing sector- or location-specific wage.[16]

If we assume that employment expands at a fixed sector-specific wage and wish to simulate the impact of an increase in demand then we need a way of moving people into and out of jobs. It is clearly rather unrealistic to suppose that all of these new jobs will be filled from the ranks of the previously unemployed; in many cases people will switch from one job to another in order to take advantage of the differences in sectoral wage rates. Nicita *et al.* (2002) provide a useful approach to calculating who is likely to gain from an expansion in employment. They calculate the probability of being in different forms of employment using a multinomial logit, rank households according to these probabilities and then put them into jobs in the order of their probability. This approach fits nicely with the intuition that, when formal sectors grow it is often not the poor who get the jobs, or at least not at first. In addition, if the new wage 'allocated' to a household on getting a job is determined by a wage equation which takes into account sectoral wage differentials then it will be possible for there to be discrete changes in income when a person gets a job.

This approach has been applied in the Integrated Framework studies for a number of different countries. For example, the study for the Republic of Yemen (2002) simulates the impact of a 6 per cent increase in female participation in the labour market. Since poorer households are more likely to participate in the labour market in Yemen, two-thirds of the households affected by the increase in employment opportunities are in the bottom three expenditure deciles. Furthermore, the average impact for those households that have a new entrant to the labour force is equivalent to 30 per cent of total household expenditures. Similarly in Malawi, Ajwad, Aksoy and Sivri (2002) simulate the poverty impact of a 30 per cent increase in employment in manufacturing, construction and mining. Because of the characteristics of those employed in these sectors they find that this large increase in employment has no effect upon the poorest quintile, whilst the richest quintile gains by 4 per cent. In Cambodia, Nicita, Olarreaga and Soloaga (2002) show that the impact of an increase of 50,000 employees in the industrial sector would have a large positive impact on rural households in the lowest expenditure decile with at least one member switching to the sector. But because of the relative probability of obtaining such jobs, the overall benefit to rural households is lower than the gain experienced by urban households.

A similar but somewhat more sophisticated methodology is used by Bourguignon and others in micro-simulation models of distribution changes (Bourguignon, Fournier *et al.* 2001). Bourguignon *et al.* estimate an individual level wage equation correcting for selection bias using the Heckman method. They then estimate wage and farm labour participation equations sequentially for each member of the household (starting with the household head) as a multinomial logit choice between (i) inactivity, (ii) wage work, (iii) work on the family farm, (iv) work in non-farm businesses, and (v) a combination of (ii) and (iii). The multinomial logits incorporate variables reflecting household characteristics which may have an influence upon individual participation decisions.

The advantage of both of the above methods of modelling employment and wage income is that they only require readily available household survey data. In particular all that is needed is information on employment by sector, wages (or employment income and the quantity of labour supplied) and household characteristics. Using only this information it is possible to 'allocate' individuals to jobs and determine their likely wage, given a known increase or decrease in employment.

However, the extent of the employment change is exogenous using the above approach. Ideally, the expansion or contraction of each sector resulting from reform could be predicted by a general equilibrium model, but, as noted above, the resources required to construct a CGE model may preclude this option in many countries. One therefore needs a mechanism for estimating the potential employment impact of a structural reform. There are two components to this problem: firstly, it is necessary to estimate the impact of the price change induced by reform on sectoral output; and secondly it is necessary to estimate the impact of the change in output upon employment and wages.

One ad hoc approach to the first part of the problem would be to use investment climate surveys to obtain estimates from senior managers of companies in each sector about the sort of growth rates they anticipate and what difference they might expect policy reforms to make. Such estimates are of course highly subjective at an individual level, but assuming that knowledge of the prospects for growth is reasonably common across each industry, aggregate estimates of growth expectations may be at least as accurate as historical or model-based estimates. Furthermore, if detailed firm-level surveys are available it may be possible to cross-check whether growth expectations are 'reasonable' given the margins and financing structure of firms within the industry.

Alternatively, if estimates of aggregate supply elasticities are available, then these may be used to estimate the impact of price reforms on the output of affected sectors. By its nature this approach will not take into account general equilibrium effects, but if the reforms do not affect too many sectors simultaneously then this may provide an adequate approximation of the output change.

Estimating the impact of the change in output upon employment and wages can be addressed in a number of ways without resorting to a CGE analysis. If the sector of employment is indicated in the household survey, then it is possible simply to scale employment up or down by the sectoral growth rate (if one is assuming an infinite elasticity of labour supply) or to scale wages up or down for existing employees (if one is assuming that the labour supply elasticity is zero).

If it is reasonable to assume excess capacity and unemployment so that exogenous changes can be satisfied through an increase in output without having any effect on prices, then a more theoretically defensible approach is given by Niimi, Vasudeva-Dutta and Winters (2002). They attempt to estimate the employment impact of the growth in exports and imports in Vietnam between 1993 and 1998 using the Vietnam input–output matrix. They simply calculate labour coefficients for each sector (in terms of jobs per dollar of output) by dividing the total labour cost in each sector by the value of gross output (to give labour cost per dollar) and then dividing by the average wage.[17] Using this approach one can simulate the employment impact of any assumed sectoral growth rate by simply multiplying the change in output by the labour coefficient for the sector. Since this approach ignores the second-round expenditure effects associated with the demand for intermediates, it provides a lower bound of the employment changes resulting from growth.[18] Niimi, Vasudeva-Dutta and Winters also use 'total labour coefficients' to take into account the effect of growth on the demand for intermediates.[19] This provides an upper bound of the employment changes. Of course the lower and upper bounds are rather crude approximations to the employment changes, but the advantage of this approach is that it only requires an input–output matrix (and preferably information about sectoral wage rates).

Analysing remittances

Finally, in many countries remittances form an important part of income for many groups of households. If this is the case then one needs to think about the determinants of remittance income since it is not satisfactory to treat this as exogenous. There are a number of ways in which this might be done. At the very least, if one has estimates of the sectoral growth rates likely to result from reform (or a set of scenarios about what such growth rates might be), and if the sectoral source of the remittance is indicated in the data, then it is straightforward to scale up or down household remittance incomes accordingly. This is similar to the inelastic labour supply assumption above in that it is assumed that the wage rises in the growing sector benefiting existing employees and therefore increasing remittances. To account for the idea that growing sectors will employ new people who may then remit income it may be better to estimate the probability of receiving remittances from different sectors and the level of remittance received/sent against a set of household characteristics (see Republic of Yemen, 2002 for an example). Then one can scale up or down employment in the different sectors using the probability of involvement in exactly the same way as suggested for labour income above.

This simple approach does not take into account that whether households receive remittances often depends on an earlier decision by one or more household member to migrate in search of work. If data are available on sectoral employment and wage rates as well as the characteristics of those employed, then it is possible to adopt a somewhat more sophisticated approach by modelling the decision to migrate. Consider a simple model of a household with n adult members – n^r are in the rural household (which is receiving the remittances), n^u are in the urban area sending remittances. For simplicity suppose that the members in rural areas are guaranteed a return on their labour of w^r, whereas those in the urban area may receive a higher return w^u but with a probability that depends upon overall labour demand and their individual characteristics. Assume each household maximizes its household income (i.e. the total income of its members in both the rural and urban areas).

In this simple model, maximizing income simply involves deciding how many people to send to the urban area to try and get a job. If the sectoral wage and the way in which the probability of getting a job depends on characteristics is known, then each household can allocate the optimal number of people to finding employment in the urban area. In the case of households with members with 'poor' characteristics, it may not be worth their while sending someone to urban areas to get a job, but if for any household member w^u. Prob(Employment) is greater than w^r, then sending that member to obtain employment will increase expected household income, and, if the household is risk-neutral, it will also increase its welfare. Finally, if a household does send one or more members to the urban area to obtain employment, then one has to determine how much remittance income they will send back. One approach is to assume (or calculate from the data) an average saving rate and assume that they remit a fixed proportion of their income. An alternative might be to assume a 'social compact' within the household that the migrant would not live at a higher per adult equivalent level of consumption than the members of the sending household, i.e. that they would remit that amount which would make them as well off as the receiving household (after taking into account the remittance).

If one were to exploit a simple 'Harris–Todaro' model of this kind, estimating the returns to different activities and the parameters of the probability of employment from the data, then it should be possible to simulate the impact of growth in a particular sector upon the supply of migrant labour and therefore upon the level of remittances, whilst taking into account the loss of income resulting from their departure from rural areas.

Modelling the household

The sections above have described ways of separately incorporating quantity responses into each element of income and consumption, i.e. production and consumption substitution, expansions or contractions of labour employed, and shifts in remittance income. However, in practice these responses happen simultaneously within the household. It would be useful therefore to have a mechanism for modelling the impact of price changes upon households when they are allowed to simultaneously respond by changing production, consumption and labour sale decisions to maximize their overall welfare. This suggests the use of simple 'household models' in the Singh, Squire and Strauss (1986) tradition. Such models assume that households are faced with an exogenous set of prices but can re-allocate their resources between different activities to maximize overall household welfare. Lofgren and Robinson (1999) have developed a sophisticated non-separable farm household model to explain non-linearities in the supply response of households to a variety of policy reforms. Their approach is quite data and resource intensive. However, it is possible to construct a very simple version of this model which allows one to take account of household level responses:

Equation	Example	
Utility	$U = \prod_i (q_i^C)^{\alpha_i}$	(1.6)
Production function	$q_i^X = a_i \cdot \prod_f (qf_{fi}^I)^{\beta_{fi}}$	(1.7)
Commodity balance	$q_i^X + q_i^P = q_i^C + \sum_j q_{ij}^I + q_i^S$	(1.8)

Factor balance
$$qf_f^E + qf_f^P = \sum_i qf_{fi}^I + qf_f^S \qquad (1.9)$$

Cash constraint
$$\sum_i p_i^P q_i^P + \sum_f p_f^P qf_f^P = \sum_i p_i^S q_i^S + \sum_f p_f^S qf_f^S \quad (1.10)$$

Suppose that a household maximizes its utility (given here by a simple Cobb–Douglas function of the goods which its members consume – equation (1.6)) subject to a set of constraints. The first constraint is the production technology which they have (given above by a simple Cobb–Douglas function of the primary factors – equation (1.7)); the next two constraints are simple commodity balances – the quantity of any commodity produced plus the amount purchased must equal the amount consumed plus the amount used as inputs and that sold (equation (1.8)) – similarly the total endowment of a factor which the household may have plus that which is purchased (e.g. labour hired in) must be equal to that used in production and that sold (equation (1.9)); finally, the household is subject to a cash constraint so that its total purchases of commodities and factors cannot exceed the value of its sales of commodities and factors (equation (1.10)).[20]

Given a set of exogenous purchase and sales prices for commodities and factors (if necessary unit prices from the household survey may be used), households will choose how to allocate their factors between different activities in order to maximize their incomes, consumption and utility. The model requires a small set of parameters (the a_i, α_i, and β_{fi} for each commodity i and factor f) which can either be taken from existing studies or estimated from the data. It is therefore possible in principle to construct a 'household level' SAM for each household in the dataset and to estimate the impact of a price shock on household behaviour for each household separately.

Table 1.6 gives an example of a simple stylized household SAM. This household undertakes two activities: subsistence crop production and cash crop production. These activities use labour, land and capital as well as fertilizer. These activities 'sell' their output to the commodity accounts (SUB-C and CASH-C) respectively. In addition the commodity accounts 'import' some of the subsistence crop from the 'rest of the world' (recall that this is a household level SAM so that the rest of the world (ROW) here simply means all other households; 'imports' in this context are simply purchases from outside the household) as well as fertilizer and non-food commodity. The household also sells their output of the cash crop to the ROW – their cash constraint means that the value of their imports (subsistence crop, fertilizer and non-food) must match the value of their exports (cash crop). The household's endowment of labour, capital and land 'pays' the household account which then spends its income on food and non-food.

In a practical example the household may have many more activities and there will be many more commodities. In addition, if the data allows, factors of production can be broken down (e.g. by gender, age, experience, education, etc). The model may also allow some factors to be tradable (e.g. labour) whilst others may not be (e.g. land). More significantly, the determination of whether a commodity or factor is tradable can be endogenous. Our model allowed the possibility of

Table 1.6 A stylised household SAM

		Activities		Commodities				Factors			Household	ROW	Total supply/income
		1	2	3	4	5	6	7	8	9	10	11	
		SUB-A	CASH-A	SUB-C	CASH-C	INPUT-C	NONF-C	LAB	CAP	LAND	HH	ROW	
Activities													
1. Subsistence activity	SUB-A			40									40
2. Cash crop activity	CASH-A				75								75
Commodities													
3. Food crop	SUB-C										60		60
4. Cash crop	CASH-C											75	75
5. Fertilizer	INPUT-C	10	20										30
6. Non-food	NONF-C										25		25
Factors													
7. Labour	LAB	10	20										30
8. Capital	CAP	10	20										30
9. Land	LAND	10	15										25
Household													
10. The household	HH							30	30	25			85
Other institutions													
11. Rest of the world	ROW			20		30	25						75
Total demand/expenditure		40	75	60	75	30	25	30	30	25	85		75

Notes
Expenditures go from column to row (or equivalently, sales go from row to column). The row totals therefore represent the income of each account; column totals represent total expenditures of the accounts.

differences in the purchase and selling prices arising from transaction costs. This can result in households choosing not to trade goods which, were such transaction costs reduced, they would trade.[21]

It may not be realistic to construct a full household level SAM for every household in the dataset (although this is not impossible – indeed Cogneau and Robilliard, 2000, and Robilliard, Bourguignon *et al.*, 2001) have embedded all the households in the survey into a full country level CGE). However, it is relatively straightforward to construct a set of SAMs for 'representative households' and estimate the impact on each of these representative households separately.

The household modelling approach has the attraction that it can allow for all the above substitution effects within a consistent theoretical framework, whilst only requiring information typically available from a household survey. However, it has the important disadvantage of remaining a fixed price model. Indeed it is perfectly possible for each of the representative households simulated to simultaneously supply more labour to the market as a result of a structural reform without this having any effect upon the wage. Similarly, household production responses change the supply and demand for commodities in the economy, but in these household models this has no effect upon the prices of these commodities. In some circumstances this does not matter – if prices are likely to remain fixed or if the nature of the changes can be assumed exogenously then it is not necessary to complicate the model by incorporating assumptions about the ways in which markets clear and prices adjust. However, in other circumstances, accounting for the likely changes in the prices of some key commodities (notably staple foods) and some key factors (notably the unskilled wage) is important. One way in which these can be accommodated without moving to a country level CGE model is to employ a multi-market model.

Multi-market models

All the above assumes that prices are exogenous. In some circumstances this may be reasonable – such as homogenous tradable goods whose price will be determined by the world price. But the literature on growth linkages (Haggblade, Hazell *et al.*, 1989; Hazell and Haggblade, 1991) points clearly to the fact that many of the goods which matter to the poorest people are non- or at least not very readily tradable. In such situations prices are going to be determined by local market clearing.

Multi-market models model the impact of household supply and demand decisions upon the prices of key commodities and thereby on household income (see Braverman and Hammer, 1986, for an early exposition; Arulpragasam and Conway, 2002, provide a practical guide to the use of such models). Rich and Lundberg (2002) describe the application of a multi-market model to the analysis of policy reforms in Malawi. Their model contains explicit supply and demand equations for a limited set of commodities using supply and demand elasticities estimated from previous studies. However, the key difference from the household model above is the inclusion of a set of price equations linking domestic producer and consumer prices for each commodity with import and export prices given estimates of various transport and transaction costs and taxes. Producer and consumer prices are then made endogenous by the inclusion of a market clearing equilibrium equation which ensures that the overall supply and demand for each commodity is equalized. Household agricultural income is determined by the value of the commodities produced by each of four household types minus their costs of production; non-agricultural income is exogenous to the model.

Minot and Goletti (2000) present an interesting variation of this approach by constructing a spatial multi-market model for Vietnam. This is similar to the model of Rich and Lundberg but with a number of innovations. Most significantly they estimate supply and demand elasticities for several different regions of the country, rather than for different household groups. Markets in their model follow rules of spatial arbitrage – that is, trade between two regions occurs when the price difference between them reaches the transfer cost (the full cost of transporting and marketing the good from one region to the other). The model generates estimates of the impact of changes in transaction costs and export quotas upon production, consumption and prices of a set of commodities as well as average incomes in each region. In order to estimate the distributional and poverty impact of these changes, the price changes predicted by the model, along with the estimated supply and demand elasticities, are applied to household data on production and consumption to predict the change in net income for each household using the basic methodology described above.

Multi-market models are a useful tool for the analysis of reforms if those reforms are likely to give rise to supply and demand responses which may significantly change prices. However, multi-market models are heavily dependent on being able to obtain reasonable estimates of income elasticities and price elasticities of demand and supply. Furthermore, multi-market models, like the household model described above, have no factor markets (indeed, unlike the household model above, they have no factors at all since income is determined by the value-added of own production). It is therefore impossible to examine the impact of supply and demand responses on wage rates. Indeed non-agricultural income is often exogenous and models where this is the case are clearly not appropriate for the analysis of situations in which non-farm income is important. Given that the consumption of non-tradable services in rural areas can be important (Hazell and Hojjati, 1995) this is a particularly serious omission, although there is no reason in principle why non-tradable services cannot be added as a commodity within a multi-market model if suitable data are available. Nonetheless, multi-market models can be valuable if endogenous price changes resulting from responses in several different markets are likely to be the main drivers of welfare changes.

Allowing for growth

The omission of growth from the basic methodology is a particularly serious omission because the size of the impact on poverty resulting from a typical simulation which does not incorporate growth tends to be rather small. Consider a large shock such as a 50 per cent increase in the price of rice in Cambodia. Table 1.1 shows that rice production is 21.4 per cent of the income of the poorest decile; Table 1.2 shows that rice consumption is 28.4 per cent of their expenditure – thus their net consumption of rice is 7 per cent of their income. Thus the percentage change in net income of the poorest decile when faced with this large shock will be at most 3.5 per cent of their net income (7 per cent times 50 per cent price change). Furthermore, if poor households are able to adjust at all, either by producing more rice or consuming other foods, then the impact on their net income will be less. Of course this is an aggregate figure – individual households or groups of households may be more severely affected – but the fact remains that the aggregate impact (positive or negative) upon the poor from such simulations tends to be rather small.

The generally small value of predicted impact is in direct contrast with the claims of two different actors in the process of reform. Activists, NGOs and organizations representing those most severely affected often claim that the negative effects from structural reforms are large; whilst governments and international organizations often claim that the benefits from such reforms are large. These differing perspectives can be understood when one allows for aggregation and growth (Kanbur, 2001). For example, claims of strong negative effects on some groups are often true – some households or groups can be badly hit by particular reforms – but when the impact on such groups are aggregated along with the smaller negative or positive impact on other households the overall effect can be quite small. Resolving this is a political rather than an economic issue – policymakers need to decide on the extent to which policy should be determined by its impact on the worst affected as against the impact on the general population. Claims of strong positive effects from structural reforms usually rely on (sometimes correct) assumptions about the impact of reform on growth. In the medium- to long-run the impact of enhanced productivity and growth on poverty tend to dominate the impact of redistribution caused by reforms (see Demery, Sen and Vishwanath, 1995), and poverty can be substantially reduced if reforms actually do have the assumed impact on growth.

How might one incorporate growth within our simple methodology? In the absence of a model linking policy reform to sectoral growth rates one is forced to rely upon projections based upon historical performance. It is straightforward to incorporate a steady reduction in particular transaction costs, or productivity growth in line with that experienced in the past (see World Bank, 2001b). Furthermore, if separate studies give some indication of how such parameters may be changed by policy reforms then these new values may be used instead. Certainly this approach leaves much to be desired, but it does have the advantage that, since the 'growth' rates are exogenously determined, it is possible to conduct sensitivity analysis so that policymakers can see the likely distributional outcome for any set of growth rates which they deem to be plausible.

Other ideas for methodological development

In the longer term there are a number of other ways in which the analysis of the linkages between structural reforms and poverty could be improved. These are grouped under two themes: dynamics and risk; and qualitative approaches.

Dynamics and risk

Poverty is not a static phenomenon. A large number of studies from both developed and developing countries show that there is a great deal of movement in and out of poverty (see Baulch and Hoddinott, 2000, for a selection of papers on poverty dynamics in developing countries). However, much 'poverty profile' analysis is based upon static regressions between income/consumption and a set of household and economic characteristics. Unsurprisingly we find that the poor have high dependency ratios, are poorly educated, have few assets and live in poor areas – in other words, they are poor! The policy implications resulting from such associations are much less clear: 'removing' children or the elderly from households with high dependency ratios is not a policy option; neither in most cases is supplying significant private assets to poor households, while the problems associated with 'moving' households to better areas are well known. Education *is* a key policy option, but even here, it is not certain that, if everyone's educational level rises, the poor will be much better off, even if they are better educated.

Interventions based upon such static analysis may therefore be less effective than expected in reducing poverty. If, instead, we think of poverty as a dynamic process, then the 'equilibrium' poverty rate can be reduced either by reducing the probability of falling into poverty, or by increasing the probability of exiting poverty (or both). For example, if the most important reason why households fall into poverty is illness of a major income earner in the household, then appropriate primary (and curative) health care can be prioritized; similarly if the principal reason for exiting poverty is obtaining a job, then employment creation can be emphasized. It is therefore important that poverty analysis should attempt to understand the most important reasons for falling into and exiting from poverty. In particular, it is important for us to know the extent to which price reforms are a cause of entries into or exits from poverty.

How might this analysis be achieved? When there is only one survey available for a country there is little that can be done. This said, it is surprising that in addition to collecting large quantities of quantitative data about the *status* of the household, most household surveys do not also ask the simple qualitative question 'what happened?'. Households that have fallen into poverty usually know the reason why – analysis of this qualitative information would be extremely valuable and it is important that future surveys should provide for a mix of both quantitative and qualitative information about causality.

In some situations more than one survey exists – usually for different years, but sometimes within one year. In this situation there is more that can be done. Where the multiple surveys are repeated cross-sections, these are typically used to look at aggregate trends in poverty. However, they also offer the possibility of understanding something about the dynamics of poverty by examining pseudo-panels. For example, one might look at how different cohorts have fared, possibly disaggregated by region, sector or skill (see Deaton, 1997). Although the extent of disaggregation may be limited by the need to maintain reasonable standard errors, such analysis can be very useful in painting a picture of how different groups in society have actually fared as a result of known price shocks. Credible explanations of what has actually happened in previous reform episodes can be more convincing to policymakers than simulations based upon single snapshots in time.

Furthermore, in a few cases panel data is available. In these situations much more comprehensive analysis of the impact of economic reforms is possible. The classic methodology is outlined by Dercon (2000) for Ethiopia. But panel data sets are available and have been analysed for Peru (Glewwe and Hall, 1998), Zimbabwe (Alwang, Mills *et al.*, 2002; Hoddinott, Owens *et al.* 1999), South Africa (Carter and May, 2001), China (Jalan and Ravallion, 2000), India (Walker and Ryan, 1990), Pakistan (McCulloch and Baulch, 2000) and Vietnam (Justino and Litchfield, 2002). In other cases intra-annual panels may be available (i.e. the same households were recorded at multiple times during the year, but households are different across years). Thus, in addition to exploring how poverty has changed between years, using the intra-annual data to 'correct' for seasonality, it may be possible to analyse how seasonality itself moves people into and out of poverty within the year. Seasonality is well documented as one of the most important concerns of the poor (Narayan, Chambers *et al.*, 2000). Furthermore the seasonality of price variation can be influenced by interventions such as warehouse receipting systems and buffer stocks mechanisms. Thus understanding the impact of price fluctuations on poverty can give an indication of the potential benefits of behind-the-border trade interventions.

Closely related to the issue of poverty dynamics and the impact of shocks is the issue of risk and uncertainty. Sometimes economic policy analysis ignores the substantial risk aversion of poor households. But security is a central concern of the poor (World Bank, 2001b). The reason is quite clear; poor households not only have less – they are much more vulnerable to being in poverty in any given year. They consequently make great efforts to minimize this vulnerability and these efforts can undermine their ability to benefit from reforms and their long-run growth. For example, poor households sometimes plant lower yielding but more drought resistant crops despite the fact that they could substantially increase their incomes with higher yielding crops if they had an effective means of dealing with the risk of crop failure. Thus it is useful to consider issues of risk and vulnerability when analysing structural reform, not just for the purpose of designing social safety nets for those negatively affected, but also because better social protection policies may enable more poor households to participate in the benefits of reform.

There are a number of ways in which a risk analysis may be undertaken. Firstly, in many cases surveys record both consumption and income. In cases where there is just one survey it is useful to look at how much narrower the cross-sectional consumption distribution is than the income distribution.[22] Where a panel (or pseudo-panel) is available it is possible to calculate the extent of consumption smoothing as well as the degree of persistence in both consumption and income. Studies which have done this have shown that the poor are rather less well insured than the better off (Jalan and Ravallion, 1999). This begs the interesting policy question – what sorts of interventions are likely to affect the vulnerability of households to poverty, given that domestic institutions can be important indirect providers of social protection (e.g. agricultural marketing boards which provide guaranteed prices, or enterprises providing transfers to existing and former employees)? In order to answer this question it is necessary to have a measure of vulnerability. Several studies have constructed vulnerability measures (see Christiaensen and Boisvert, 2000; Pritchett, Suryhadi *et al.*, 2000; McCulloch and Calandrino, 2003) and then attempted to understand the determinants of vulnerability. An analysis of how reforms affect vulnerability could therefore enrich the analytical framework used above.

A second, and more comprehensive approach to incorporating risk into our analysis, would be to incorporate a stochastic element into the household modelling approach discussed above. Household models provide solutions for the optimal allocation by households of the productive factors at their disposal. Including risk in such models would allow one to capture the idea that households tend to allocate resources in order to maximize the return to and minimize the risk from their entire 'portfolio' of activities.[23] This would allow the impact of reforms that changed the volatility of prices to be simulated. For example, the removal of a variable rate tariff is likely to create more domestic price volatility than previously (along with a change in the average price). A model which incorporated risk could therefore analyse the impact of *both* these effects upon poverty and vulnerability.

Qualitative approaches

The above discussion has focused on technical economic methodological issues. However, poverty is about much more than just income and consumption so it is essential to take a multi-dimensional approach to poverty analysis. A multi-dimensional approach does not necessarily mean a qualitative approach; other dimensions of poverty can be quantified and analysed using the same tools as those applied to income and consumption. For example, there is no reason why one cannot report educational level, access to medical facilities, distance from markets, extent of soil degradation, etc by decile or plot their cumulative distributions just as is done for income and consumption. Furthermore, several surveys contain subjective measures of wellbeing and almost all surveys contain information on assets and durables enabling the construction and comparison of welfare indices based on these variables (see Sahn and Stifel, 2000, for an example using the Demographic and Health Surveys in Africa).

However, aside from the technical literature, there is a vast amount of qualitative literature on poverty and the impact of reform on poverty in developing countries. Such material does not have the advantages of quantitative surveys in terms of providing a statistically representative picture of a whole country. But it can provide enormously valuable insights into the processes of destitution, the structural social relationships which provide the context in which economic activity takes place, the nature and functioning of key institutions, the dynamics of intra-household and community behaviour, the political processes which determine the success of reform, and much more. Of particular importance is the role which qualitative studies can place in uncovering the causal pathways through which reforms may influence different dimensions of wellbeing. For example, if a reform increases the price of a cash crop typically produced by women, but social norms dictate that women are also responsible for household maintenance and childcare, then the reforms may simultaneously increase incomes and reduce the welfare of poor women due to the additional pressures on their time. Quantitative household surveys rarely capture such processes making it important to perform analysis using both quantitative and qualitative sources.[24]

One key resource here is the large volume of participatory material which is now available for many countries. In situations where quantitative surveys are of debatable quality, such participatory analyses can provide key information on the relative importance of different sources of income to different groups within the society. Also, although it is difficult to obtain good measures of the *level* of welfare from participatory assessments making comparisons across groups difficult, such exercises do generally provide useful indications of the direction of *changes* in welfare over time. They can also provide information about: the key causes of poverty; the dimensions of poverty which matter to the poor in that country; the nature and extent of the risks faced by the poor; the policies and institutions which have the largest impact upon their lives; the role and timing of seasonal shocks; the agro-climatic conditions faced by different groups and so forth. They can therefore provide a valuable input into the analysis of the impact of structural reform on poverty.

Summary and conclusions

This chapter has outlined a simple methodology for linking structural reforms and poverty using household survey data from developing countries. As is always the case, the nature of the appropriate model for analysing such linkages must depend upon the precise question being asked and upon the data and time resources available. If the intention is to analyse the short-run impact of exogenous price changes, then the basic methodology, which assumes that all quantities remain fixed, can be used to provide a first-order approximation to the likely change in net income for each household. Furthermore, if the nature and size of the transport and transaction costs determining producer and consumer prices are known then it is possible to simulate the impact of exogenous changes in these costs.

If it is desired to look at the medium-run outcome of such exogenous policy changes then it is necessary to account for the possibility of substitution in both consumption and production. Ideally this should be done by the econometric estimation of price elasticities of supply, and income and price elasticities of demand if suitable data are available. If this is not possible within the available time or data constraints, then estimates can be selected from other studies of the same or 'similar' countries, or, at worst, parameters can be chosen which reproduce the observed output levels given an assumed functional form. Experience from several countries suggests that many households tend to be more specialized in production than in consumption, so that the incorporation of substitution possibilities in production has a greater impact upon the final results than the incorporation of substitution in consumption.

In many circumstances, households earn an important share of their income from the labour market. The basic methodology's assumption of fixed quantities may not always be appropriate here, since exogenous price shocks resulting from reforms may give rise to changes in employment levels in different sectors rather than only changes in wages. If excess labour means that it is reasonable to assume that employment can change without changes in wage rates and the sector of employment is indicated in the household survey data, then employment can be scaled up or down by the sectoral growth rate. Alternatively, labour coefficients from an input–output matrix may give an indication of the employment changes resulting from exogenous changes in output.

If employment changes can be calculated or assumed, then it is still necessary to allocate (or take away) the jobs to individuals. Here it is possible to draw upon the household survey data to estimate the probability of an individual being employed in a variety of different activities based upon their characteristics and those of their household. In this way one may account for the fact that the growth resulting from a reform may not directly benefit the poor if there is no corresponding rise in the unskilled wage.

Similarly, in circumstances where remittance income is important it may be desirable to have a somewhat deeper analysis of the impact of reform from this source. If estimates are available for the sectoral growth rates likely to result from the reform and the sector source of remittance income is known then it is possible to scale up or down household remittances pro rata. Alternatively, one may estimate the probability of receiving remittances based upon household characteristics and increase or decrease employment (and therefore remittances) on this basis. Better still, if suitable data are available, it may be possible to model the decision to migrate based upon the expected remittance returns and then simulate the change in income resulting from a shift in the probability of employment in particular sectors.

One may also attempt to integrate the above extensions of the basic methodology in the form of a simple household model. Such a model can allow a household to allocate their resources between a number of different activities (including wage labour) in order to maximize their utility when faced with an exogenous set of prices. One can then simulate the manner in which households change their resource allocations when prices change as a result of reform.

Alternatively, if reforms are likely to give rise to supply or demand responses with significant knock-on effects for domestic prices, then it is possible to endogenize the process of price formation through the use of a multi-market model. However, such models can require substantial additional data and resources and are often inappropriate for analysing circumstances where non-agricultural income is important.

Other potential methodological developments include greater attention to the dynamics of poverty and the ways in which reforms may cause entry into or exit from poverty. Furthermore, with suitable data it may be possible to simulate the impact of structural reforms on price volatility and the consequential impact upon household vulnerability.

Efforts may also be made to analyse the quantitative aspects of non-income dimensions of poverty. However a proper analysis of the linkages between reform and other dimensions of poverty will require an exploration of the qualitative poverty material in each country.

All of the approaches described above have focused on ex ante prediction of welfare effects resulting from structural reforms. This is, of course, what policy-makers are most interested in. However, it is worth noting that ex ante analysis can also be usefully informed by the application of the same techniques ex post to see if the predicted effects actually did occur. Such ex post analysis can point to weaknesses in the modelling methodology and provide information on the relative importance of different effects upon welfare, allowing future modelling to take these into account. More generally, it is important that the effects of structural reform are monitored during implementation and adjustments made if it becomes clear that the predicted and actual effects are far apart.

In conclusion, the choice of technique for modelling the link between structural reforms and poverty should be determined by the precise nature of the question, the data available and the characteristics of economic activity and poverty in the country in question – there is no single 'best' model. This chapter has presented a basic methodology which can be applied using only household survey data and limited time resources, along with a set of elaborations upon this methodology which may be adopted as circumstances and resources dictate.

Acknowledgements

This chapter was written while the author was a consultant at PREM Trade in the World Bank. The author is grateful to Ataman Aksoy for making this work possible and for providing numerous helpful comments and suggestions, and to Baris Sivri for producing several helpful tables. Thanks are also due to Burcu Duygan, Stephen Matteo Miller, Yvonne Tsikata and other members of PRMTR and the Trade and Poverty Cluster in the World Bank Trade Department as well as to Alessandro Nicita, Marcelo Olarreaga and Isidro Soloaga upon whose methodology this chapter is based. The views expressed are those of the author and do not necessarily reflect the views of the World Bank Group.

Notes

1 See Cornia, Jolly and Stewart (1987) for an early critique of structural adjustment reforms.
2 See Ahmad and Stern (1991) for a comprehensive review of the issues raised by taxation in developing countries. Deaton (1997) provides a succinct statement of some of the methodological problems.
3 See also http://web.worldbank.org/WBSITE/EXTERNAL/TOPICS/TRADE/0,, contentMDK:20097501~menuPK:207649~pagePK:148956~piPK:216618~theSite PK:239071,00.html for a selection of papers. The World Bank also provide a 'toolkit' of methods for conducting poverty and social impact analysis – see http://www1.worldbank.org/prem/poverty/psia/tools.htm.
4 For example, the International Food Policy Research Institute (IFPRI) has conducted numerous studies of this kind – see http://www.ifpri.org/.

5 The Integrated Framework (IF) was established under the World Trade Organization (WTO) in October 1997 to facilitate the coordination of trade-related technical assistance to least developed countries (LDC) and to promote an integrated approach to assist these countries in enhancing their trade opportunities. The work programme includes the preparation of country-specific Diagnostic Trade Integration Studies (DTIS) most of which include chapters on the linkage between trade and poverty (see www.integratedframework.org for more details). DTISs have been prepared for Burundi, Cambodia, Djibouti, Ethiopia, Guinea, Lesotho, Madagascar, Malawi, Mauritania, Mozambique, Nepal, Senegal and Yemen. The draft DTIS for Mali will be ready soon. New studies are being prepared for Benin, Chad, Sao Tome and Principe, Lao PDR, Mali, Rwanda, Tanzania and Zambia.

6 The basic methodology is based on 'A simple methodology to assess the poverty impact of economic policies using household data'. An application to Cambodia is described by Nicita, Olarreaga and Soloaga (2002). See Annex 1 for details.

7 Transfer income is harder to disaggregate in this way – see the section on remittances below.

8 Given by money metric utility – see Annex 1 for details.

9 See Minot and Goletti (2000) Appendix 2 for a full derivation.

10 We also assume no change in transfer income – see Annex 1 for an expanded expression with transfer income.

11 In the simple case shown in equation (1.2) the percentage change in the household price will be equal to $\alpha t/(1-t)$ where α is the percentage change in the tariff on an input; or $-\alpha t/(1-t)$ for an output.

12 The percentage change in producer prices will be given by $E^d t/(1-E^d t)$; the percentage change in consumer prices will be given by $E^s t/(1-E^d t)$ where $E^d = \varepsilon^d/(\varepsilon^s - \varepsilon^d), E^s = \varepsilon^s/(\varepsilon^s - \varepsilon^d), \varepsilon^d$ is the demand elasticity, ε^s is the supply elasticity and t is the ad valorem tax rate.

13 See poverty chapters of the Diagnostic Trade Integration Studies mentioned above.

14 Even here there may be difficulties: price information is often not well recorded (often one has to rely on unit prices rather than community price surveys); similarly wage information is often absent so that wages have to be inputed from earnings and hours worked; and transfers data often gives no indication of the source of the transfer (what sector was the person working in) or the determinants of the size of the transfer.

15 The superscripts from equation (1.1) have been omitted since this expression applies to all elements of that equation (except remittances). See Minot and Goletti (2000) for a derivation.

16 Or at least that the formal sector wage is higher than the subsistence wage.

17 Ideally the average sectorial wage should be used, but in their case this was unavailable.

18 Assuming no changes in wages.

19 This is similar to the technique of using Social Accounting Matrix (SAM) multipliers to simulate the impact of exogenous income shocks upon different household groups – see Decaluwe, Patry, Savard and Thorbecke (1999) for an excellent exposition.

20 For simplicity we have set up the commodity and factor balance constraints and the cash constraints as equalities – it is possible to specify them as inequalities so that not all factors or commodities have to be used.

21 More precisely, production and consumption decisions become non-separable so that the household is in fact responding to an endogenously determined shadow price rather than to the market prices.

22 Although the difference will be a mixture of consumption smoothing and differences in measurement error variances between consumption and income.

23 More precisely one might model them as maximizing their expected utility taking into account their risk aversion.

24 See Kanbur, Chambers, *et al.* (2001) for a collection of notes on mixing quantitative and qualitative approaches.

References

Ahmad, E. and N.H. Stern (1991) *The Theory and Practice of Tax Reform in Developing Countries*, Cambridge: Cambridge University Press.

Ajwad, M.I., A. Aksoy and B. Sivri (2002) 'Trade and Poverty in Malawi', Mimeo, PREM Trade, World Bank.

Ajwad, M.I., B. Duygan and B. Sivri (2002) 'Trade and Poverty in Armenia', Mimeo, PREM Trade, World Bank.

Alwang, J., B. Mills, *et al.* (2002) 'Changes in Well-being in Zimbabwe, 1990–1996: Evidence Using Semi-parametric Density Estimates', Journal of African Economies (U.K.) 11(3): 326–64.

Arulpragasam, J. and P. Conway (2002) 'Partial Equilibrium and Multi-market Analysis', in PSIA Toolkit, World Bank <http://www1.worldbank.org/prem/poverty/psia/tools.htm> (accessed 6 June 2005).

Baulch, B. and J. Hoddinott (2000) 'Economic Mobility and Poverty Dynamics in Developing Countries', *Journal of Development Studies* 36(6): 1–24.

Bourguignon, F., M. Fournier, *et al.* (2001) 'Fast Development with a Stable Income Distribution: Taiwan, 1979–1994', *Review of Income and Wealth*, 47(2): 139–163.

Braverman, A. and J. Hammer (1986) 'Multi-market Analysis of Agricultural Pricing Policies in Senegal', in I. Singh, L. Squire and J. Strauss (eds) *Agricultural Household Models: Extensions, Applications and Policy*, Washington DC: World Bank.

Carter, M.R. and J. May (2001) 'One Kind of Freedom: Poverty Dynamics in Post-apartheid South Africa', *World Development*, 29(12): 1987–2006.

Chen, S. and M. Ravallion (2004) 'Welfare Impacts of China's Accession to the World Trade Organization', *World Bank Economic Review*, 18(1): 29–57.

Christiaensen, L. and R.N. Boisvert (2000) 'On Measuring Household Food Vulnerability: Case Evidence from Northern Mali', Department of Applied Economics and Management, Cornell University.

Cogneau, D. and A. Robilliard (2000) 'Growth, Distribution and Poverty in Madagascar: Learning from a Microsimulation Model in a General Equilibrium Framework', Washington DC, IFPRI, Trade and Macroeconomics Division.

Cornia, G.A., R. Jolly and F. Stewart (1987) *Adjustment with a Human Face*, Oxford: Clarendon Press for the United Nations Children's Fund.

Deaton, A. (1997) *The Analysis of Household Surveys: A Microeconometric Approach to Development Policy*, Baltimore and London, John Hopkins University Press for the World Bank.

Deaton, A. and F. Grimard (1992) 'Demand Analysis for Tax Reform in Pakistan', LSMS Working Paper 85, Washington DC: World Bank.

Decaluwe, B., A. Patry, L. Savard and E. Thorbecke (1999), 'Poverty Analysis Within a General Equilibrium Framework', Working Paper 9909, CREFA 99–106, University of Laval.

Demery, L., B. Sen and T. Vishwanath (1995) 'Poverty, Inequality and Growth', ESP Discussion Paper series 70, World Bank, Washington DC.

Dercon, S. (2000) 'The Impact of Economic Reforms on Households in Rural Ethiopia 1989–1995', Centre for the Study of African Economies, Oxford University.

Glewwe, P. and G. Hall (1998) 'Are Some Groups More Vulnerable to Macroeconomic Shocks than Others? Hypothesis Tests on Panel Data from Peru', *Journal of Development Economics* 56: 181–206.

Haggblade, S., P. Hazell, *et al.* (1989) 'Farm–Nonfarm Linkages in Rural Sub-Saharan Africa', *World Development*, 17(8): 1173–1201.

Hazell, P.B.R. and S. Haggblade (1991) 'Rural–Urban Growth Linkages in India', *Indian Journal of Agricultural Economics* 46(4, October–December): 515–529.

Hazell, P.B.R. and B. Hojjati (1995) 'Farm/Non-farm Growth Linkages in Zambia', *Journal of African Economies* 4(3): 406–435.

Hoddinott, J., T. Owens, *et al.* (1999) 'Revisiting Forever Gained: Income Dynamics in the Resettlement Areas of Zimbabwe, 1983–1997', Centre for the Study of African Economies, Oxford.

Jalan, J. and M. Ravallion (1999) 'Are the Poor Less Well Insured? Evidence on Vulnerability to Income Risk in Rural China', *Journal of Development Economics* 58(1): 61–81.

Jalan, J. and M. Ravallion (2000) 'Is Transient Poverty Different? Evidence from Rural China', *Journal of Development Studies*, 36(6): 82–99.

Justino, A.P. and J.A. Litchfield (2002) 'Poverty Dynamics in Vietnam: Winners and Losers during Reform', PRUS Working Paper No. 10, University of Sussex.

Kanbur, R. (2001) 'Economic Policy, Distribution and Poverty: the Nature of the Disagreements', *World Development* 29 (6): 1083–1094.

Kanbur, R., R. Chambers, *et al.* (2001) 'Qualitative and Quantitative Poverty Assessment: Complementarities, Tensions and the Way Forward', New York, Cornell University.

Lofgren, H. and S. Robinson (1999) 'Non-separable Farm Household Decisions in a Computable General Equilibrium Model', *American Journal of Agricultural Economics*, 81(3): 663–670.

Matusz, S.J. and D. Tarr (1999) 'Adjusting to Trade Policy Reform', World Bank Working Paper 2142.

McCulloch, N. and B. Baulch (2000) 'Simulating the Impact of Policy upon Chronic and Transitory Poverty in Rural Pakistan', *Journal of Development Studies* 36(6): 100–130.

McCulloch, N. and M. Calandrino (2003) 'Vulnerability and Chronic Poverty in Rural Sichuan', *World Development*, 31(3): 611–628.

McCulloch, N., Winters, L.A. and Cirera, X. (2001) 'Trade Liberalisation and Poverty: A Handbook', Centre for Economic Policy Research, London.

Minot, N. and F. Goletti (2000) 'Rice Market Liberalization and Poverty in Viet Nam', IFPRI Research Report 114, IFPRI, Washington DC.

Mundlak, Y. (1963) 'Estimation of Production and Behavioural Functions from a Combination of Cross-section and Time-series Data', in Carl F. Christ (ed.) *Measurement in Economics: Studies in Mathematical Economics and Econometrics in Memory of Yehuda Grunfeld*, Palo Alto, CA: Stanford University Press.

Narayan, D., R. Chambers, *et al.* (2000) *Voices of the Poor: Crying out for Change*, New York, Oxford University Press for the World Bank.

Nicita, A. (2004) 'Efficiency and Equity of a Marginal Tax Reform: Income, Quality and Price Elasticities for Mexico', World Bank Working Paper 3266.

Nicita, A., M. Olarreaga and I. Soloaga (2002) 'A Simple Methodology to Assess the Poverty Impact of Economic Policies using Household Data, an Application to Cambodia', Washington, DC: World Bank.

Niimi Y., P. Vasudeva-Dutta and L.A. Winters (2002) 'Trade Liberalisation and Poverty Dynamics in Vietnam', paper presented at Globalisation, (In)Equality, and Regionalism Conference at the University of Warwick, 15–17 March 15-17, 2002 (Chapter 2 of this volume).

Pritchett, L., A. Suryhadi, *et al.* (2000) 'Quantifying Vulnerability to Poverty: A Proposed Measure with Application to Indonesia', Washington DC, World Bank.

Reimer, J.J. (2002) 'Estimating the Poverty Impacts of Trade Liberalization', Policy Research Working Paper 2790, World Bank.

Republic of Yemen (2002) *Diagnostic Trade Integration Study*, Component Reports Chapter 6, Ministry of Industry and Trade.

Rich, K. and M. Lundberg (2002) 'Multimarket Models and Policy Analysis: an Application to Malawi', Personal Communication.

Robilliard, A., F. Bourguignon, *et al.* (2001) 'Crisis and Income Distribution: A Macro–Micro Model for Indonesia', International Food Policy Research Institute, Paper prepared for the ESRC Development Economics/International Economics Conference, Nottingham University, 5–7 April 2001.

Sahn, D.E. and D.C. Stifel (2000) 'Poverty Comparisons over Time and Across Countries in Africa', *World Development*, 28(12): 2123–55.

Singh I., L. Squire and J. Strauss (1986) *Agricultural Household Models: Extensions and Applications*, Baltimore, MD, Johns Hopkins University Press.

Walker, T. and J. Ryan (1990) *Village and Household Economies in India's Semi Arid Tropics*, Baltimore, Johns Hopkins.

Winters, L.A. (2002a) 'Trade liberalisation and Poverty: What are the Links?' *World Economy*, 25(9): 133913–1367.

Winters, L.A. (2002b) 'Trade Liberalisation and Poverty: Two Partial Empirical Studies', Mimeo, University of Sussex, Brighton.

World Bank (2001a) *Diagnostic Trade Integration Study for Madagascar*, Volume 1, Washington, DC: World Bank.

World Bank (2001b) *Attacking Poverty*, World Development Report 2000/2001, Washington, DC: World Bank.

Annex: The basic methodology

The basic methodology draws on the approach of Nicita, Olarreaga and Soloaga (2002) in their study of the impact of trade reform in Cambodia. Let the income Y of a household be given by:

$$Y = \left(\sum_j p_j^O q_j^O - \sum_k p_k^I q_k^I\right) + \sum_f w_f L_f + \sum_m \sum_n T_{mn} \tag{1A.1}$$

where p_j^O is the price of output j, q_j^O is the quantity of output j; p_k^I and q_k^I are the corresponding input prices and quantities; w_f is the wage rate for factor f; L_f is the net sale of factor f by the household; and T_{mn} is the net transfer received by household member n from source m.

Note that the first term in equation (1A.1) is the value-added of all production (whether from farming or non-farm enterprises). This includes both marketed production and own consumption. The second term is the value of net factor sales by the household – in the case of most poor households this simply means net labour sales (i.e. employment income minus payments for hired labour) since the only factor which most poor households can sell is their own labour. The final term represents the net transfers received by the household.

Similarly we can write the consumption of the household simply as:

$$C = \sum_i p_i^C q_i^C \tag{1A.2}$$

where p_i^C is the buying price of good i and q_i^C is the quantity consumed of good i. Note that q_i^C includes own consumption as well as goods purchased from the market.

It is then possible to simulate the impact on household income of price changes induced by structural reforms. In the short run we can assume that all quantities remain fixed so that

$$\Delta Y = \left(\sum_j \Delta p_j^O . q_j^O - \sum_k \Delta p_k^I . q_k^I \right) + \sum_f \Delta w_f . L_f + \sum_m \sum_n \Delta T_{mn} \quad (1A.3)$$

Similarly the change in consumption assuming that quantities remain fixed is

$$\Delta C = \sum_i \Delta p_i^C . q_i^C \quad (1A.4)$$

It is possible to show that a first-order approximation of the change in money metric utility resulting from a change in the price of a commodity can be given by[1]

$$\Delta MMU = \Delta Y - \Delta C \quad (1A.5)$$

This makes intuitive sense: an increase (say) in the price of a good which is both produced and consumed will increase income and also increase the cost of achieving the original level of consumption – the difference between these is therefore an approximation to the welfare change.

Note that we can combine equations (1A.1), (1A.2), (1A.3) and (1A.4) to write equation (1A.6):

$$\frac{\Delta MMU}{Y} = \left(\sum_j BS_j^O \frac{\Delta p_j^O}{p_j^O} - \sum_k BS_k^I \frac{\Delta p_k^I}{p_k^I} \right) \quad (1A.6)$$
$$+ \sum_f BS_f^w \frac{\Delta w_f}{w_f} + \frac{\sum_m \sum_n \Delta T_{mn}}{Y} - \sum_i BS_j^C \frac{\Delta p_j^C}{p_j^C}$$

where BS_j^O indicates the budget (or income) share of output revenue in total income, BS_j^I is the budget share of input costs, BS_j^w is the income share of net factor income from factor f, and BS_j^C is the budget share of good j in consumption. Thus the first-order percentage change in net income can be approximated by the budget shares of income and expenditure on each item times the percentage changes in prices experienced.[2]

Notes

1 See Chen and Ravallion (2004) for an exposition of the theory.
2 See Minot and Goletti (2000) Appendix 2 for a full derivation.

2 Linking trade liberalisation and poverty

An illustration from Vietnam in the 1990s

Yoko Niimi, Puja Vasudeva-Dutta and L. Alan Winters

Introduction

Winters (2002) provides a conceptual framework with which to trace the links between trade shocks, including trade liberalisation, and household poverty. The Winters framework is predicated on the view that, while in the long run the critical causal link is economic growth, in the short run one needs to consider links via the product and labour markets and government revenue, considering both short-term adjustment issues and medium-term secular changes. The framework has figured in several subsequent discussions of trade and poverty but has so far received virtually no formal empirical application and testing. Although it is difficult to isolate the effects of trade shocks from those of other shocks and to attribute changes in the economy solely to trade liberalisation, this chapter addresses this absence.

Since the start of the *doi moi* reforms in 1986 the Vietnamese economy has been undergoing a gradual transition from a centrally planned socialist to a market-oriented economy. While the process is certainly not complete – see, for example, van Donge, White and Nghia (1999) – the transition has been accompanied by high growth, macroeconomic stability, significant structural change and a general improvement in the standard of living (Niimi *et al.*, 2003). This chapter aims to identify the international trade reforms that have occurred and plot their transmission through to poor households.

The chapter comprises five further sections. First we explain the analytical framework and then we review the major external sector reforms undertaken in Vietnam during the 1990s. The main mechanisms through which these macro reforms impact households – the price and labour market channels – are analysed in section 4. In particular we explore the consequences of the trade changes for net labour demand in a standard factor content of trade analysis. Section 5 explores the production link between trade liberalisation and poverty using household survey data, estimating a multinomial logit model of the transition between poverty and non-poverty. The household survey data come from the Vietnam Living Standard Measurement Surveys (VLSS) and refer to the years 1992–93 and 1997–98. For consistency we focus on these years throughout. Section 6 concludes.

Trade liberalisation and poverty: a theoretical framework[1]

Winters (2002) develops a framework for exploring the links between trade shocks and poverty[2] by considering its effect on the prices of tradable goods and thence to changes in household and individual welfare. The key tool of analysis is the so-called 'farm household' – a household which potentially makes production as well as employment and consumption decisions. Economic growth is the critical causal link between openness and poverty alleviation in the long run, and there is a strong presumption that liberalisation results in higher growth (see Winters, 2004) and that economic growth relieves poverty (Dollar and Kraay, 2001). In the medium and short term, however, static effects are also important. These are explored via their direct effects on product and factor markets, and indirectly through changes in government revenues and social spending, all of which have implications for poor households. In addition, there is usually a short-term adjustment period before the long-term gains from trade are realised. Unfortunately, such adjustment problems cannot be examined separately from more permanent static effects given that our data contain only two observations per household. We therefore concentrate our analysis on the following two channels, namely price and employment effects.

Lowering tariff barriers will normally reduce the price of importables in the domestic market, while export liberalisation will raise those of exportables. The effect of a price change on a household's welfare depends on its net supply position: an increase in the price of something of which it is a net seller (labour, good, service) will increase its welfare, while a decrease will reduce it. The strength of this effect will depend on the transmission of the price change from the border to the household via the distribution channels. It will also depend on the household's ability to adjust to the new prices. In addition to changing prices, trade liberalisation can both create and destroy markets. A drastic fall into poverty is often associated with the disappearance of a market while rapid escapes are associated with the creation of markets for previously non-traded goods.

The other major channel through which foreign shocks are transmitted to poverty is through factor markets. The changes in product prices that accompany trade reform could lead to changes in the composition of output, and hence in the bundle of factors used in production. Presuming that the poor have only their labour to sell, the focus for poverty studies is usually on unskilled labour and wages. There are two ways that trade-induced changes in the factor market can alter the labour income of households – through employment changes or through wage changes.

If the labour supply is taken as fixed (as in traditional trade theory), then changes in demand will result in changes in wages. On the other hand, if the labour supply is perfectly flexible then factor market changes would result in changes in employment. Whether these increases reduce poverty depends on whether the poor are heavily dependant on the type of labour for which demand has risen and (for head-count poverty indices) on whether the changes move families from one side of the boundary to the other.

Economic reform and trade liberalisation in Vietnam[3]

The process of 'economic renovation' or *doi moi* was set in motion in 1986 and gathered momentum in the early 1990s with the objective of transforming Vietnam from a centrally planned to a market economy. The institutional reforms during this period included the encouragement of the private sector and establishment of legal basis for contract, banking and financial sector reforms, taxation reforms, establishment of economic courts, the consolidation of property rights, land reform, and the rationalisation of state-owned enterprises (SOEs).

External sector reform

An important facet of the renovation process was the dramatic change in external sector policy from inward-oriented import substitution to outward-orientation. Vietnam's major external sector reforms included:

- The removal of constraints on trade outside the CMEA bloc:[4] by 1993 all foreign transactions were in convertible currency;
- The rationalisation and unification of the exchange rate in 1989 and further liberalisation of foreign exchange controls;
- The relaxation of import and export controls and a move towards a tariff-based system of trade management;
- Export promotion and the establishment of export processing zones;
- The relaxation of controls on entry into foreign trading activity and the simplification and eventual elimination in 1998 of the licensing procedure;
- The initiation of an 'open door policy' to promote foreign investment and the creation of a legal framework to approve and regulate foreign direct investment (FDI); and
- Integration with the world economy via regional and multilateral trading agreements.

Despite these reforms the maximum and average tariff rates (especially on consumer goods) have remained high to date, and although the average tariff rates do not seem out of line with those in other developing countries, most of the items imported are in the high tariff bracket (between 30 per cent and 60 per cent). In addition, there have been several retrogressive measures in the form of rising export taxes, temporary prohibitions on imports of consumer goods, and other barriers introduced as anti-smuggling measures. Overall, both the import tariff and export tax systems are complex and suffer from frequent changes (CIEM, 2001), so that despite all the reforms, Vietnam's trade regime must be considered to remain quite restrictive and interventionist (IMF, 1999).

The complexity of Vietnam's trade policy regime makes it very difficult to trace the effects of tariff and other policy changes on households and for this chapter we are thrown back on analysing outcomes – prices and quantities – rather than policies directly, in order to identify the impact of trade liberalisation. Measures such as the openness of the Vietnamese economy have changed quite dramatically over the 1990s, so there is a reasonable presumption that the external sector will have had significant effects on poverty and that many changes in policy noted above have influenced the outcomes significantly.

In what follows we clearly identify significant trade effects and it is perfectly reasonable to assume that at least a significant proportion of the trade shock originated in trade policy changes.

Macroeconomic outcomes

Despite their incompleteness, the impact of the reforms on the Vietnamese economy has been tremendous. The economy grew at approximately 7–8 per cent p.a. between 1990 and 2000 and over 5 per cent even following the Asian crisis in 1997. Firm domestic credit policies, tight monetary policies and interest rate reforms stabilised the hyperinflation of the 1980s. The exchange rate has remained relatively stable after the rationalisation of the multiple exchange rate system and successive devaluations (CIE, 1998). Vietnam's 'open door' policy in 1987 led to large FDI inflows averaging 9 per cent p.a. of GDP between 1993 and 1997, though this declined after the 1997 Asian crisis. The data on FDI are weak, but the broad picture is that there is a distinct import-substitution bias and that the employment impact of these enterprises is low – the average FDI project in 1998 employed just 112 workers (IMF, 1999).

The share of trade in GDP increased from about 52 per cent to 71 per cent between 1993 and 1998 (GSO statistics).[5] Exports grew strongly for a number of commodities in which Vietnam apparently has a comparative advantage:[6] the share of agriculture, forestry and fisheries in exports fell steadily, being off-set by an increase in that of handicrafts and light industrial goods (IMF, 1998, 2000). By 2000 the combined exports of the textile and garments industry and the footwear industry were higher than those of the four chief agricultural exports – rice, coffee, rubber and marine products (CIEM, 2001). One of the most dramatic changes was in the opposite direction, however: pre-*doi moi* Vietnam was a net importer of rice, but by 1996 she was the world's second largest exporter of rice by volume (Nielsen, 2002b), see below.

Imports continued to be dominated by machinery and intermediate goods (amounting to approximately 70 per cent of total imports), reflecting both the industrialisation of the Vietnamese economy and the structure of protection with a bias against imports of consumer goods (IMF, 1998, 2000).

Since it figures prominently in the subsequent analysis, we consider briefly, here, the rice market, see Niimi *et al.* (2004) for more detail. Institutional reform in agriculture, domestic price liberalisation coupled with general and rice-specific trade reforms resulted in increased domestic rice production and exports and rising rice prices accompanied by falling fertiliser prices (Nielsen, 2002b). It is difficult to divide credit for the improvement in the rice economy precisely between the domestic and the trade policy reforms. However, while the domestic reforms clearly impinged on farmers more directly than did the trade reforms, it was the latter that allowed Vietnam to operate in world markets and hence see both prices and quantities increasing so strongly.

To summarise, the *doi moi* economic reforms generated high growth during the 1990s characterised by increasing exports and foreign investment, expanding private sector as well as state enterprise activity, and declining inflation. The relatively egalitarian distribution of land, the stress on agriculture and the subsequent high growth of the economy suggest that the restructuring of the economy might have had a favourable impact on the poor in Vietnam. Glewwe *et al.* (2000) find that, based on the World Bank poverty line, absolute poverty incidence declined from 58.1 per cent to 37.4 per cent between 1992–93 and 1997–98.[7] The next section attempts to trace the channels through which the trade reforms might impact poor households using the Winters framework sketched in Section 2.

Trade liberalisation and poverty: an empirical application

We analyse the mechanisms through which these macro-level reforms impact households by applying the Winters framework to the Vietnamese economy, focusing on the period between 1992–93 and 1997–98. A five-year period is not long enough to distinguish between the various contributors to economic growth so we focus on the first two static effects – prices and labour markets.

The price channel

Given the remarkable development of Vietnam's export sector and import liberalisation during this period, we would expect to observe significant changes in the prices of some tradable commodities. Data on proportionate changes in the real retail prices of selected consumer goods and services (from GSO statistics) confirm this and reveal that Vietnam's leading export products such as rice and marine products saw relatively higher price increases during this period than did other products.[8] Rice is extremely important, being the most important single source of income for the majority of Vietnamese households and accounting for about 30 per cent of household income in 1998 (World Bank, 1999). Rice prices rose by 21–26 per cent for different types of rice. Although price data are not available for coffee, which was another leading export commodity in Vietnam over our sample, secondary sources – e.g. Minot (1998) – suggest a favourable effect of liberalisation-induced price changes on producers. It is not possible to insist that these various price increases were due solely to trade liberalisation, but there seems very likely to be a strong trade component.

In contrast to their benefits for producers, price increases, especially of rice, will hurt net consumers. We calculate that in 1992–93, rice accounted for 44 per cent of total food expenditure, and Minot and Goletti (1998) find that it comprises about 75 per cent of the total calorific intake of the typical Vietnamese household. The analysis in this chapter does not allow us to identify adequately the differential effect of rice price increases depending on household consumption patterns,[9] but in Niimi *et al.* (2004) we find that they make little difference.[10]

Employment and wages

In order to assess the impact of trade liberalisation on the labour market, in this section we analyse the trends in employment and wages in Vietnam. In the next, we explore how trade shocks have been transmitted through the labour market. Although the impact of trade reforms via the labour channel is expected to be limited because the bulk of the labour force in Vietnam is self-employed (Gallup, 2002), it is still of sufficient potential interest to warrant attention.

The *doi moi* reforms had a substantial impact on the sectoral composition of output growth. The industrial and services sectors grew rapidly, outpacing the growth in the agricultural sector during the 1990s. Despite the high output growth, however, total employment apparently grew by only about 2–3 per cent in this entire period (IMF, 1998, 2000) and was characterised by the absence of job creation in the industrial sector despite its being the fastest growing sector (MOLISA statistics provided by CIEM).[11] Probably related is the fact that the state sector is still predominant in the Vietnamese economy, especially in the industrial and services sectors. Despite the large output share at around 40 per cent of the GDP (GSO statistics), the share of the state sector in total employment is only about 10 per cent.[12] Both unemployment and underemployment in urban and rural areas declined until the Asian crisis hit Vietnam in 1997, reaching about 6.9 per cent and 1.4 per cent respectively in 1998, although with considerable regional variations (CIEM, 2000; World Bank, 1999).[13] Estimates from the VLSS data reveal that wage employment expanded marginally from 24 per cent to 25 per cent of the labour force between 1993 and 1998 (Gallup, 2002).

There is some disagreement about wage movements given the paucity of wage data. Chandrasiri and de Silva (1996) use ILO data to argue that real wages fell following liberalisation, while the IMF (1998, 2000) seems to suggest that real earnings (broader concept including perks etc.) increased strongly. The VLSS data indicate that real hourly earnings grew rapidly at about 10.5 per cent p.a. between 1993 and 1998. There are wide regional differences, however, with Ho Chi Minh City and Hanoi having higher earnings and experiencing faster growth in earnings (Gallup, 2002).

There are considerable earning differentials by sector of employment, education, and region (Chandrasiri and de Silva, 1996; O'Connor, 1996). Although minimum wage levels have been prescribed for both domestic and foreign-invested enterprises, average unskilled wages are about three times higher than the minimum in all forms of employment, and exceed the minimum even in small household enterprises (Belser, 2000).

The trade–labour link

This section tries to identify the significance of the trade–labour link. We use mirror statistics from the UN Comtrade system[14,15] in order to identify industries that showed the biggest absolute increase in export and import flows between 1993 and 1998 at the Standard International Trade Classification (SITC-R2) 2-digit level.[16] Light industrial products such as footwear, garments and electrical parts, and primary commodities including rice, coffee, seafood and petroleum are the main export growth commodities, while imports are dominated by capital and intermediate products. This seems to accord with a factor endowment view of comparative advantage.

For such changes in trade patterns to have a positive poverty impact, however, they must actually be reflected in the labour market. We start by calculating the consequences of the trade changes for net labour demand in a standard factor content of trade analysis.[17] This takes as given the input structure of Vietnamese industries and assumes that every unit of exports generates demand for the average input bundle of its producing industry and that every unit of imports displaces a unit of demand for domestic output and thus eliminates demand for the average bundle of inputs. This is far from a convincing way of looking at the economy as we discuss below, but it does at least aggregate information from the whole vector of trade flows. We use both direct labour coefficients, which is appropriate if all intermediate goods are imported (as, for example, assumed by effective protection exercises), and total labour coefficients based on the whole of the input–output table which would be appropriate if no intermediates were imported. Because it disaggregates labour-inputs by skill (low/medium/high skills), we conduct this accounting exercise on the 1997 Social Accounting Matrix (SAM) reported in Nielsen (2002a).[18] This is similar to the official SAM for 1996 (from GSO), but incorporates changes in structure as well as the desired more detailed factor break-down.

The first task is to create vectors of exports and imports corresponding to the I–O table's 97-sector classification.[19] As we found ourselves unable to replicate the trade data in the SAM, even allowing for our restricted set of partner countries, we conduct the exercise on two sets of data: those using our own mapping (which we refer to as unadjusted – set B below) and also adjusting our data to reflect, so far as possible, those of the SAM (set A). The latter applies growth factors over 1993 and 1998 derived from our mapping to the levels of exports and imports given in the SAM. We first calculate:

$$f_i = x_i^{\mathrm{SAM}}/x_i^{\mathrm{NVW}}$$

from the 1997 data, in which i refers to sector, x_i^{SAM} is the export of i reported in the SAM, and x_i^{NVW} is our unadjusted export data for sector i. Thus f_i reflects not only differences due to commodity mappings, but also due to our narrower partner country coverage, the treatment of the cif-fob adjustment, and any other SAM manipulations.

Given f_i, we calculate the 1993 and 1998 adjusted data as:

$$x_i^{\mathrm{ADJ}}(t) = f_i^* x_i^{NVW}(t) \qquad t = 1993, 1998$$

A similar procedure is followed for imports.

Trade policy affects the size and composition of export and import flows not, in the long run, their net balance. Hence to reflect its effects on labour demand, it is

Table 2.1 Labour demand per $1 of trade, 1993, 1998 direct labour coefficients

	EX93	IM93	NET93	EX98	IM98	NET98	NET93-98
(A) Direct labour coefficients (direct labour demand per $1 of trade). Adjusted data.							
Unskilled	0.1415	0.0859	0.0556	0.1270	0.1009	0.0261	−0.0295
Medium-skilled	0.0285	0.0330	−0.0045	0.0275	0.0313	−0.0038	0.0007
Highly-skilled	0.0015	0.0027	−0.0012	0.0015	0.0027	−0.0012	0.0000
Total	0.1715	0.1216	0.0499	0.1560	0.1349	0.0211	−0.0288
(B) Direct labour coefficients (direct labour demand per $1 of trade). Unadjusted data.							
Unskilled	0.1249	0.0801	0.0448	0.1251	0.0854	0.0397	−0.0051
Medium-skilled	0.0348	0.0312	0.0036	0.0392	0.0319	0.0073	0.0037
Highly-skilled	0.0018	0.0028	−0.0010	0.0020	0.0028	−0.0008	0.0002
Total	0.1615	0.1141	0.0474	0.1663	0.1201	0.0462	−0.0012
(C) Total labour coefficients (total labour demand per $1 of trade). Adjusted data.							
Unskilled	0.3950	0.3424	0.0526	0.4263	0.3814	0.0449	−0.0077
Medium-skilled	0.0937	0.1095	−0.0158	0.0987	0.1145	−0.0158	0.0000
Highly-skilled	0.0137	0.0127	0.0010	0.0137	0.0134	0.0003	−0.0007
Total	0.5024	0.4646	0.0378	0.5387	0.5093	0.0294	−0.0084
(D) Total labour coefficients (total labour demand per $1 of trade). Unadjusted data.							
Unskilled	0.3665	0.3899	−0.0234	0.4046	0.4090	−0.0044	0.0190
Medium-skilled	0.1004	0.1245	−0.0241	0.1156	0.1278	−0.0122	0.0119
Highly-skilled	0.0147	0.0147	0.0000	0.0145	0.0151	−0.0006	−0.0006
Total	0.4816	0.5291	-0.0475	0.5347	0.5519	-0.0172	0.0303

Source: Calculations based on the SAM 1997.

best to normalise the data in order to calculate the factor demands of, say, a typical $1 of exports and a typical $1 of imports. Since average wage data (required to convert incomes into employment) are unavailable we leave the current exercise in terms of labour incomes.

Table 2.1 part A reports the direct labour requirements for producing $1 worth of exports spread across sectors in the proportions observed in total exports, and for replacing $1 worth of imports (allocated as in the total) in 1993 and 1998. Direct labour coefficients assume that labour demand increases only in the final producing sector of an export, the material inputs it requires being imported. This is not an inappropriate assumption for Vietnam's manufacturing exports, since cloth for garments and parts for electronics are substantially imported (electrical and electronic machinery and parts (SITC (2R) 77) shows the fifth largest increase in exports and the second largest in imports). Thus, column 1 of block A shows that in 1993 a dollar of visible exports with the composition predicted by our adjusted export vector would generate 17c. of labour income, with the lion's share going to unskilled workers. Unfortunately we cannot distinguish male and female workers, but the latter are known to be very important to garment exporting. Interestingly displacing a typical dollar of imports also appears to make large demands on un-skilled labour (column 2). This reflects the relatively high reported inputs of the latter into machinery and instrument production – presumably assembly opera-tions. Of course, the bundle of goods produced in Vietnam under the heading, say, informatics, is actually quite different from that imported, so the comparison is flawed. Vietnam could not replace many of the imported inputs domestically at any price and one actually might think of them better as non-competing imports that boost employment, rather than competing ones that erode it. We return to this below. Continuing with the model for now, however, the net effect (column 3) is that a balanced increase of $1 in both exports and imports – theoretically the consequence of trade liberalisation – would, in 1993, have increased the demand for labour by about 5c.

Columns 4–6 of Table 2.1 repeat the exercise for $1-worth of 1998 exports and imports. The export bundle has become less labour intensive since 1993, while the import bundle has become more so. Together they imply that by 1998 a balanced increase in trade would increase employment incomes by only 2c.

This decrease in the apparent net employment effects of trade is potentially rather alarming, for Vietnam remains a very poor and labour abundant country. It is largely due, however, to changes in trade in the category 'other crops n.e.s.' which is very highly unskilled-labour-intensive in Vietnam, but subject to some data concerns. Our crude data record its share of visible exports falling from 6.0 per cent in 1993 to 2.7 per cent in 1998, but since we underestimate its share in 1997 relative to the SAM by over 100 per cent, these shares translate into 12.3 per cent and 6.4 per cent respectively in the adjusted exports series. The adjusted import share, on the other hand, increases from 4.8 per cent to 7.2 per cent. Thus this one sector accounts for a decline of 3.7c. in the demand for unskilled labour, while changes in all other sectors increase demand by about 0.7c.

Turning to block B, our unadjusted data suggest similar net trade effects for unskilled labour in 1993, and also positive net effects for the semi-skilled. More interestingly, however, they hardly change by 1998, suggesting that trade continues to have strong pro-labour effects.

Jenkins (2002) also presents a factor content exercise for manufacturing in Vietnam in 1998. He uses UNIDO production data and an alternative series of mirror trade statistics to derive jobs per $1 million of trade: 213.6 for exports as opposed to 96.0 for imports. The differences between his estimates and ours partly reflect the lower wages paid in export industries than import industries (about 12 per cent lower when UNIDO's implied wages are averaged over the 1998 vectors of manufactured trade). In the main, however, they lie in the different labour and labour income coefficients implied by the SAM and the UNIDO data. The SAM's labour shares are, on average, 30 per cent higher, which may indicate a conceptual

Table 2.2 The effects of actual trade on employment income

	1993	*1998*
Aggregate trade flows ($millions)		
Exports	2985	9360
Imports	3924	11499
Net	−939	−2139
Labour income – direct coefficients ($millions)		
From exports	512	1460
From imports	477	1551
Net	35	−91
Labour income – total coefficients ($millions)		
From exports	1500	5042
From imports	1823	5856
Net	−323	−814

Source: Calculations based on the SAM 1997.

difference, but the striking statistic is the correlation between the two labour shares series which, over the manufacturing sectors they have in common, is only 0.19. This seems low, even given the difficulties of matching the classifications. It is not clear a priori which source is correct, so this remains a job for further research.

Blocks C and D of Table 2.1 repeat the factor content exercise but with total labour coefficients constructed on the (questionable) assumption that no extra intermediates are imported when a sector increases its exports. The adjusted data continue to suggest that exports are more labour intensive than imports and that their unskilled labour intensity has increased. The unadjusted data suggest that imports are more labour intensive, but decreasingly so, so that the change through time has been benign.

Table 2.2 combines the 'per-dollar' coefficients reported in Table 2.1 with the aggregate visible trade data to estimate the actual impact of trade on employment income. As noted above, however, these aggregates reflect macro-economic factors more than trade-policy ones. The table suggests that, if the model is to be believed, the rapid growth of imports has destroyed more jobs than the export boom has created. As we noted above, however, for a low-income economy many imports are likely to be complementary and hence employment enhancing (even if not extremely labour-intensive).

Modelling complementary imports is a difficult task in the absence of detailed sectoral case studies. However, it is not difficult to imagine imported inputs being essential to their user industries. This is especially true for the two largest import growth sectors – textiles and electrical parts – for which we have anecdotal evidence on the user industries, but also for the others such as machinery, iron and steel and plastic sectors – for which imports supply very large shares of apparent consumption. To explore the possibilities that these imports are (partly) employment generating, we consider the following informal experiments.

First, it is not an uncommon complaint that Vietnam's exports are imported-input intensive. Taking this at face value, our estimated increase of $807 million in exports of clothing between 1993 and 1998, for example, calls for $311 million of inputs of fibres and cloth (via an input–output coefficient of 0.385). Of these, applying an average import intensity of 0.36 would imply that $112 million of the imports of textiles (25 per cent) is explained by this industry alone. Generalising this calculation to other sectors, assuming that all exports have their sector's average imported-input intensities, the direct input requirements of the increase in exports between 1993 and 1998 accounts for $1.07 billion (14 per cent) of the increase in imports. If we took the use of direct labour-input coefficients seriously and assumed that all additional material inputs were imported this would increase to $3.58 billion (47 per cent of the total).

Second, one might recognise that imports are necessary to the growth of all output, including that directed toward the booming domestic market. We can then explore how many jobs the imports would support if they relaxed the critical constraint on output. We define as 'critical' those inputs for which imports provide a major share of total use and which make a significant contribution to other activities' gross output. Table 2.3 considers the five largest import growth commodities (i) and asks in which sectors (j) they constitute more than 20 per cent of all inputs or more than 40 per cent of material inputs; writing z_{ij} for the value of input i into sector j, that is sectors for which $z_{ij}/\sum_m z_{mj} \geq 0.2$ if m counts across all inputs, or ≥ 0.4 if m refers only to material inputs. For these sectors it then calculates their access to additional imports if the increase in imports is spread among uses according to the corresponding row of the SAM ($= \Delta m_i z_{ij}/\sum_l z_{il}$), where Δm_i is the increase in imports and l includes final demand as well as intermediate demand.[20] It finally calculates the labour income in sector j associated with a unit of input of $i (= w_{kj}/z_{ij})$, where w_{kj} is activity j's total payment to labour of type k, and then takes the product of these three terms to derive the change in labour income k from industry j that is supported by a relaxation of a constraint on input i by Δm_i:

$$\Delta L^{kij} = \frac{w_{kj}}{z_{ij}} \frac{z_{ij}}{\sum_l z_{il}} \Delta m_i$$

Clearly this is all very heuristic and depends crucially on the assumption that these major inputs are the binding constraints on output. Nevertheless, Table 2.3 suggests significant additional incomes especially for unskilled labour and especially from fertiliser imports. It is clearly implausible to argue that both export demand and import supply have had only employment-creating effects, but this discussion does suggest how imports may have increased labour income.

Whatever we believe about job or income creation, translating these results into poverty impacts is not straightforward. Even assuming that employment levels were unchanged and that all the changes in demand were converted into wages changes, the net effects would depend on household composition. However, in

Table 2.3 Major imported inputs

i: input sectors	j: user sectors	Imports/apparent consumption	Change in imports (US$m)	$z_{ij}/\sum_i z_{il}$	$z_{ij}/\sum_m z_{mj}$ materials	$z_{ij}/\sum_m z_{mj}$ all inputs	Labour income increase (US$m) unskilled	medium skilled	highly skilled
61 Fibres, thread and weaving cloths	61 Fibres, thread and weaving cloths	0.36	449.84	0.17	0.57	0.34	26.60	5.72	0.16
	62 Ready-made clothes, sheets	0.36	449.84	0.49	0.65	0.40	48.61	17.84	0.62
60 Ferrous metals and products, except machinery and equipment	57 Electrical machinery	0.63	392.68	0.09	0.36	0.23	10.54	6.03	0.62
	60 Ferrous metals and products, except machinery and equipment	0.63	392.68	0.10	0.53	0.30	18.77	6.70	0.50
58 Machinery and equipment used for broadcasting, television and information technology	58 Machinery and equipment used for broadcasting, television and information technology	0.58	318.69	0.17	0.74	0.46	10.26	5.87	0.60
46 Plastics	47 Other plastic products	0.84	256.37	0.32	0.42	0.30	6.74	2.23	0.31
41 Fertiliser	1 Paddy	0.79	202.21	0.63	0.49	0.18	304.63	19.91	0.66
	3 Coffee beans	0.79	202.21	0.09	0.73	0.31	19.45	1.27	0.04
	5 Other crops	0.79	202.21	0.17	0.49	0.11	191.85	12.51	0.42

Source: Calculations based on the SAM 1997.

fact it is likely that some of these changes would be reflected in employment (see Winters, 2002), whereupon it becomes important to know not only household composition, but also the relative sizes of wages and the poverty line and the wages that workers earned before taking these 'trade-related' jobs or after losing them. Overall, however, we would argue that these data tend to suggest that trade changes have contributed positively to real wage increases or wage bill increases in Vietnam.

Econometric analysis of household poverty[21]

This section tests whether the observable liberalisation-induced changes identified above have contributed to poverty alleviation using the formal analysis of household data by means of a multinomial logit model. Specifically we ask whether production characteristics that would a priori dispose a household towards an escape from poverty actually do so. This is of interest per se, but also as a means of testing the operational significance of the framework provided by Winters (2002).

Multinomial logit (MNL) models analyse the probability of being in a particular state out of several unordered alternatives. We examine the poverty transition between 1992–93 and 1997–98 in terms of multiple (unordered) choices – (1) being poor in both periods (P→P), (2) starting non-poor and becoming poor (NP→P), (3) starting poor and becoming non-poor (P→NP), and (4) being non-poor in both periods (NP→NP). The MNL model requires us to define one category as a 'base' and then calculates the probabilities of an observation being in one of the other categories relative to being in the base. In most of our work outcome 1 (the household is poor in both periods) is used as base, because we are primarily concerned to see whether trade helps households to escape from poverty. The multinomial logit is most easily interpreted as giving conditional probabilities. Given that (P→P) is the base category, the coefficients for (P→NP) (outcome 3) tell us the probabilities of moving out of poverty relative to being poor in both years.

The VLSS contains two waves of data: 4,800 households in 150 communes surveyed over October 1992 to October 1993 and 6,000 households in 194 communes surveyed over December 1997 to December 1998.[22] The samples are believed to be representative and, critically, a panel of 4,302 households are identifiably surveyed in both waves. The poverty line used in this work is the official poverty line, which is based on the ability to afford a specific basket of goods designed to provide a given calorie intake, plus some non-food expenses – see World Bank (1999) or Glewwe *et al.* (2000).[23]

The modelling is related to that in Justino and Litchfield (2002b) and Glewwe *et al.* (2000), but differs from these in that we focus closely on the trade effects and explore both urban and rural populations. In addition, there are some differences in the sets of independent variables. Starting from a 'standard' demographic view of household poverty dynamics, we add a number of additional variables to reflect the trade links: rice production, coffee production, land and fertiliser use, and the ratio of household members working in the leading export industries (seafood, food processing, garments and shoes) to the number of adults in the household.[24]

Table 2.4 Odds ratios from the 'trade-related' multinomial logit model OR for escaping from poverty – i.e. for (P→NP) relative to base (P→P)

	A	B
Agricultural variables		
Quantity of rice production	***1.55	***1.75
In Mekong River Delta		**0.60
In Red River Delta		**0.85
Quantity of coffee production	***3.00	***2.31
Quantity of fertiliser – rice		***1.46
Quantity of fertiliser – non-rice		*1.70
Employment variables		
Ratio of household members working in export sectors	*1.11	***1.25
Change in the above ratio (export sectors)		**1.17
Pseudo R^2	0.26	0.27

Note: *** significant at 1% level; ** significant at 5% level; * significant at 10% level in the single equation reported. The export sector includes seafood, food processing, garments and shoes (rubber and plastic products).

Source: Calculations based on the VLSS 92–93 and VLSS 97–98.

With one exception all the variables refer to households' characteristics or activities in the initial period. This is partly to avoid problems of simultanety and partly a desire to test the conceptual framework as a predictive tool, that is, to see how well the framework would predict the effects of trade reform if it were applied ex ante using only the information available in the initial period.

The results of the 'basic' model with no trade variables, which explains poverty dynamics as a function of region, ethnicity, demography, human capital (education), occupation, health, infrastructure and seasonality, are reported in Niimi *et al.* (2003). Location, education and occupation of the household head, and infrastructure variables were among the major factors that increased the probability of escaping poverty, while belonging to a minority ethnic group and illness of the household head increased the probability of falling into poverty.

The trade effects are largely orthogonal to the 'basic' effects and so we report only the trade effects in Table 2.4. We report the results as odds ratios (OR), which give the ratio of the probability of each outcome relative to the probability of the base category, and all data have been standardised.

Our basic 'trade-inclusive' model (column A) includes among the regressors the household's initial production of rice and coffee and the proportion of workers initially holding jobs in export sectors. All have positive effects, the first two are strongly significant, both in the system as a whole (i.e., for the three equations as the system together) and in explaining just the escape from poverty, whereas the last is significant for the system as a whole and only at 10 per cent for escape from poverty alone. For example, ceteris paribus, a one standard deviation increase in a household's initial production of coffee more than doubles its chances of escaping from poverty in 1998, while a one standard deviation increase in rice output increases it by over 50 per cent. Adding these three variables to the 'basic' model increases the pseudo-R^2 of the system from 0.23 to 0.26.

Column B reports our preferred 'trade-inclusive' equation.[25] One important refinement is the regional dimension to the rice result. The production effect is weaker in the Mekong Delta than elsewhere.[26] As well as being the major producing region for rice exports, the Mekong is also characterised by larger farms and a much greater use of hired labour (Minot, 1998). Thus, as production increases, less accrues to the householder as a producer and more to the labour he hires; correspondingly, household income owes more to wages deriving from others' rice production than it does elsewhere in Vietnam. A similar, although less easily explained, attenuation is also evident in another major rice area, the Red River Delta. Once these two regional variants are permitted the rice production effect elsewhere in the country increases somewhat.

A second refinement adds variables for the initial use of fertiliser. As fertiliser prices fell heavy users could sustain material increases in real consumption – a straightforward income effect. We distinguish between rice and non-rice fertiliser effects, because the latter may reflect greater opportunities for exploiting the fall in price as farmers can switch between crops rather than just increase use for a single crop. The table shows strong positive effects from fertiliser use although non-rice use is significant only at 10 per cent.

The third major dimension of the trade liberalisation operates via the employment market. There are at least three ways of making a link between initial employment in an export sector and the escape from poverty. Existing workers could get either wage increases, or longer hours, or it may be that initial employment indicates a location close to exporting firms and hence better chances of the household obtaining more jobs as the firms expand.

In order to explore these possibilities more closely, we break our rule of using only initial values as explanatory variables, and add the change in the proportion of adults with employment in export sectors. This captures the third hypothesis above whereby an export boom generates more jobs but at constant real wages. Given the stock of workers in agriculture and the state-owned enterprises, and the relatively low skills required for most manufacturing export jobs, there is little reason to expect that new workers will be less productive than incumbents over the five years between our surveys. According to our results, incumbency does have advantages in escaping poverty (via wages or hours presumably, neither of which we can test because the data are so noisy), but so too does a household's ability to supply new workers. Methodologically the lesson here is that for predicting the poverty effects of trade liberalisation, agricultural shocks may be well captured by initial activity in the affected sector because mobility is relatively low in these sectors.[27]

For manufacturing, however, although initial employment captures some of the likely effects, some will be less predictable because mobility into manufacturing jobs is high.[28]

While the trade effects appear to be estimated sufficiently precisely to reject the hypothesis that they have arisen by chance, we also should consider their contribution to explaining poverty dynamics by asking how much better we can explain the observed outcome if we recognise the trade component. The increase in the pseudo-R^2 from 0.23 (pertaining to the unreported 'basic' model with no trade variables) to 0.27 (pertaining to our preferred 'trade-inclusive' model) suggests that trade adds a further 14 per cent to the explained variation in poverty experience but that much variation remains unexplained. The proportions of correct predictions from the model tell a similar story. The basic model classifies 59.9 per cent of households correctly, over-predicting no-change outcomes and strongly under-predicting the changes. Adding the trade variables improves the overall success rate by about 1.5 percentage points or 2.5 per cent and materially improves the predictions for escapees from poverty.

The results so far offer convincing evidence that international trade reform has affected individual household poverty dynamics in Vietnam, and that by taking it into account we are better able to predict which households prosper and which do not. This lends considerable weight to the analytical framework proposed and to the view that 'trade matters'. It does not, however, tell us directly whether trade reform reduced poverty. For that, we need to create a counterfactual – '1998 without trade reform' – and it is here that the uncertain division of responsibility between trade policy, other policies and exogenous shocks really takes its toll.

Our approach above identifies characteristics that predispose a household to escape from poverty between 1993 and 1998. They do so because they equip households to benefit from changes in their environments occurring over that period, including trade liberalisation. To calibrate the effects of trade liberalisation we suppose that these characteristics have only 'average' effects by setting the 'trade-related' coefficients to zero (the corresponding OR to unity) and recalculating the predicted changes in poverty.[29,30] For some effects, of course, the characteristic matters for reasons other then trade, so we also consider reductions of one-half in these coefficients.

If none of the trade effects had applied, about 250 fewer households (out of 4,302) would have escaped from poverty and 668 more would have been in poverty in 1998. If trade effects are set to half the estimated coefficients, the contribution of trade reform is still large – nearly 100 additional households escaping from poverty (about 10 per cent of those that did) and nearly 300 fewer households in poverty (about 10 per cent again). There are reservations about exactly how well we are capturing these effects, see Niimi *et al.* (2003), but overall these are quantitatively important effects.

The results just described allow us some confidence that we have located the effects of trade reform in the dynamics of individual households. Two caveats are in order, however. First, the trade effects included in this exercise are not exhaustive: there will be other channels through which trade has impacted poverty dynamics.

This is not a problem with the regression results, unless these other factors are correlated with our included effects. We have identified systematic effects and these will continue to exist even if there are others. It is a problem for calculating the net effect of trade reform on poverty because the omitted effects could be either reinforcing or offsetting to our included effects. All we claim is that the channels we have identified had a beneficial effect. The second caveat is that while it would be desirable to control for unobserved household characteristics that may influence poverty transitions, it is not possible to do so as there are only two waves of data. Despite these caveats, the econometric analysis suggests that the trade reforms of the 1990s influenced the poverty transitions of Vietnamese households. The significant effects chosen accord well with the shocks identified in the discussion of trade policy (although not all those identified could be included), and given that we use only initial variables we are free from worries about endogeneity.

Conclusion

This chapter has argued that despite its incompleteness and hesitancy, the reform process in Vietnam over the 1990s had significant effects. Exports and imports boomed and the prices of some tradable goods increased strongly. The changes stimulated the demand for labour somewhat and the benefits of export orientation are evident in the household data, with the real incomes of the poor tending to increase as a result of the increases in rice prices and the boom in exports. Our results are subject to some caveats, but they represent, we think, the first time that trade variables have been formally traced through into poverty statistics *ex post*.

Acknowledgements

This chapter is part of the project 'The Impact of Trade Reforms and Trade Shocks on Household Poverty Dynamics' (ESCOR-R7621) funded by the UK Department for International Development, for the benefit of developing countries, as part of their Globalisation and Poverty Research Programme. The views and opinions expressed in this chapter are, however, those of the authors alone. We are grateful to the World Bank for making the trade data available for the DFID-funded Globalisation and Poverty Research Programme's projects on Vietnam. The chapter draws freely on work by and discussion with our colleagues in the Poverty Research Unit, Sussex, Patricia Justino and Julie Litchfield. We are also grateful for comments on earlier drafts from colleagues in the Economics Subject Group at Sussex, participants in the University of Warwick's Conference on 'Globalisation, Growth and (In)Equality', March 2002, the DFID Seminar on Globalisation and Poverty in Hanoi, September 2001, and the OECD Development Centre Conference on 'How are Globalisation and Poverty Interacting?' in Paris, December 2002, and from Bob Baulch, Rhys Jenkins, Patricia Justino, Julie Litchfield, Andy McKay, Neil McCulloch, David O'Connor, Line Song, Finn Tarp, Shujie Yao, and Linxiu Zhang.

Notes

1 This section draws freely on Winters (2002).
2 For simplicity, the poverty measure employed in this framework is absolute income or consumption poverty.
3 See Niimi *et al.* (2003) for a more detailed review.
4 The Council of Mutual Economic Assistance consisting of the former Soviet Union, Eastern European socialist countries and Cuba.
5 There are discrepancies in trade data between various sources, possibly due to the treatment of transit centres like Singapore, North Korea and Hong Kong (Apoteker, 1998). However, all sources tell the same sort of story about the increase in openness.
6 These include rice, coffee, rubber, marine products, garments and footwear.
7 Justino and Litchfield (2002a) find that alternative poverty lines also imply strong declines in poverty.
8 See Niimi *et al.* (2003) for details.
9 This is because of the way in which we measure poverty: following the World Bank, poverty is defined relative to the cost of a standard consumption basket – 2,100 calories per day per head plus minimal non-food expenditures.
10 Niimi *et al.* (2004) also report certain caveats about the rice data.
11 There is some debate about employment trends according to different sources. All sources, except the World Bank (1999), put industrial employment as a constant share of total employment. We use data from MOLISA (unless otherwise indicated).
12 These relative sizes are hard to explain and raise concerns that the two sources of data (GSO and MOLISA, respectively) are incompatible.
13 'Underemployed' is defined as working less than 40 hours per week, and 'severely underemployed' as working less than 15 hours per week.
14 We thank Azita Amjadi of the World Bank for assistance with these data.
15 Partner data are used because Vietnamese data are not available in sufficient detail. These data account for approximately 90 per cent of Vietnam's total exports and imports (GSO statistics) for each year. The list of partners used includes Australia, Austria, Belgium, Canada, China, Czech Republic, Germany, Denmark, Finland, France, Hong Kong, Hungary, Indonesia, India, Italy, Japan, South Korea, Sri Lanka, Madagascar, Malaysia, the Netherlands, the Philippines, Poland, Romania, Russia, Senegal, Singapore, Sweden, Thailand, Taiwan, the UK, the USA and Venezuela. We preferred to use a defined set of partners rather than requesting data on 'all partners', because the Comtrade database from which the data are derived tends to show considerable variation through time in the set of countries included in such a category. As some CMEA countries did not report to the Comtrade system until 1992 (1996 for Russia) to the extent that trade with CMEA was significant in 1992–93 our data could miss declining sales. However, even the largest CMEA partner (Russia) accounted for only about 3.5 per cent of Vietnam's exports in 1993.
16 We repeated the exercise for the SITC 4 and 5 digit level to obtain the more detailed description of commodities where necessary.
17 A major challenge with these exercises is that trade, input–output, and employment data have different classifications (SITC, International Standard Industrial Classification (ISIC) and International Standard Classification of Occupation (ISCO) respectively) with the additional problems that the Vietnamese Input–output Table (GSO, 1999) does not exactly follow the ISIC and different occupation codes were utilised in the VLSS 92–93 and VLSS 97–98. In the absence of readily available converters between these data we have matched them as precisely as possible from their textual descriptions.
18 We are grateful to Chantal Nielsen and IFPRI for supplying the complete SAM.
19 Of the 97, 73 refer to visible commodities (goods) which are our focus here.
20 The assumption that marginal imports are allocated proportionately to average use of the input is very conservative, probably significantly understating the role of imports in increasing output and employment.

21 This section draws on some of the analysis in Niimi *et al.* (2003).
22 Justino and Litchfield (2002a) give more detail.
23 Its value is 1.160 million dong in 1992–93 and 1.790 million dong in 1997–98 (World Bank, 2001).
24 We also measure various non-trade effects in slightly different ways from Glewwe *et al.* (2000).
25 Niimi *et al.* (2003, 2004) report more equations and the inferences leading to column B.
26 The rice production effect in the Mekong in column B of Table 2.4 is an increase of 5 per cent in the chance of escaping = 100*(1.75*0.60-1).
27 By the same token negative shocks will hit hard in agriculture, as, for example, the decline in coffee prices since 1997 is reported to have done in Vietnam's Central Highlands.
28 We also experimented by looking at employment and change in employment effects in import sectors and in manufacturing in general. Neither added much to the model (see Niimi *et al.*, 2003 for the results).
29 Because we standardised the variables in the regression equation, we also need to subtract $\beta\bar{x}/s$ from the constant to ensure that the equations go through the same mean point as before, where $\bar{x}$ is the mean value of the trade variable, s its standard deviation and β the trade coefficient set to zero.
30 This exercise is essentially a simulation. We are comparing predictions under two sets of conditions, not actual and predicted values. Thus the results are predicated on the relevance of the estimated model.

References

Apoteker, T. (1998) *Vietnam: Trade and Investment Analysis: 1998 Update*, A Report for the European Commission, Vietnam.

Belser, P. (2000) 'Vietnam: On the Road to Labour-Intensive Growth?', background paper for the Vietnam Development Report 2000, *Vietnam: Attacking Poverty*, Washington, DC: World Bank.

Chandrasiri, S. and Amala de Silva (1996) 'Globalisation, Employment and Equity: The Vietnam Experience', Regional Office for Asia and the Pacific: Bangkok, ILO/EASMAT project.

CIE (1998) *Vietnam's Trade Policies 1998*, Canberra and Sydney: Centre of International Economics.

CIEM (2000) *Vietnam's Economy in 1999*, Central Institute for Economic Management, Hanoi: Statistical Publishing House.

CIEM (2001) *An Overview of Vietnam's Trade Policy in the 1990s*, Central Institute for Economic Management, processed. An updated version of 'An Overview of Vietnam's Trade Policies', by The Technical Group of TLCV in *Vietnam's Socio-Economic Development*, No.19, Autumn, 1999.

Dollar, D. and A. Kraay (2001) 'Growth is Good for the Poor', World Bank Policy Research Working Paper 2587, Washington, DC: World Bank.

Gallup, J.L. (2002) 'The Wage Labour Market and Inequality in Vietnam in the 1990s', World Bank Policy Research Working Paper 289, Washington, DC: World Bank.

General Statistics Office (GSO) (various issues) *Statistical Yearbook*, Hanoi: Statistical Publishing House.

General Statistics Office (GSO) (1999) *Input–output Table 1996*, Hanoi: Statistical Publishing House.

Glewwe, P., M. Gragnolati, and H. Zaman (2000) 'Who gained from Vietnam's boom in the 1990s?: an analysis of poverty and inequality trends',World Bank Policy Research Working Paper 2275, Washington, DC: World Bank.

International Monetary Fund (IMF) (1998) 'Vietnam: Selected Issues and Statistical Appendix', *Staff Country Report 98/30*, Washington, DC: IMF.

International Monetary Fund (IMF) (1999) 'Vietnam: Selected Issues', *Staff Country Report 99/55*, Washington, DC: IMF.

International Monetary Fund (IMF) (2000) 'Vietnam: Statistical Appendix and Background Notes', *Staff Country Report 00/116* Washington, DC: IMF.

Jenkins, R. (2002) 'Globalisation and Employment in Vietnam', presented at the DFID Seminar in Hanoi, September 2002.

Justino, P. and J. Litchfield (2002a) 'Poverty Reduction in Vietnam: What Do the Numbers Tell Us?', PRUS Working Paper No.8, Poverty Research Unit at Sussex.

Justino, P. and J. Litchfield (2002b) 'Poverty Dynamics in Vietnam: Winners and Losers during Reform', PRUS Working Paper No.10, Poverty Research Unit at Sussex.

Minot, N. (1998) 'Competitiveness of the Food Processing Sector in Vietnam: A Study of the Rice, Coffee, Seafood and Fruits and Vegetables Subsectors', Appendix I of the *Industrial Competitiveness Review*, Vienna: UNIDO.

Minot, N. and F. Goletti (1998) 'Export Liberalisation and Household Welfare: The Case of Rice in Vietnam', *American Journal of Agricultural Economics*, 80: 738–749.

Nielsen, C.P. (2002a) 'Social Accounting Matrices for Vietnam 1996 and 1997', TMD Discussion Paper No.86, Washington, DC: IFPRI.

Nielsen, C.P. (2002b) 'Vietnam in the International Rice Market', *Fodevareokonomisk Institute Rapport*, 132, Copenhagen: Fodevareokonomisk Institute.

Niimi, Y., P. Vasudeva-Dutta, and L.A. Winters (2003) 'Trade Liberalisation and Poverty Dynamics in Vietnam', PRUS Working Paper 17, Poverty Research Unit at Sussex.

Niimi, Y., P. Vasudeva-Dutta, and L.A. Winters (2004) 'The Storm in a Rice Bowl: Rice Reform and Poverty in Vietnam in the 1990s', *Journal of the Asia Pacific Economy*, 9(2): 170–190.

O'Connor, D. (1996) *Labour Market Aspects of State Enterprise Reform in Viet Nam*, Paris: OECD Development Centre.

van Donge, J.K, H. White, and L.W. Nghia (1999) *Fostering High Growth in a Low Income Economy*, Stockholm: SIDA.

Winters, L.A. (2002) 'Trade, Trade Policy and Poverty: What Are the Links', *The World Economy*, 25: 1339–1367.

Winters, L.A. (2004) 'Trade Liberalisation and Economic Performance: An Overview', *Economic Journal*, 114(493): F4–F21.

World Bank (1999) *Vietnam Development Report 2000: Attacking Poverty*, Donor-NGO Working Group, Consultative Group Meeting for Vietnam, 14–15 December 1999.

World Bank (2001) *Vietnam Living Standards Survey 1997–98: Basic Information*, Poverty and Human Resources Division, World Bank, April 2001.

3 Globalisation and poverty

Implications of South Asian experience for the wider debate

Jeffery I. Round and John Whalley

Introduction

Substantial heat and in some ways limited light surrounds the linkages between globalisation and poverty. Despite the allegations and concerns that globalisation adversely affects the poor (Khor, 2002; Watkins, 2002), and especially so in poorer countries, and counter-claims that it has 'supported' poverty reduction (World Bank, 2002), conclusive evidence on the linkages and the magnitude of effects is difficult to find. There is extensive literature discussing the possible channels through which globalisation and poverty are linked[1] and a body of theoretical and empirical literature seeming to provide evidence either in one direction or the other (O'Rourke, 2001; McKay, Winters and Kedir, 2000; Dollar and Kraay, 2001; Weller and Hersh, 2002), so the outcomes are, at best, ambiguous.

Precise definitions of globalisation are elusive, but it is usually perceived as a process of increased integration between and within countries, manifested through an increase in the movement of commodities, labour, capital (financial and physical), and technology. The wide-ranging nature of these globalisation processes and the inherent difficulties in identifying and measuring them, in terms of either their initial shocks or their impacts on various parts of the economic system (especially their impact on welfare and poverty) creates a number of analytical and empirical challenges. Even if we focus on just one kind of globalisation shock, trade liberalisation, and consider the consequences analytically (via a modelling framework) the shock might be seen to have quite different effects in different models, under different configurations of otherwise similar models, and based on different experiments (e.g. using different replacement taxes to make tariff reductions revenue neutral).

Equal care is required when clarifying the poverty side of the globalisation and poverty link. It can be interpreted as 'money-metric'-based poverty or expressed in terms of more broadly-based social indicators (Ravallion, 1993). Clearly the measure of poverty used matters because different poverty indices do not correlate perfectly. Monetary-based measures also vary according to the choice of relative or absolute numbers below poverty lines, on nominal or real incomes, the reference unit (households, individuals, household subgroups); or they may rely on measures of relative poverty based on skilled/unskilled wage differentials, or on the relative incomes of population subgroups. Data on poverty is often fragmentary, and where available data may be inconsistent when one source is compared with another, so inferences are quite difficult to make.[2]

Many of these analytical difficulties have been addressed in an attempt to identify some linkages between globalisation and poverty in four South Asian economies in a project involving researchers from Bangladesh, India, Pakistan, and Sri Lanka.[3] Each researcher executed modelling work aimed at quantitatively evaluating the sign and significance of key elements of linkage; for example, how capital flows and changes in foreign remittances occurring simultaneously with tariff changes influence the results of tariff/inequality studies; how significant export surges in garment industries have been in reducing gender inequality; how the separate influences of trade and technical change occurring under globalisation can be measured; and other such targeted analyses.

In the course of executing this work, broader questions have also been considered. Just what has been the record on poverty and inequality change in these countries as globalisation processes have occurred? When did major globalisation shocks (such as trade liberalisation) occur, and how did inequality measures seemingly respond and when? What does a crude data-based analysis of linkage suggest? What are some of the pitfalls in using data in model-based counterfactual analyses in trying to unearth directions and size of linkage mechanisms? These issues are addressed here by considering some of the broader themes and results that emerge from the project.

In assessing the role of various elements of linkage, a number of points can be made. First, the choice of poverty measure matters. This is not simply a matter of distinguishing between relative and absolute poverty. Outcomes may differ as between measures based on income, consumption, health and education, and other dimensions of human well-being. Second, the structure of models used to unearth linkage is critical. Models with specific immobile factors have localised rents that change in a narrow and prescribed way with trade liberalisation; models with mobile factors do not have this feature. Quotas (if unauctioned) confer rents which liberalisation takes away; quotas which are auctioned or sought (rent-seeking) do not have these features. Third, trade policies that raise revenues (tariffs), if replaced by similar revenue-raising instruments (a progressive income tax, or a VAT), may see their perceived inequality effects largely determined by the replacement policies. These are not just abstract, analytical issues, although they can be addressed using models. They reflect differences in economic circumstances that will influence the impact of trade liberalisation on poverty.

Many other pitfalls exist in such analyses, to the point that one can argue that meaningful discussion of the globalisation–poverty linkage can only take place if very precise contours for the discussion exist. Is globalisation inequality-worsening in a particular model of a particular economy using certain assumptions and conducting a precise experiment? Without such specificity, precise answers to the linkage conundrums cannot be given; with any small change in setup the answers could change, often dramatically. On top of this, globalisation is likely to impact on economies in different ways because the appropriate 'contours' differ between countries; and because of other factors, such as the influence of institutions and of policy impacts other than those that are directed at liberalisation, which affect the 'other things being equal' assumptions modellers are obliged to make.

In taking this perspective, this project differs from the DFID Handbook on *Trade Liberalisation and Poverty* (McCulloch, Winters and Cirera, 2001) that provided the background framework for the DFID White Paper on globalisation. The authors argued that 'in general, trade liberalisation is an ally in the fight against poverty' (McCulloch *et al.*, 2001: 3). It did not draw a clear distinction between relative and absolute poverty, although the impacts might be quite different. While it focused on impacts on goods prices, wages, and employment, and outlined alternative detailed pathways through which trade liberalisation might have a direct effect on poverty, the study acknowledges that the total effect might be ambiguous, and this accords with our own experience. McCulloch *et al.* also suggested that agriculture and services were key sectors for poverty alleviation, although they provided limited intersectoral analysis and did not stress the many pitfalls in assessing the nature and magnitude of such a linkage.

The rest of this chapter is organised into three sections. Section 2 briefly considers the evidence and some of the difficulties (both conceptual and practical) in determining when liberalisation occurs and at what speed, and the apparent changes in poverty during the period of liberalisation. In two of the countries (Sri Lanka and Pakistan) liberalisation was gradual, whereas in India and Bangladesh liberalisation was much more rapid. Section 3 then draws together some experience from the simulation exercises. There is considerable variety in terms of both the experiments and the modelling approaches. We purposely do not use one single generic model and apply it to each country. Instead, the models range from small, stylised, and more transparent models to much larger, computable general equilibrium (CGE) models embracing macro and micro closures. The final section draws some conclusions about the broad effects of globalisation on poverty from these experiments.

Assessing the evidence

Dating globalisation shocks in four South Asian economies

As 'globalisation' and 'liberalisation' are terms which are open to such wide interpretation, it is not surprising that there is little consensus about identifying dates when countries may be said to have 'globalised' or 'liberalised'. This issue pervades much of the literature, most notably in the recent paper by Dollar and Kraay (2001) in which they attempt to subdivide a sample of developing countries into 'post-1980 globalisers' and the rest (i.e. essentially 'non-globalisers'). Their aim was to consider the relative growth and poverty performance of the two groups. Dollar and Kraay identify post-1980 globalisers in terms of two simple, trade-related measures:

(i) an outcome measure, based on the growth in trade relative to GDP;
(ii) a policy input measure, based on the decline in average tariff rates.

Each measure has some deficiencies and Dollar and Kraay acknowledge certain anomalies in the resulting classifications.

A further measure, the Sachs–Warner index (Sachs and Warner, 1997) is more to do with the timing of liberalisation than with the aim of producing a binary classification of countries. Their measure is based on five tests: (1) average tariff rates below 40 per cent; (2) average quota and licensing coverage of imports of less than 20 per cent; (3) a black market exchange premium of less than 20 per cent; (4) no extreme controls (taxes, quota and state monopolies) on exports; and (5) not considered a socialist country by the Kornai standard (Sachs and Warner, 1997: 339). An economy is deemed to be open to trade if all five tests are satisfied. In principle of course, the Sachs–Warner index could be used to identify the *speed* as well as the timing of liberalisation, by observing how rapidly the five tests are satisfied. However, each test is scored on a pass/fail basis so it would give no indication of how rapidly average tariff rates or average quota coverage are reduced. It would only indicate the rate at which the cumulative position on the five tests has been attained.

Some countries are generally believed to have liberalised more quickly than others in terms of key indicators (especially trade and financial indicators). Nevertheless, these different indicators of liberalisation give differing results. The four South Asian countries considered here are a case in point. India and Bangladesh satisfy both of Dollar and Kraay's criteria as 'post-1980 globalisers' and are included in their list; Pakistan passes the first criterion (tariff reduction) but not the second (and Dollar and Kraay seem unconvinced by its inclusion anyway); and Sri Lanka does not appear at all in their classifications. However, in the original Sachs–Warner index the picture is a little different. Sri Lanka and India are included in the list of developing countries that had 'opened' by 1994 (after initial closure) and Bangladesh and Pakistan are in the list of countries that were still closed by 1994. But all four countries have now liberalised, at least to a large degree. What really distinguishes them is the speed at which they have liberalised.

A detailed examination of the evidence in relation to trade, based on changes in tariff rates and quota coverage (input measures) and openness ratios (outcome measures), suggests the following. Pakistan has been relatively slow in liberalising trade, commencing in the late 1980s and through the 1990s. In contrast, a series of liberal policy reforms, involving both trade and financial liberalisation and privatisation, were introduced in Bangladesh in 1990, leading to significant reductions in tariff and quota reductions during the following decade, although in terms of other facets of liberalisation (e.g. financial direct investment, and financial integration) the reform process has been much slower.

In India, through the 1990s, tariff levels were reduced quite significantly, and quotas also experienced some relaxation. But economic reform in India involved more than trade liberalisation. The devaluation in 1991 was also significant, as were the relaxation of exchange controls previously applying to both capital and current accounts, and restrictions on FDI inflows. In contrast, Sri Lanka embarked on a series of trade reform measures much earlier – in 1977, when exchange control was dismantled, tariffs were reduced and quota restrictions began to be removed. The main feature of Sri Lanka's liberalisation is not so much the degree and intensity of reform but the relatively long time horizon over which the reforms were introduced.

Identifying poverty responses in an era of globalisation

The broad picture on the changes in absolute and relative poverty experienced during the last two decades in each of the four South Asian countries under study can be set against the background of their records on globalisation. As discussed above (Section 1) it is often quite difficult to provide a clear and unequivocal assessment of either levels or changes in poverty. Even when a money-based measure of poverty is used, many alternative poverty measures exist to measure and assess changes in poverty. So a first aim is to provide some broad overall indications of the magnitude and directions of change, distilled from the individual project material. In most cases the evidence accumulated is predominantly based on the contributing researchers' own poverty assessments carried out under the MIMAP project (see endnote 3).

In broad terms, evidence on poverty in the South Asian countries suggests that major change has occurred in terms of absolute poverty (expressed as a headcount index, that is, the numbers below the poverty line) and that this change has accelerated as growth performance has picked up post-liberalisation. However, the results are far from unidirectional. It is now generally agreed, in the light of some mixed evidence, that absolute poverty has declined in India during the 1990s, and a similar picture has emerged in Bangladesh. This underlines the broad evidence for South Asia as a region. In Pakistan, however, following a decline in poverty in the early 1990s there has been some volatility in the poverty ratios, though set against a rising trend. In Sri Lanka, after some apparent increase in absolute poverty during the early 1980s, and a decline in the second half of the 1980s, there was a further increase in the 1990s.

With regard to relative poverty (inequality) in the region over the last few decades, the broad picture is that it has remained relatively unchanged (at least until recently) in spite of major trade liberalisation in the late 1980s and early 1990s. Still, from the evidence available, there are some differences between countries; increasing inequality in Pakistan post-liberalisation; a period of slightly increasing and then falling inequality in Bangladesh post-liberalisation; a similar increasing then falling inequality in Sri Lanka, though this occurs over a much longer horizon; and some evidence of sharper increases in inequality in India in the late 1990s. However it is difficult to ascribe precise reasons for these different outcomes.

Evaluating the mechanisms of globalisation–poverty linkage in South Asia

Against this mixed and uncertain picture of dating globalisation shocks and assessing changes in absolute and relative poverty, the next step is to assess what form the linkages actually take. Globalisation shocks in South Asia appear worthy of careful study because, to the outside observer, they appear to have occurred dramatically and to be concentrated over a relatively short time period. The view might be that if there are discernible impacts of globalisation on poverty, then surely they could show through in these cases. However, the central difficulty is that the statistical outcome observed reflects the combined influence of several factors, some of which are seemingly unconnected with liberalisation per se. For example, work on poverty reduction in Vietnam (Niimi, Vasudeva-Dutta and Winters, 2003) in the period following liberalisation suggests that trade liberalisation accounts for a small share of overall poverty reduction, with changes in domestic policy being more important. Therefore, some form of counterfactual analysis is needed to isolate the component of the overall change that is attributed to globalisation influences. Considering trade liberalisation, primarily in the South Asian countries but also in OECD export markets, a number of channels of influence on poverty and inequality can be identified.

Tariff-based liberalisation

The central form of linkage to poverty from tariff-based liberalisation discussed in the theoretical literature is from relative goods prices that change as tariffs fall relative to factor prices. These effects are associated with Stolper and Samuelson (1941) who provided conditions under which the factor that is intensive in the production of importables would lose out. Stolper–Samuelson effects in the South Asian case would therefore appear as a reduction in the relative return to labour used in protected sectors, typically being more skilled labour. These effects are widely thought to be pro-poor.

Many other factors influence the way trade liberalisation impacts on poverty. If the rich purchase relatively more of the imported good, then reductions in tariffs will be more beneficial to them on the demand side. If there are fixed, or specific, factors used in production, then the owners of these factors rather than owners of factors more generally will be the losers. Depending upon how tariff revenues are, or are not, replaced, various distributional effects will follow. Replacing revenues using a progressive income tax will have different effects from a VAT or payroll tax, for instance. If tariffs are reduced while quotas remain in place, the effects of the tariff reductions are only lump sum since they merely increase the value of the quota rents. Other distortions in the economy may be germane too. For example, if labour in the traditional (agricultural) sector is paid its average product, and the price of labour in the modern sector is determined by its marginal product, then tariffs can affect these distortions and intersectoral migration patterns may well be affected by the policy change.

Quota-based liberalisation

The South Asian economies were characterised, pre-liberalisation, by extensive use of quotas and other trade restraints, as well as tariffs. However, quotas, when changed, might produce quite different effects on poverty compared with tariffs. A number of sub-cases can be identified. One case is where import quotas are merely allocated by national governments, so recipients of quotas also receive quota rents. In this case, trade liberalisation that removes the quotas also takes away the quota rents. If quotas are allocated to the rich, such liberalisation becomes pro-poor in its income redistribution effects, in addition to having the relative goods and factor prices effects that were noted above for the tariff case. A second case is where the quotas are auctioned by governments, so that in this case revenues accrue very much like in the tariff case. In these situations, the poverty implications of tariff and quota based liberalisation become very similar.

A third case is where quotas are sought after via rent-seeking behaviour that uses real resources. Examples would be taking on surplus labour to demonstrate unemployment in the enterprise so that a licensing board will allocate quotas for imports of machinery. Such instances are discussed for India pre-liberalisation in Mohammed and Whalley (1984) who, for India in the 1970s, estimated rent-seeking costs for all major policy interventions in India (i.e. not just trade) at 15–40 per cent of GDP. If rent-seeking accompanies trade-based quotas, then, on the removal of these quotas, real resources are saved, potentially leading to positive income effects.

Economy-wide models

The ways in which these elements of linkage can be investigated usually involve the use of numerical simulation models, typically of the general equilibrium variety. Econometric methods are unable to deal with the richness and detail of the under-lying structural forms involved and generally are not used. Parameter estimates based on past behaviour or existing structure may not give adequate clues at to what might be the case after the policy 'shock'. Therefore, numerical simulation and computable general equilibrium modelling approaches are much more useful for counterfactual analysis – that is, to examine the likely (or possible) consequences from some change in the initial situation. This implies that most analyses are *ex ante*: they are attempts to examine 'what' might be the economy-wide responses 'if' some exogenous change (a policy change) were to take place.

The typical procedure is to build a model with goods and factors, with trade in goods but no trade in factors. Such models are usually calibrated to a base year data set around which counterfactual equilibrium analysis is performed (see Shoven and Whalley 1992). The counterfactuals typically involve the removal or reduction of tariffs and quotas, with an equal yield replacement tax in the tariff case (often a VAT surcharge).

Increasingly, these models are being used in double calibration mode with calibration taking place to two separate years of data. In this case the models are being used *ex post* rather than *ex ante*; the aim being to see how important one or other of a number of components of a combined change are for a change that has already occurred (such as a change in inequality). The methods used for this are discussed in Abrego and Whalley (2002).

Many issues arise with using these numerical simulation models. One is that the precise structural form used can, to a large degree, predetermine the conclusions.

First, models with fixed factors, that is for instance, where labour and/or capital cannot move freely between sectors, tend to yield concentrated outcomes from liberalisation, while models with mobile factors yield smaller but broader economy-wide effects. So in reality, the degree of mobility of factors is important to the effects of liberalisation. This has implications for policy, in that labour market policies that promote migration, micro-credit, etc, which more generally increase the mobility of labour and capital, may spread the effects of liberalisation more widely. Second, short-run models with adjustment costs can produce sharply different implications from those of longer-run models without them (see Edwards and Whalley 2002). Third, results are highly parameter dependent. Typically, a subset of key model parameters is pre-selected (such as key elasticities of substitution) and it can be observed that liberalisation impacts change as parameter values change, often quite sharply. General results are thus typically not generated by numerical simulation; the results are therefore indicative rather than definitive, and it is orders of magnitude and directions of effect rather than precise numerical outcomes that are achieved from the analyses.

Yet another issue is how poverty is analysed using these approaches. Some models tend to analyse factor price effects (such as the differential between skilled and unskilled wage rates) rather than a broader concept of income including capital income and transfers and taxes. Siddiqui and Kemal's (2002a) data for Pakistan suggests a high income share for capital income (perhaps 30 per cent in aggregate) indicating how partial this approach is. Others are large models based on social accounting matrices. Some modelling efforts (such as Cockburn 2001) have attempted to add micro-simulation detail to conventional factor income-type analyses. These approaches allow for calculations of movement of individual incomes above and below the poverty line, and other broader measures of income change, but rely heavily on ad hoc assumptions and assumed parameter values.

Results from the models

In Table 3.1, we have attempted to summarise some of the results from a sample of numerical simulation models used to analyse globalisation–poverty linkages, mainly in the South Asian countries, but with Vietnam added due to its policy relevance.

Three of the papers (Weerahewa, 2002a; Mujeri and Khondker, 2002; Pradhan, 2002a) use double-calibration techniques for simple models of Sri Lanka, Bangladesh and India respectively to analyse the relative importance of trade, technical change, and endowment change as determinants of inequality change. They take liberalisation to be given by the actual tariff and quota changes for the years that are analysed, looking at revenue-preserving change.

A feature of these models is that they all embody some degree of factor specificity. This is due to a general model feature that if models capture all factors as being fully mobile across sectors then typically only a relatively small range of factor price changes can be accommodated as resulting from a goods price change without encountering problems of equalisation. These problems are also

Table 3.1 Recent numerical models evaluating linkage between trade liberalisation and poverty

Author(s)	Country	Type of model	Base year data used in calibration	Conclusion
Weerahewa (2002a)	Sri Lanka	Static 2-sector Ricardo–Viner type model	Double calibration to pairs of years (1977, 1994, 2000)	Trade plays no essential role in explaining poverty change (either relative or absolute). Technical change and endowment changes are the main drivers.
Mujeri and Khondker (2002)	Bangladesh	Static 2-sector Ricardo–Viner type model	Double calibration to 1985 and 1996 data	Trade is the minor determinant of poverty change compared with technical change and endowment growth.
Siddiqui and Kemal (2002a)	Pakistan	Static 11-sector Ricardo–Viner type model	Single calibration to data for 1989–90 and forward projections	Non-globalisation variables are key to understanding how globalisation affects poverty measures. Model runs including or excluding remittance changes alter the sign of effects.
Pradhan (2002b)	India	Static 13-sector Ricardo–Viner type model	Single calibration to data for 1994 and forward projections	Trade policy change has small impact on poverty effects.
Chan and Dung (2001)	Vietnam	Static 12-sector fixed factor model	Single calibration to data for 1997 and forward projection	Trade policy change is pro-rich, since in Vietnam consumption data suggest the rich buy proportionately more imports than the poor.

noted in Johnson (1966) and Abrego and Whalley (2002) and are widely accepted in the modelling literature. As a result, pure Stolper–Samuelson effects do not show through from these models because rewards to fixed factors are involved. Nonetheless, these studies all point to the conclusion that the influences of trade-based liberalisation, and of trade in general, on both absolute and relative poverty (i.e. inequality) are quite small. This is the strong and broad conclusion from these studies.

Other results shed further light on this conclusion. Siddiqui and Kemal (2002a) show how, in the Pakistan case, there is a clear and potentially major role for excluded variables in the analysis of linkage. As noted earlier, in the early 1990s both absolute and relative poverty increased in Pakistan. But this occurred along with a reduction in remittances that previously went primarily to the poor (as a percentage of income). Thus if the remittance change is removed from the analysis then trade changes alone generate an opposite effect in terms of both absolute and relative poverty.

Table 3.1 also refers to results from a Vietnam model project, which, while not part of the South Asia project, is also germane to the cases here. These results show trade policy changes to be pro-rich based on household budget data that show expenditure shares on imports to be significantly higher for the rich than for the poor. Other studies, not cited in Table 3.1, shed further light on these linkages. Pradhan (2002a) analysed both tariff-based and quota-based liberalisation in India, showing how impacts on inequality measures under liberalisation change. Siddiqui and Kemal (2002b) analyse the poverty impacts of trade liberalisation under scenarios where capital flows are also liberalised at the same time, concluding that relatively little added impact occurs. Weerahewa (2002b) analyses how outward trade surges in textiles and apparel from Sri Lanka impact on the relative male–female ratio, concluding that outward orientation has served to partially lower the gap in this case. Bussolo and Whalley (2002) show how in the Indian case, reductions in transaction costs[4] that occur contemporaneously with trade liberalisation also serve to impact on relative wage inequality, and may help to explain a reduction in the relative wage gap between skilled and unskilled labour in the early period of liberalisation in India.

Conclusions

To assess the effects of globalisation shocks in South Asia we have examined four cases of Pakistan, Sri Lanka, India and Bangladesh during the 1980s and 1990s. At first sight, they seem to be cases of declining absolute poverty, which accelerates some time after liberalisation, and relatively constant inequality. There are departures from this situation, rising absolute and relative poverty in Pakistan, and a few years of increasing relative poverty in Bangladesh. All in all, at a broad sweep of the brush the picture seems to be one of almost no impact on relative poverty (i.e. inequality) and some acceleration (through higher growth) in the decline of absolute poverty. However, separating out the linkages from other effects and influences, many problems are encountered. There are conceptual problems with measuring and dating liberalisation. These are measurement and data problems in ascertaining exactly what has happened to poverty changes over the time period, especially with regard to different measures and income concepts. There are problems with model-based analyses. Model structures make a difference, as does the precise liberalisation experiment used. Hence, even in a case where, at first sight, the linkages between globalisation and poverty are seemingly exposable, conceptual, data, and modelling issues preclude overly firm conclusions. Specificity of experiment, of the model, and other factors all matter greatly.

The general and overriding conclusion from these analyses is that the debate on globalisation and poverty linkages appears to be pitched at too general a level – even in these country cases – to be able to draw firm conclusions. There is no firm theoretical link between globalisation and poverty; the empirical evidence is difficult to disentangle, not least because so many events occur contemporaneously. Numerical simulation methods and models are useful in separating effects but usually under strict 'other things being equal' conditions of one form or another. So policy conclusions are necessarily severely constrained by circumstances and are heavily conditioned as a result.

Acknowledgements

This chapter is a revised version of an overview paper of an ESCOR project 'Exploring the Links Between Globalisation and Poverty in South Asia' which is part of the Globalisation and Poverty Programme, funded by the Department of International Development (DFID) UK. We wish to thank John Humphrey, the Programme Director, for valuable comments on an earlier draft and for his support to the project as a whole. Statistical details have been excluded although these may be obtained from the earlier version, Round and Whalley (2002).

Notes

1 For example, McCulloch, Winters and Cerera (2001) review the transmission channels of trade liberalisation on poverty.
2 Throughout this chapter inequality is referred to as 'relative poverty' in order to reflect the income or well-being of one group (e.g. the poor) relative to another (e.g. the rich).
3 The researchers are: Jeevika Weerahewa (Sri Lanka), Rizwana Siddiqui and A.R. Kemal (Pakistan), Bazlul Khondker and Mustafa Mujeri (Bangladesh), and Basanta Pradhan (India). The project was also co-linked to MIMAP, an IDRC-funded network of researchers on poverty analysis and modelling in these and other countries in Asia and Africa.
4 Transaction costs in this context refer to several forms of impediments to transactions between buyers and sellers. These include the costs of transportation, communication, and information transfer and include policy-induced restrictions and controls.

References

Abrego, L. and Whalley J., 2002, 'Decomposing wage inequality change using general equilibrium models', NBER Working Papers 9184, Washington, DC: National Bureau of Economic Research.

Bussolo, M. and Whalley, J., 2002, 'Globalisation in developing countries: the role of transaction costs in explaining economic performance in India', DFID project paper, http://www.oecd.org/dataoecd/59/22/2503649.pdf (accessed 9 October 2003).

Chan, N. and Dung, T.K., 2001, 'Development of a CGE model to evaluate tariff policy in Vietnam', MIMAP Modelling Meeting, Singapore, http://www.bellanet.org/mimap/dynamic/dyn_workinpr2/vnpaper2-10.doc ?OutsideInServer=rules (accessed 7 October 2003).

Cockburn, J., 2001, 'Trade liberalisation and poverty in Nepal, a computable general equilibrium micro simulation analysis', CREFA, Université Laval Québec, Canada http://www.crefa.ecn.ulaval.ca/cahier/0118.pdf (accessed 7 October 2003).

Dollar, D. and Kraay, A., 2001, 'Trade, growth and poverty', paper presented to the WIDER conference on Growth and Poverty, May (http://www.wider.unu.edu/conference/conference-2001-1/dollar%20and%20kraay.pdf) (accessed 7 October 2003).

Edwards, T.H. and Whalley, J., 2002, 'Short and long run decompositions of OECD wage inequality changes', NBER Working Paper 9265, Washington, DC: National Bureau of Economic Research.

Johnson, H.G., 1966, 'Factor market distortions and the shape of the transformation curve', *Econometrica*, 34: 686–698.

Khor, M., 2002, 'A perspective of globalisation and its implications for developing countries', paper presented to the CSGR conference on Globalisation, Growth and (In)Equality, University of Warwick, March 2002 (http://www.warwick.ac.uk/fac/soc/CSGR/PKhor.pdf) (accessed 7 October 2003).

McCulloch, N., Winters, L.A. and Cirera, X., 2001, *Trade Liberalisation and Poverty: A Handbook*, London: Centre for Economic Policy Research.

McKay, A., Winters L.A. and Kedir A.M., 2000, 'A review of the empirical evidence on trade, trade policy and poverty', a report to DFID prepared as a background document for the Second Development White Paper (http://www.globalisation.gov.uk/BackgroundWord/EmpiricalEvidenceOnTrade AndrewMcKay.doc) (accessed 7 October 2003).

Mohammed, S. and Whalley, J., 1984, 'Rent-seeking in India: Its costs and policy significance', *Kyklos*, 37(3): 387–413.

Mujeri, M. and Khondker, B., 2002, 'Decomposing wage inequality change in Bangladesh: an application of the double calibration technique', DFID project paper, http://www.gapresearch.org/production/MusafaDecomp.pdf (accessed 9 October 2003).

Niimi, Y., Vasudeva-Dutta, P. and Winters, L.A., 2003, 'Trade liberalisation and poverty dynamics in Vietnam', PRU Working Paper 17, Brighton: Poverty Research Unit, University of Sussex.

O'Rourke, K., 2001, 'Globalisation and inequality: Historical trends', CEPR Discussion Paper 2865, London: Centre for Economic Policy Research.

Pradhan, B., 2002a, 'The role of education in wage inequality change in India: 1988–97', DFID project paper, http://www.gapresearch.org/production/Pradhan-EdJN02.pdf.

Pradhan, B., 2002b, 'Debating the effects of trade liberalisation on poverty: how experiment specificity determines the conclusions', DFID project paper, http://www.gapresearch.org/production/BasantaPov.pdf (accessed 9 October 2003).

Ravallion, M., 1993, 'Poverty comparisons', *Fundamentals of Pure and Applied Economics*, Vol 56, Chur, Switzerland: Harwood Academic Press.

Round, J.I., and Whalley, J., 2002, 'Globalisation and poverty: Implications of South Asian experience for the wider debate', DFID project paper (http://www.gapresearch.org/production/JJoverview.pdf) (accessed 7 October 2003).

Sachs, J.D., and Warner, A.M., 1997, 'Sources of slow growth in African economies', *Journal of African Economies*, 6(3): 335–76.

Shoven, J. and Whalley, J., 1992, *Applying General Equilibrium*, Cambridge: Cambridge University Press.

Siddiqui, R. and Kemal, A.R., 2002a, 'Remittances, trade liberalisation and poverty in Pakistan: the role of excluded variables in poverty change analysis', DFID project paper, http://www.gapresearch.org/production/RizwanaRemittR2.pdf (accessed 9 October 2003).

Siddiqui, R. and Kemal, A.R., 2002b, 'Poverty inducing or poverty reducing? A CGE-based analysis of foreign capital inflows in Pakistan', DFID project paper, http://www.gapresearch.org/production/RizwanaFKI2.pdf (accessed 9 October 2003).

Stolper, W.F. and Samuelson, P.A., 1941, 'Protection and real wages', *Review of Economic Studies*, 9: 58–73.

Watkins, K., 2002, 'Making globalisation work for the poor', *Finance and Development*, 39(1): 24–26 (and a response by Dollar and Kraay, 27–28).

Weerahewa, J., 2002a, 'Assessing the impacts of globalisation on poverty using decomposition methods', DFID project paper, http://www.gapresearch.org/production/JeevikaPov.pdf (accessed 9 October 2003).

Weerahewa, J., 2002b, 'Globalisation and male–female inequality in Sri Lanka: Short-run and long-run impacts', DFID project paper, http://www.gapresearch.org/production/JeevikaTex.pdf (accessed 9 October 2003).

Weller, C. and A. Hersh, 2002, 'The long and short of it: Global liberalisation, poverty and inequality', Washington, DC: Economic Policy Institute (http://www.zei.de/download/zei_wp/B02-14.pdf) (accessed 7 October 2003).

World Bank, 2002, *Globalisation, Growth and Poverty: Building an Inclusive World Economy*, New York: Oxford University Press for the World Bank.

4 Globalisation in developing countries

The role of transaction costs in explaining economic performance in India

Maurizio Bussolo and John Whalley

Introduction

The quest for large numbers has been going on in international trade economics for some time. Models of trade liberalisation using numerical simulation methods in multilateral, regional or single-country contexts have consistently produced results that, when compared *ex post* to real world data, show the right sign but the 'wrong' magnitudes. These quantitative assessments normally use general equilibrium models based on the theory of comparative advantage and the positive effects they usually produce originate from static resource reallocation and disappearances of dead-weight loss triangles. Dissatisfied by these meagre estimates of benefits, economists have built new models that better explain the large gains observed for internationally integrating countries. The models have mainly progressed along two directions, into dynamics and into non-convexities (that is, economics of scale and imperfect competition).[1]

New models have incorporated the insights of a large literature that emphasises the important role of 'openness' in boosting economic performance and growth. In a variety of theoretical approaches, a liberal external policy, facilitated by financial and trade flows, helps an economy in various ways, in particular to: get its domestic prices right, allocate its resources to their best uses, acquire new technologies, increase its primary factor productivity, increase competition and X-efficiency, reduce rent-seeking, and even improve its domestic governance. However, the strength of the links between trade policy and some of these positive effects has been challenged by some authors. Indeed, the debate is still open, although models that include some of these dynamic and non-convex features have produced larger numbers.

This chapter pursues a complementary approach by considering reductions in transaction costs as an important factor explaining developing countries' performance in the real world. This approach has also recently been advocated to explain the development failures of numerous African countries. According to Collier (1997, 1998) many African countries face unusually high, and often policy-induced, transaction costs that, by generating comparative disadvantages in manufactured exports, lower growth performance. Elbadawi, Mengistae and Zeufack (2001) and Elbadawi (1998) argue that this transaction costs hypothesis is supported by empirical evidence, even when specific geographic and endowment variables are controlled for. This chapter – rather than presenting econometric estimates of transaction costs from reduced-form equations, as in the studies cited – explicitly introduces transaction costs in a system of structural form equations within a general equilibrium simulation model. A primary objective of this study is, therefore, to produce a clear mapping of the analytical channels through which changes of transaction costs may affect the economic performance of an economy.

Additional to the effect on aggregate income (the large number issue) this chapter examines how transaction costs influence income distribution or, put more explicitly, how they affect relative factor prices. In the simplest Heckscher–Ohlin–Samuelson (H-O-S) model of comparative advantage, trade liberalisation leads to a reallocation of resources and to the specialisation of production in those sectors that use intensively the country's most abundant factor. This model predicts that production shifts towards goods intensive in low-skilled labour, increases the demand for unskilled workers, and increases their wage rates relative to other factor rewards. However, several authors have emphasised that empirical evidence conflicts with this prediction. An increase in the relative wages of skilled to unskilled labour is observed in many developing countries.[2] Without rejecting the H-O-S model, most studies explain this puzzling widening wage gap by suggesting skill-biased technological change to be the primary cause, attributing only a minor role to trade.[3] By considering the distributional effects of a reduction in transaction costs in addition to those due to productivity changes, some fresh insights into the trade and wage gap debate are offered here.

Beyond the analytical motivation for this exercise, the direct exploration of the effects of transaction costs on aggregate incomes and relative wages has valuable policy relevance. First, by showing that a reduction in transaction costs may be an important channel through which trade liberalisation affects incomes, policy makers may gain support for an outward-oriented development strategy. Second, domestic as well as international trade policies can influence transaction costs. Given that these policies are often implemented as a part of comprehensive packages, their correct co-ordination becomes essential to their success. Because of the scope of indirect effects, the signs and magnitudes of induced adjustments are difficult to ascertain and the need for numerical simulation models of the type presented here becomes evident.

This study focuses on India; a series of trade models with transaction costs are calibrated to Indian data for the mid-1990s. This country undertook extensive market liberalisation towards the end of the 1980s and began opening its economy to world trade soon after. Extensive controls have been removed and rent-seeking activity has reduced considerably. Our approach attempts to quantify the nature of this deep structural transformation.

The chapter is organised as follows: the next section discusses the transaction cost approach by using a simple partial equilibrium model, followed by a brief review of the theoretical pedigree of the notion of transaction costs and concluded by some evidence of its empirical relevance. Section 3 presents the structure of general equilibrium models used to study the effects of transaction cost reductions, their calibration to Indian data and the main numerical results achieved. Section 4 summarises the main conclusions. An appendix briefly surveys Indian economic policies likely to have generated transaction costs and the recent major policy reforms.

Transaction costs: basic theory and empirical evidence

A simple transaction costs model

The following four equations representing demand, supply and equilibrium conditions in a generic market illustrate a simple partial equilibrium model with transaction costs: .

$$P_d = a - bQ_d \text{ (demand function)}$$
$$P_s = c + dQ_s \text{ (supply function)}$$
$$Q_d = Q_s \qquad \text{(market equilibrium)}$$
$$P_d = P_s + T \quad \text{(transaction cost mark-up)}$$

In the last equation transaction costs represent a wedge between the supply and demand price that is a fixed mark-up equal to T and paid by the purchaser on each unit of the good exchanged. The equilibrium quantity Q_e can easily be calculated as a function of T and of the other parameters as follows:

$$Q_e = \frac{a - c - T}{b + d}$$

and the basic comparative static result is:

$$\frac{\partial Q_e}{\partial T} = -\frac{1}{b + d}$$

Thus it clearly shows that the quantity exchanged is reduced by increasing transaction costs and that it can go to zero if these reach or exceed the value $(a - c)$, which is called the autarky limit. On the other hand, and depending on the initial level of transaction costs, their reduction may create a market or may simply increase the quantity exchanged.

In this simple set-up, if T is thought of as if it were an excise tax, the following crucial question should arise: what happens to the *revenues* $(Q_e T)$ collected from this tax? If these revenues simply disappear, then clearly a reduction in T would be similar to a windfall with positive effects. If, instead, other agents in the economy receive these revenues, then the net effect of a reduction in transaction costs should be calculated by considering the effects on both winners and losers.

A first important point should already be apparent: a reduction in transaction costs corresponds to a reduction in *rectangles* and thus will have larger impacts than the usual reduction of dead-weight loss *triangles*. A model including transaction costs can therefore fit the large numbers observed in reality either with or without recourse to exogenous or endogenous technological change, but what about the effect on income distribution? Before answering this second important question fully, let us consider a brief digression on the productivity (technological change) approach.

Technology and relative poverty

The reason why technological progress can have a strong distributional and poverty effect is intuitive: if a new technology increases the efficiency of a certain factor of production over that of the others, then it directly confers higher economic rewards to the owners of this more efficient factor given that its demand will increase proportionally more than that of the other less efficient factors. More formally, consider an economy where goods are produced using just two factors, skilled and unskilled labour, and that unskilled workers represent the poor. Firms demand the two categories of labour up to the point where the value of the production of an additional worker covers the cost of employing her. This is:

$$L_d = P.MPL$$

This equation states that labour demand is equal to the value of the marginal product of labour (MPL). Factor rewards are determined by the equality between their demands and supplies. To keep things very simple, we assume full employment: this is equivalent to having fixed labour supplies.

In this framework we can consider two types of technological shocks. In the first, the shock affects the efficiency of skilled and unskilled (i.e. poor) workers to the same extent (factor-neutral case); in the second, technological progress is skill-biased and one factor becomes more efficient than the other (factor-biased case). Relative poverty effects are easily traceable since they correspond to the wage ratio of skilled to unskilled workers:

$$\frac{W_S}{W_U} = \frac{P.MPL_S}{P.MPL_U} = \frac{MPL_S}{MPL_U}$$

Clearly, with factor neutrality, the same change affects both marginal productivities thus leaving the wage ratio equal to its initial equilibrium value. The whole economy becomes more efficient, goods production goes up (with the same quantity of resources), and the rewards go to the poor in the same way as they go to the non-poor. If, due to the new higher wage, a hypothetical poverty line were exceeded then poverty would no longer exist in this simple economy.

With factor bias, and supposing that the new technology makes skilled labour more efficient, inequality would rise given that the wage ratio would be higher after the technological shock. However, notice that this particular increase in inequality does not translate into an increase in *absolute* poverty, given that the wage rate of the poor (unskilled) goes up as well.

A straightforward variation of this simple framework can be used to construct a case where technological progress, even in its factor-neutral form, can indeed increase relative as well as absolute poverty. The variation consists of moving from a partial equilibrium approach exemplified above to a general equilibrium setting where there are two sectors of production that employ skilled and unskilled labour with different intensities. Consider, for instance, an economy with an advanced and a traditional sector, and that the former uses proportionally more skilled workers than the latter. Assume now that a new factor-neutral technology is introduced in this economy and that it is initially adopted by the advanced sector and not by the other. Production in the advanced sector becomes more profitable and more firms enter the sector. Its expansion occurs at the expense of a contracting traditional sector, now less profitable. Given the different factor intensities of the two sectors, skilled workers, employed in the advanced sector at a rate exceeding that at which they are released by the traditional sector, experience high demand for their services and rising wages; the opposite situation affects unskilled workers whose demand in production as well as wages are decreasing. If unskilled workers were initially above the poverty line and the wage decrease leaves them below, then absolute poverty would have been caused by a factor-neutral sector-biased technological change.

Numerous variations of this basic set-up have been provided in the literature. One can think of production that requires more than two factors and where some factors are complements and others are substitutes. A realistic case may involve firms adopting a technology that uses simultaneously more of capital and skilled labour thus leaving less capital available for unskilled labour and reducing its productivity and wage. Another extension considers more sophisticated modelling of labour supply including either education and training, or migration. In such models, the larger the initial wage ratio the larger the incentive to acquire education or to migrate; the equalising forces ensuing from an increasing supply of skilled workers, would probably take time to materialise. Finally international flows of goods, factors, and technologies may be considered.

The transaction costs approach used here shows that, even by abstracting from these productivity effects, transaction costs shocks can have similar distributional effects. In a more complete model these can then be added in or netted out from the above-cited productivity effect. But before showing how a standard general equilibrium trade model can be modified to take account of transaction costs, the remainder of this section provides a brief description of their theoretical pedigree and empirical relevance.

Transaction costs theory

Since the seminal work of Coase (1937), transaction costs economics has tried to resolve the apparent inconsistency in the co-existence of markets and firms or, in current terminology, of markets and institutions. Coase observed that if markets were perfect in organising production and exchange there would be no reason for multiple firms to exist. Alternatively, by turning the argument around, if firms had advantages over markets why should we not observe a single giant firm producing all that is demanded? His fundamental intuition was that differential transaction costs generate situations where both firms (or institutions) and markets are observed. In terms of the simple model above, there are certain types of activities for which transaction costs are above the autarky limit and exchanges take place inside institutions, and other types for which a market exists because transaction costs are below that limit. This has been an extremely significant contribution and it is probably one of the founding ideas of the voluminous transaction costs and institutional economics literature that followed.[4] This literature is not free from criticism. In particular, sceptics point out the difficulty in making the concept of transaction costs operational. In Goldberg's words, explaining economic phenomena by appeals to transaction costs 'is the all encompassing answer that tells us nothing' (Goldberg, 1985).

Another approach uses the concept of transaction costs in a less abstract and perhaps less interesting way but it may be more helpful for the purpose of understanding how changes in transaction costs may explain developing countries' performance. The crucial difference of this approach is that, rather than being concerned about changes in transaction costs close to the breaking point of the autarky limit, it considers how exchanges already taking place in the market may be affected by variations in transaction costs.

The antecedents to this approach may be found in general equilibrium theory and international trade. In an effort to enrich the theory of general equilibrium as formulated by Arrow and Debreu,[5] a few authors[6] have studied how this should be modified to incorporate transaction costs and what would be the consequences of such a modification on the major predictions of the standard theory. In Foley's words 'the key aspect of the modification I propose is an alteration in the notion of 'price'. In the present model there are [. . .] a buyer's and a lower seller's price [and their] difference yields an income which compensate the real resources used up in the operation of the markets' (Foley, 1970). This can be considered as an initial answer to the question posed above: where do transaction costs revenues go? When the operation of a market needs intermediaries that provide information or other services to buyers and sellers so that they can realise an exchange, then these intermediaries would receive the income generated by charging a transaction *fee* (= cost).

Another form of transaction costs has been considered in international trade and explicitly incorporated into models since Samelson's paper on transport costs (Samuelson, 1954). The basic idea here is that trade involves transaction costs and that these may be simply thought of as a fraction of the traded good itself, as if 'only a fraction of the ice exported reaches its destination as un-melted ice' (Samuelson, 1954). This 'iceberg model' provides another answer to the basic question on the fate of the transaction costs revenues and it clarifies how a reduction in transaction costs saves real resources and makes an economy more efficient.

Transaction costs: empirical basis

Real-world situations present numerous examples of transaction costs, however it is possible to group them into three broad categories, namely, geography/infrastructure-, technology/infrastructure-, and institution-/policy-related transaction costs. Notwithstanding that these categories overlap, they allow us to organise a large and diverse body of empirical evidence.

A major example of the first category is given by transportation margins. These are also probably the easiest to observe and possibly the easiest to measure. In an international context they can be measured by the c.i.f./f.o.b. ratio giving the 'carriage, insurance and freight' costs of countries' imports. Henderson, Shalizi, and Venables (2001) estimate that they can 'range from a few per cent of the value of trade, up to 30–40 per cent for the most remote and landlocked (and typically African) economies'. Limao and Venables (2001) find that being landlocked raises transport costs by more than 50 per cent and that the level of infrastructure development is an important variable in explaining differences in shipping costs. Estimates for within-country trade and transport costs are not easily available, however, even if smaller, distances may still play a role in generating transaction costs in national markets. In a recent study on Africa, Elbadawi *et al.* (2001) show that domestic transportation costs are an even stronger influence on export (and growth) performance than international transport costs.

Additionally, in developing countries, poor people usually living in rural or remote areas are often victims of high transaction costs that partially disconnect them from the rest of the society. Jalan and Ravallion (1998) find that road density was one of the significant determinants of household-level prospects of escaping poverty in rural China.[7] Any technological advance that provides the poor with better and cheaper access to national and international markets should, at least in principle, be beneficial.

The second category of transaction costs includes those related to technology and infrastructure. It is clear that drastic technological innovations affecting the whole infrastructure of an economy and having the potential to be used in a variety of sectors, such as steam power, electricity, telecommunications, can have profound effects on transaction costs and hence indirectly on an economy's growth and poverty record.[8] A clear example of technology/infrastructure transaction costs can be seen in the information and communication sector. The Internet explosion and its connected technologies have dramatically reduced exchange and search costs in most OECD countries. Although only indicative and not directly transferable to developing countries, some estimates for the cost savings (i.e. reduction in transaction costs) due to B2B electronic commerce are available for a few sectors of the US economy and are reported in Table 4.1.

Related to the above, an interesting working paper by Freund and Weinhold (2000) finds that, when introduced in a standard gravity model of trade flows, cyber-mass (i.e. Internet hosts per capita) is a significant positive variable that, while increasing the overall explanatory power of the regression, does not reduce the magnitude and significance of the physical distance.

Indirect evidence of technology/infrastructure-related transaction costs is found in the level of manufacturing inventories across countries. Guasch and Kogan (2001) report on huge inter-country differences in inventory levels. Table 4.2, taken from Guasch and Kogan (2001), reports on the very large disadvantage of Latin American economies vis-à-vis the USA with respect to inventories: on average these countries hold twice as much raw material and finished products as the USA. According to the authors, higher transaction costs explain a relevant part of these inventory discrepancies: Latin American countries faced with uncertain demand, longer delays in shipments, and larger costs for small frequent shipments, choose to maintain larger reserves. Considering that the cost of capital is normally higher in Latin America than in the USA, the authors point out that these high inventory

Table 4.1 Potential cost savings from B2B electronic commerce in the US

Industry	Potential cost savings %	Industry	Potential cost savings %
Electronic components	29–30	Chemicals	10
Machining	22	MRO	10
Forest products	15–25	Communications	5–15
Freight services	15–20	Oil and gas	5–15
Life sciences	12–19	Paper	10
Computing	10–20	Healthcare	5
Media and advertising	10–15	Food ingredients	3–5
Aerospace machining	11	Coal	2
Steel	11		

Source: Goldman Sachs (1999) cited in KPMG report *The Impact of the New Economy on Poor People and Developing Countries* for DFID.

Table 4.2 Latin American ratios to US inventories (all industries)

Raw materials inventory level ratios: ratio to US level by industry (average of all available data for 1990s)

	Chile	Venezuela	Peru	Bolivia	Colombia	Ecuador	Mexico	Brazil
Mean	2.17	2.82	4.19	4.20	2.22	5.06	1.58	2.98
Minimum	0.00	0.30	0.10	0.11	0.52	0.86	0.42	0.80
1st Quartile	0.36	1.87	1.25	1.39	1.45	2.55	1.06	1.60
Median	1.28	2.61	2.30	2.90	1.80	3.80	1.36	2.00
3rd Quartile	2.66	3.12	3.90	4.49	2.52	5.64	2.06	3.10
Maximum	68.92	7.21	31.10	34.97	13.59	20.61	3.26	7.10

Final goods inventory levels: ratio to US level by industry (average of all available data for 1990s)

	Chile	Venezuela	Peru	Bolivia	Colombia	Ecuador	Mexico	Brazil
Mean	1.76	1.63	1.65	2.74	1.38	2.57	1.46	1.98
Minimum	0.01	0.10	0.39	0.11	0.19	0.67	0.35	0.75
1st Quartile	0.17	0.87	1.17	1.13	1.05	1.67	0.82	1.10
Median	0.72	1.60	1.54	2.02	1.28	1.98	1.36	1.60
3rd Quartile	1.38	2.14	2.11	3.18	1.63	2.86	2.14	2.00
Maximum	31.61	5.29	3.87	21.31	5.31	7.94	4.91	5.20

Source: Guasch and Kogan (2001)

levels translate into considerable costs and ultimately into lower competitiveness and diminished growth.

The last category of transaction costs includes those related to institutions or economic policies. Rent-seeking is probably the most well-known example, however, even by just considering trade policy, a few others are worth mentioning.

A well-established literature finds that an international border has a large dampening effect on trade. This has also been termed the 'home bias' in trade. Most of the literature is focused on the Canada–USA trade, but this empirical puzzle applies to any region of the world. Obstfeld and Rogoff (2000) label the home bias in trade one of the 'six major puzzles in international macroeconomics'. Recent literature considers various explanations: Evans (2000) confirms the hypothesis that the home bias is due to the border itself rather than to inherent differences in domestic and foreign goods; Obstfeld and Rogoff (2000) argue that empirically reasonable trade (i.e. transaction) costs can explain much of the home bias; and Anderson (2000) suggests that information costs and imperfect contract enforcement can be important factors.

Deep policy switches such as the creation of the common European market in 1992 have also induced researchers to evaluate their economic impacts. A large collection of studies known as the 'Costs of Non-Europe', supported by the European Commission, mainly consists of detailed estimations of the costs of the borders in Europe. The most-cited reference is the Checchini report that finds that these costs are considerable up to a small percentage of the European GDP. Harrison, Rutherford and Tarr (1996) explicitly model these costs in a general equilibrium framework and reach similar conclusions.

Another more recent example of trade-policy related transaction costs is found in Hertel, Walmsley and Itakura (2001). The particular trade liberalisation policy evaluated in their study includes a series of measures intended to lower non-tariff trade costs between Japan and Singapore. In fact, by imposing the adoption of computerised procedures, an explicit objective of this policy was a reduction of the costs of customs clearance, a clear policy-related transaction cost. For the case of the Japan–Singapore FTA, the effect of linking the two customs' systems is expected to generate additional reductions in effective prices amounting to 0.065 per cent in Japanese imports from Singapore and 0.013 per cent in Singaporean imports from Japan, and these cost savings refer solely to the cost of reduced paperwork, storage and transit expenses. However, in addition to the direct cost savings, there are indirect savings associated with the elimination of customs-related delays in merchandise flows between these two countries. Hummels (2001) emphasises that such time-savings can have a profound effect on international trade by reducing both 'spoilage' and inventory holding costs. He argues that spoilage can occur for many types of reasons. The most obvious might be agricultural and horticultural products that physically deteriorate with the passage of time. However, products with information content (newspapers), as well as highly seasonable (fashion) goods may also experience spoilage. Hummels points out that inventory costs include not only the capital costs of the goods while they are in transit, but also the need to hold larger inventories to accommodate variation in arrival time. He finds that the average value of firms' willingness to pay for one day saved in trade is estimated to be 0.5 per cent ad valorem (i.e., one-half per cent of the value of the good itself). This value of time-savings varies widely by product category, with the low values for bulk commodities and the highest values for intermediate goods.

In summary, even if in identifying empirical estimates for transaction costs we have stretched their definition to include quite different things, it seems clear that geographic characteristics, poor transportation and communication infrastructure, and bad economic policies may directly affect transaction costs, and that their presence can be documented in a variety of ways. For numerous examples of India specific transaction costs, refer to the appendix of this chapter and the references cited therein.

Transaction costs: some theory-consistent numerical simulations for India

This section considers two different ways of modelling transaction costs and several analytical structures to test how these modelling choices affect the evaluation of the effects on aggregate income and relative poverty of a reduction in transaction costs. The ultimate objective is to draw conclusions on the main channels of transmission from transaction costs reduction to income determination (its level and distribution) and their likely empirical relevance in the real world; and to do that, different model versions are parameterised for India.

Transaction costs are modelled as either a mark up on the seller's price or as icebergs melting à la Samuelson. With the former approach transaction margins generate income and they are fully comparable to transportation margins, with the latter they simply produce costless inefficiencies. Besides these, costs can affect transactions in the goods market as well as in the factor markets.

The basic general equilibrium model used here represents a small price-taking economy and it is implemented here in three main versions: the first version is a standard Heckscher–Ohlin international trade model with homogeneous goods, the second introduces intermediate consumption, and the third considers a model with differentiated goods which generalises the Heckscher–Ohlin structure. This helps towards achieving the main objective of the chapter – to show how differences in structural models matter for the estimation of the effects of transaction cost reductions.

The Indian economy: stylised facts of a South Asian developing country

The crucial characteristics of our initial data for India are shown in Table 4.3, where it is possible to observe some of the stylised facts of a typical developing country. The economy has been aggregated into two sectors: an export-oriented sector (*exportables*) and an import-competing sector (*importables*). The first two rows in the table show the relative size of the two sectors and their trade intensity (measured as ratios of exports, or imports, over production). As expected, by observing that India is relatively abundant in unskilled labour, its exportables sector uses it more

Table 4.3 Initial 1994 data – main characteristics

	Sectors		
	Exportables	*Importables*	*Economy-wide*
Production shares %	46	54	
Trade intensity %	10	8	
Skill abundance (unskilled/skilled)			7.4
Skill intensity (unskilled/skilled)	65.9	11.1	
Wage gap (skilled/unskilled)			4.7
Intermediates as % of production	50.6	50.3	
Transaction costs sector allocation	45	55	
Transaction costs ad valorem %	15.0	13.0	

Factor ownership shares	*Skilled labour*	*Unskilled labour*
Rural households	21	79
Urban households	59	41

Consumption Shares	*Urban household*	*Rural household*
Exportables	59	49
Importables	41	51

Source: 1994 SAM for India (B. K. Pradhan, A. Sahoo, and M. R. Saluja (1999)) and authors calculations

intensively. The initial wage gap, measured as the ratio of the average incomes of skilled to unskilled labour, is quite high – with skilled workers earning almost five times more than unskilled workers. Exportables and importables use a similar share of intermediates in production and bear an almost identical transaction cost, as shown by the 'ad valorem' estimate.

Notice also that transaction margins (when modelled as mark-ups) generate income that is allocated across sectors in the same way as total demand (45 per cent goes to exportables and 55 per cent to importables). So whenever transaction margins are reduced, the price wedge between seller and buyer is narrowed, and the total revenues generated will fall. Initially, these revenues are used to buy exportables and importables in fixed shares and these shares are chosen to reflect the structure of total demand so as to be as neutral as possible. Hence, assuming margins are modelled as mark-ups, a fall in revenues should not directly affect the overall demand structure. Clearly, another way of thinking of the sectoral allocation of transaction margin income is that transaction costs are produced using exportables and importables as inputs. The current sectoral allocation may not reflect the real world 'production structure' of transaction costs; nevertheless, in the absence of additional empirical evidence, the neutral allocation allows us to by-pass the problem without introducing unreasonable bias.[9]

Table 4.3 sets out the household shares of factor ownership and goods consumption. Households have been grouped into rural and urban households – and the factor ownership structure shows that rural households are receiving a very large share of their income from unskilled labour. Overall, consumption shares do not differ greatly between the two household groups. Most of the estimates shown in the table are direct calculations from India's national accounts and input–output tables; however, transaction costs have been estimated using raw data on geographic distances and inputs of transport/communication/distribution services.

In summary in this set-up, given similar sectoral ad valorem transaction margins, neutral revenue allocation and similar consumption pattern across households, a reduction in goods market transaction costs affects household poverty and income mainly through changes in factor rewards.

Model 1. A simple Heckscher–Ohlin homogeneous goods trade model

The model includes two tradable homogeneous commodities, two factors of production and two households.

Production. The economy produces two goods, an aggregate exportable commodity (X) and an importable commodity (M), using combinations of skilled and unskilled labour in a Cobb–Douglas constant returns to scale technology as follows:

$$Q_i = \eta_i Ls^{\alpha_i} Lu^{1-\alpha_i} \text{ with the commodities index } i = X, M \qquad (4.1)$$

where Q_i represents the quantity produced of the two goods, η_i stands for sector-specific technical level, and α_i and $(1-\alpha_i)$ are the Cobb–Douglas output elasticities with respect to skilled and unskilled labour (Ls and Lu). Factor-neutral technology shocks similar to those mentioned above would entail changes in the parameter η_i.

Factor markets. We assume full employment of fixed endowments of skilled ($\overline{Ls}$) and unskilled ($\overline{Lu}$) labour, so that their supplies will be completely inelastic with respect to their prices. These are thus determined by firms' demands that, in competitive markets, are equal to the value of their marginal products:

$$Ws = \alpha_i P_i \frac{Q_i}{Ls_i} \qquad i = X, M \qquad (4.2)$$

$$Wu = (1-\alpha_i) P_i \frac{Q_i}{Lu_i} \qquad i = X, M \qquad (4.3)$$

where Ws and Wu are the wages for the two types of labour respectively, and P_i is the producer commodity sale price.

Transaction costs. These are modelled as a mark-up on commodity prices. This is equivalent to an excise tax or a transport margin and, since they do not increase with the value of the commodity exchanged but are proportional to their quantity, they are consistent with the empirical hypotheses on transaction costs described above:

$$Pt_i = P_i + t_i \qquad i = X, M \qquad (4.4)$$

The revenues (T) generated by the wedge t_i between the seller's and buyer's prices are equal to $\sum_i t_i Q_i$, and are used to buy transaction services from both sectors of the economy according to the fixed structure described above.

Consumption. The model includes two household groups, rural households (HHr) and urban households (HHu), each receiving income from selling factor services and demanding commodities via an optimisation of a Cobb–Douglas utility function. Households are therefore differentiated by their consumption patterns and their ownership shares, with the urban household loosely representing the rich household group. Derived consumption demands are as follows:

$$Qd_{Hi} = \beta_{Hi} \frac{Y_H}{Pt_i} \text{ with the household index } H = \text{r, u and } i = \text{X, M} \qquad (4.5)$$

where Qd represents the household-specific quantity demanded, β is a utility share parameter, and Y is the household's income.

Trade and equilibrium conditions. Imports, exports and domestically-produced goods are homogeneous, so trade in either of the two goods can only be one-way (it is either an import or an export) and it originates only when domestic demand and supply differ. In equilibrium, the following trade balance will hold:

$$Pw_X X - Pw_M M = 0 \qquad (4.6)$$

Given the small country assumption, producer prices are equal to the world prices (P_w), and the quantities of exports and imports will be derived from the equality between supply and demand where demand includes final consumption as well as transaction services demands:

$$P_i = pw_i \qquad\qquad i = \text{X, M} \qquad (4.7)$$

$$Q_M + M = \sum_H Qd_{HM} + Qt_M \qquad (4.8a)$$

$$Q_X = \sum_H Qd_{HX} + Qt_X + X \qquad (4.8b)$$

Factor market-clearing conditions simply state that the sums of factor demands must equal the fixed factor endowments.

$$\sum_i L_i = \overline{L} \text{ for both skilled and unskilled and} \sum_i K_i = \overline{K} \quad i = \text{X, M} \qquad (4.9)$$

In this simple model the poverty measure is a relative poverty index equal to the ratio of skilled to unskilled labour rewards.

Model 2. A simple Heckscher–Ohlin homogeneous goods trade model with intermediate goods

This model introduces a simple variation on the previous one by including the use of intermediate goods in the production process. Intermediates are employed in fixed proportions as in a standard Leontief structure, so that equation (4.7) now becomes (4.7a), and (4.8a) and (4.8b) combine into (4.8):

$$P_i = Pw_i - \sum_j (Pw_j + tc_j)a_{ji} \qquad i = \text{X, M} \qquad (4.7a)$$

$$Q_i + M_i = \sum_H Qd_{Hi} + \sum_j Q_j a_{ij} + Qt_i + X_i \qquad i = \text{X, M} \qquad (4.8)$$

where a_{ij} are the Leontief intermediate shares; notice that P_i now become value added prices and these are equal to world prices minus the cost of intermediates which are valued at world prices plus transaction cost mark-ups.

Model 3. A heterogeneous goods trade model

This third model introduces several variants to the previous models. First, transaction costs are modelled as 'iceberg wedges', that is, the quantities sold by suppliers reach the purchasers with a fractional loss (some quantity of the commodity melts away). In this way transaction costs do not generate income (or revenue) and they are in fact denominated in the same units of measurement of the good (that is, real value or quantity). In simplified terms the quantity equilibrium in a specific market would be:

$$Q_i^S = Q_i^D \tau_i \qquad (4.10)$$

where τ is a number greater than 1 representing the 'melting' due to the transaction cost.

In addition, imports and domestically produced goods are imperfect substitutes in consumption. Of the domestically produced goods one is not traded and is therefore only consumed at home while the other is either exported or consumed domestically. These changes alter the fixed world price structure of the homogeneous goods model and allow for the price of the domestically good, which is imperfectly substitutable with the imported good, to differ from the world price. This type of model has been extensively used in the literature and its properties are well known.[10]

In this model there are three goods which enter the consumer utility function, an imported good M, a domestic non-traded good D, and an exported good X. Domestic production occurs only for D and X with a CES (constant elascticity of substitution) technology that includes only skilled and unskilled inputs (the CES function represents another difference form the earlier models).

The production function is:

$$Q_i = [\beta u_i (Lu_i)^{\rho_i} + \beta s_i (Ls_i)^{\rho_i}]^{\frac{1}{\rho_i}} \qquad i = \text{D, X}$$

The factor market equations remain unaltered apart from the obvious changes due to the new functional form. Prices for commodities M and X are fixed but the price is endogenously determined for the non-traded commodity D. In fact, the supply and demand equilibrium (as in equation (4.10)) determines the price of D.

Numerical results

These simple general equilibrium models are used to conduct a basic experiment aimed at investigating the analytical relationship between relative poverty and transaction cost and the aggregate effects of a reduction in the latter. While the following numerical results should not be considered exact estimates, they do provide indications of the potential magnitude and sign of these effects.

As already described in the introduction, for a large body of literature, both empirical and theoretical, globalisation improves an economy's performance beyond the mere disappearance of tariff dead-weight loss triangles. In this study, openness is perceived to bring innovations in transaction technology and the adoption of these innovations is modelled by decreasing transaction costs without increasing any indirect effect on the productivity of primary factors.

A first set of experiments, using the three models described above, considers exogenous reductions of transaction costs affecting the goods markets thereby generating estimates of their effects on real income and the wage gap. In terms of the model parameters, the experiments consist of a shock that reduces t_i in equation (4.4) or τ in equation (4.10). A second set of experiments considers exogenous reductions of transaction costs in the factor markets. A third experiment reverses the logic of the first two sets of experiments by applying a shock to the economy equivalent to the observed changes in real income and the wage gap (and other exogenous variables such as factor supplies, technological progress, and international terms of trade), and then estimating the change in transaction costs.

Table 4.4 shows the results for model 1 of *experiment 1*: a 50 per cent reduction of exogenous transaction costs in goods markets for all goods and all agents. Given the fixed world prices and inelastic supplies of labour, a reduction in transaction costs does not produce any change either in domestic producer prices or in factor rewards so that incentives to alter output levels do not arise and the output of both sectors stays constant. Relative poverty, interpreted as the ratio of the skilled to unskilled wage, does not change due to the fact that resources cannot move across sectors. In this model, consumption due to transaction costs revenues is substituted by households' consumption (or exports) that can increase without an accompanying increase in domestic output.

It should be emphasised that with different initial transaction costs across sectors or with a sector bias in the reduction of transaction costs, these results would not qualitatively change, in particular output and factor rewards would remain unaltered.

An important result obtained with this very simple model is that it registers increases in real incomes of more than 10 per cent. These are large numbers and their occurrence is entirely due to the elimination of the dead-weight rectangles of transaction costs (compared with the elimination of triangles associated with tariff reductions).

When intermediates are introduced in the production process as in model 2 and the same experiment is applied, that is, a reduction of 50 per cent of transaction

Table 4.4 Basic experiment of reduction in transaction costs, percentage variations with respect to initial equilibrium – model 1

Percentage variations	%		%
Output of exportables (Q_X)	0.0	Exportables demand by HHr (Qd_{HX})	13.2
Output of importables (Q_M)	0.0	Importables demand by HHr (QD_{HM})	10.8
Producer price of exportables	0.0	Exportables demand by HHu (Qd_{HX})	13.2
Producer price of importables	0.0	Importables demand by HHu (Qd_{HM})	10.8
Exports (volume)	7.5	TC-induced demand for exportables	−43.6
Imports (volume)	−5.0	TC-induced demand for importables	−44.8
Wage Skilled	0.0	Real HHr income	11.7
Wage Unskilled	0.0	Real HHu income	11.7
Ratio *Ws* / *Wu*	0.0	Total real income	11.7

HHr = rural households; HHu = urban households; TC = transaction costs

Table 4.5 Basic experiment of reduction in transaction costs, percentage variations with respect to initial equilibrium – model 2

Percentage variations	%		%
Output of exportables	0.9	Exportables demand by HHr	13.6
Output of importables	−0.8	Importables demand by HHr	12.7
Value added price of exportables	6.3	Exportables demand by HHu	13.3
Value added price of importables	5.9	Importables demand by HHu	12.3
Exports	−4.4	TC-induced demand for exportables	−46.7
Imports	−10.7	TC-induced demand for importables	−47.1
Wage skilled	5.6	Real HHr income	13.2
Wage unskilled	6.4	Real HHu income	12.9
Ratio *Ws* / *Wu*	−0.8	Total real Income	13.1

HHr = rural households; HHu = urban households; TC = transaction costs

costs mark-ups, quite different results are obtained. In this case the relative profitability of the two sectors changes; the exportables sector, using a larger share of intermediates, enjoys larger cost savings than the importables sector. This translates into a larger increase of the value-added price of exportables, 6.3 per cent in contrast with 5.9 per cent for importables, and an increase of exportables output (see Table 4.5). Exportables use unskilled labour intensively and unskilled labour now enjoys an increase in its reward, hence the relative poverty index improves by about 1 per cent.

How robust is the relative poverty result? It can be easily shown that the answer crucially depends on the sectoral differences in the Leontief a_{ij} coefficients, which

Table 4.6 Initial data – main characteristics with a non-tradable sector

	Sectors			
	Importables	*Exportables*	*Domestic*	*Economy-wide*
Production shares %		47	53	
Trade intensity %	100	24	0	
Skill abundance (unskilled/skilled)				7.4
Skill intensity (unskilled/skilled)		23.7	3.3	
Wage gap (skilled/unskilled)				4.7
Transaction wedge (goods markets)	1.15	1.15	1.13	
Transaction wedge (factor markets)				
Skilled workers		1.20	1.20	
Unskilled workers		1.20	1.20	

Source: 1994 SAM for India (B. K. Pradhan, A. Sahoo, and M. R. Saluja, 1999) and authors' calculations

directly influence the size of the cost savings due to the reduction in transaction costs. The same experiment performed on an Indian economy where all sectors were assigned the same intermediate coefficients would produce identical changes in both skilled and unskilled wages, even in the case of sectorally unequal transaction costs mark-ups. However it should be stressed that a reduction in transaction costs would bring positive increases in the wages of both labour types so that absolute levels of poverty should be reduced (and welfare increased) with a reduction in transaction costs.

Given that model 3 introduces a third (non-tradable) sector, before commenting on the experiment results, a new table with the salient characteristics of the Indian economy is given (Table 4.6).

Table 4.6 displays the main changes that affect the structure of the initial Indian data for this third model and it should be contrasted with Table 4.3. The salient features to be noted are the high skilled-labour intensity in the production of domestic non-traded goods relative to that of exportables (this is derived mainly from the production structure of non-tradable services that include a high percentage of white collar workers of the government sector, a large employer in India), and the lower transaction cost wedge (13 per cent instead of 15 per cent) associated with exchanges in this sector.

Results from the basic experiment, a reduction of 50 per cent of commodity markets transaction costs mark-ups, performed with the third model are shown in Table 4.7. The main novelty here is that a reduction in transaction costs seems to have a lower effect on aggregate income. This qualitatively different outcome can be fully explained by the initial (i.e. in the benchmark data) difference in transaction wedges across sectors. In model 1, sectoral differences in transaction cost mark-ups

Table 4.7 Basic experiment of reduction in transaction costs, percentage variations with respect to initial equilibrium – model 3

Percentage variations	%		%
Output of exportables	0.03	Household demand for importables	7.2
Output of domestic goods	−0.03	Household demand for exportables	6.9
		Household demand for domestic goods	6.1
Price of importables	0.00		
Price of exportables	0.00		
Price of domestic goods	−0.03		
Exports	7.09		
Imports	0.15		
Wage skilled	−0.06	Real household income	6.5
Wage unskilled	0.01		
Ratio Ws / Wu	−0.08		

do not matter for relative poverty, but in this model they are crucial. Because domestic goods are not perfect substitutes with importables, a sectorally different transaction cost shock alters relative prices across these categories of commodities, and triggers a series of additional effects on output levels, factor allocations and rewards. A reduction of transaction costs lowers the wedge between the quantities of each commodity demanded and supplied. Given the small country assumption, prices of 'M' and of 'X' do not change and, for these markets, the new equilibrium is reached via changes in the quantities of export and import flows. Conversely, commodity D's price is endogenous and is reduced. Moreover, a falling price results in lower profitability for this sector and gives rise to a resource reallocation. Finally, a fall in the wages of skilled workers is due to the more intensive use of this factor in the contracting sector that produces commodity D.

A second experiment applies a 50 per cent reduction of exogenous transaction costs in factor markets for all factors and all agents. Table 4.8 shows the results for this experiment conducted with a slightly modified version of model 3 in which transaction costs wedges have been introduced in factor markets. The results are self-explanatory: relative prices are not altered (goods or factors) but less of the primary resources are used in transaction costs, so the economy gains in a way that is effectively the same as an increase in factor supplies.

A third experiment with model 3 entails a factor-biased reduction, in terms of a 50 per cent reduction of exogenous transaction costs in factor markets for skilled labour across all sectors.

Table 4.9 shows the results of this experiment conducted with model 3. As in the previous case these results can be interpreted as if there had been an increase in the supply of skilled labour. Clearly, the largest beneficiaries of this windfall are producers in the domestic non-tradable sector, given that they use intensively a now more abundant factor. The production possibilities frontier shifts outwards

Table 4.8 Basic experiment of reduction in factor transaction costs, percentage variations with respect to initial equilibrium – model 3

Percentage variations	%		%
Output of exportables	9.1	Household demand for importables	9.1
Output of domestic goods	9.1	Household demand for exportables	9.1
		Household demand for domestic goods	9.1
Price of importables	0.0		
Price of exportables	0.0		
Price of domestic goods	0.0		
Exports	9.1		
Imports	9.1		
Wage skilled	9.1	Real household income	9.1
Wage unskilled	9.1		
Ratio Ws / Wu	0.00		

Table 4.9 Reduction in factor (skilled labour) transaction costs, percentage variations with respect to initial equilibrium – model 3

Percentage variations	%		%
Output of exportables	−0.7	Household demand for importables	−1.7
Output of domestic goods	7.1	Household demand for exportables	−0.4
		Household demand for domestic goods	0.0
Price of importables	0.0	Consumer price of importables	0.0
Price of exportables	0.0	Consumer price of exportables	0.0
Price of domestic goods	−6.6	Consumer price of domestic goods	−6.6
Exports	−1.7		
Imports	−1.7		
Wage skilled	−5.0	Real household income	3.2
Wage unskilled	2.7		
Ratio Ws / Wu	−7.5		
Exportables' demand for skilled labour	4.0	Exportables' demand for unskilled labour	−1.7
Domestic goods' demand for skilled labour	10.1	Domestic goods' demand for unskilled labour	3.1

Table 4.10 Reduction in factor (unskilled labour) transaction costs, percentage variations with respect to initial equilibrium – model 3

Percentage variations	%		%
Output of exportables	9.8	Household demand for importables	10.9
Output of domestic goods	1.6	Household demand for exportables	9.4
		Household demand for domestic goods	1.6
Price of importables	0.0	Consumer price of importables	0.0
Price of exportables	0.0	Consumer price of exportables	0.0
Price of domestic goods	7.2	Consumer price of domestic goods	7.2
Exports	10.9		
Imports	10.9	Real household income	5.7
Wage skilled	14.5		
Wage unskilled	6.0		
Ratio *Ws / Wu*	7.9		
Exportables' demand for skilled labour	4.0	Exportables' demand for unskilled labour	11.0
Domestic goods' demand for skilled labour	−1.0	Domestic goods' demand for unskilled labour	5.7

and more in the direction of the skilled-labour intensive product ('D'); the relative (consumer) goods price shifts in favour of this same product; and producers supply more D thanks to the lower costs of employing skilled labour. The skilled wage premium is reduced and aggregate income rises (notice that skilled labour in volume is about 12 per cent of total employment).

The results of a symmetric experiment of introducing a biased reduction in unskilled labour transaction costs are summarised in Table 4.10. It should be noted that, as in the previous case, the increased supply effect (due to the reduction in transaction costs) dominates the wage-gap change: here, more abundant unskilled workers gain more in absolute terms but *less* relative to the scarcer skilled workers.

The fourth experiment entails a 50 per cent reduction of tariffs with no change in transaction costs. Initially tariffs on importables are quite high at 46 per cent and their reduction makes imports cheaper relative to domestically produced goods. This changes the incentives for production and triggers a resource reallocation.

The results shown in Table 4.11 are completely in line with traditional modelling of trade liberalisation; in particular, it should be noticed that the real income effects are quite small (less than 1 per cent), especially when compared with results obtained through a reduction in transaction costs.

All the shocks previously examined are summarised in a final experiment, with the aim of describing the recent evolution of the Indian economy. In this case, rather than assuming exogenous changes in transaction costs and measuring their effects on the Indian economy, the model is run to 'fit' the actual data and it estimates the

Table 4.11 Basic experiment of reduction in tariffs, percentage variations with respect to initial equilibrium – model 3

Percentage variations	%		%
Output of exportables	2.0	Household demand of importables	18.4
Output of domestic goods	−1.8	Household demand of exportables	−3.1
		Household demand of domestic goods	−1.8
Price of importables	0.0	Consumer price of importables	−15.8
Price of exportables	0.0	Consumer price of exportables	0.0
Price of domestic goods	−2.2	Consumer price of domestic Goods	−2.2
Exports	18.4		
Imports	18.4	Real household income	0.9
Wage skilled	−4.3		
Wage unskilled	0.9		
Ratio Ws / Wu	−5.09		

variations in transaction costs residually. In more detail, the model is calibrated to an initial equilibrium for 1988 and, by exogenously changing factors supplies, technological change, trade policy, terms of trade shocks, it is then used to estimate a new 1994 equilibrium. The model results, in terms of the GDP growth and wage gap, do not perfectly reproduce the observed 1994 data. Hence, transaction costs are allowed to vary so that the model will correctly reproduce observations. In this way, the model provides an indirect estimate of the variation in transaction costs that ensures consistency with observed data. The observed data are summarised in Table 4.12, which shows the recent evolution of the Indian economy since it implemented its major structural reforms. The bottom panel shows a considerable spike (of almost 2 per cent per annum) in the growth rate of GDP.

In this final experiment four main exogenous changes are considered: a) change in tariff rates (Tar), b) terms of trade shock (TOT), c) changes in factor supplies (LS), d) change in total factor productivity (TFP) (applied with no sector bias).

The wage gap and GDP variations resulting from this set of experiments are shown in Figure 4.1. The tariff reduction decreases the wage gap by inducing a resource re-allocation consistent with Indian comparative advantage and this has also a mild positive effect on real income; terms of trade shocks (consisting of a 10 per cent reduction of the price of Indian exportables) produce a minor increase in the wage gap accompanied by a small real income reduction; changes in the labour supply of skilled and unskilled workers have major effects for both the wage gap and income, in particular skilled workers become relatively less scarce and their wage premium is considerably reduced; and finally, technological progress has strong positive effects on real income and minor consequences for the wage gap. Combining all these shocks together produces the results shown in the column 'All'. This compares quite well with the column 'Target', which represents the observed 1988–94 variations in the wage gap and real income, although the 'model' wage

Table 4.12 India – recent economic evolution

Variables / periods	1988	1994	1988 / 94 change
GDP constant 1988 price LCU (millions)	4,194,400	5,633,150	34.30
Skilled wage	47.1	84.6	79.70
Unskilled wage	18.8	36.1	91.92
Ratio (skilled / unskilled)	2.5	2.3	–6.36
Skilled labour (millions)	29	39	34.18
Unskilled labour (millions)	223	246	10.40
Tariff (average weighted in %)	87	46	–47.13
TFP index (economy wide)	100	115	15.00
	1960–1987	*1988–1999*	
Average yearly GDP growth rate	3.88	5.69	

gap seems to decrease much more than the 'real world' wage gap, and, conversely, real incomes increase more in observed than model-produced data.

The right-most column labelled 'All TC' shows the results for an experiment where transaction costs for the market for unskilled workers are allowed to change up to the point where the observed wage gap reduction is obtained. In this way, the model's wage gap perfectly matches the observed 6.4 per cent reduction and provides an indirect estimation for the reduction of transaction costs that are nec-essary to ensure this. These have to go down considerably – by about 65 per cent. The size of this estimation should not be surprising, especially in the light of es-timates of the costs of rent-seeking in India. Rent-seeking originating from price and quantity controls is indeed another way of looking at transaction costs, and it has been initially estimated by Krueger (1974) at 7 per cent of GNP and more recently by Mohammad and Whalley (1984) at 30 per cent to 45 per cent of GNP.

Conclusions

The experiments discussed above show that different analytical structures high-light different transmission channels and can produce quite different final results. From a static (or long-term) equilibrium point of view, the debate on whether an improvement in transaction costs should benefit the poor seems essentially to be an empirical one. The results in this chapter clearly demonstrate that transac-tion cost reductions can account for a large share of income changes normally recorded in internationally integrating economies, a novelty compared with more traditional trade models. Clearly, these conclusions echo very closely those reached

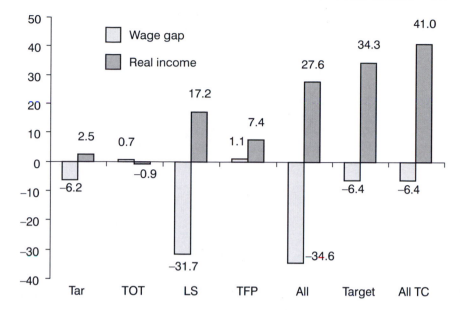

Figure 4.1 1988–94 combined shocks: tariffs, terms of trade, labour supplies and TFP

when technology advances are modelled as productivity changes, and the transaction cost approach may indeed complement that of productivity. However, unless technology is modelled endogenously, which is a daunting task, especially for developing countries, a productivity shock would represent a totally exogenous windfall, whereas a reduction in transaction costs feeds back in these models in a reduction of intermediation, and may therefore be simpler to implement empirically. Notice also that, in the models examined here, transaction costs affect not only commodity exchanges, but also factor markets. In this way it is then possible to simulate changes in education, training, health, or even migration, that originate from lower transaction costs, and even larger numbers then emerge.

Notes

1 For surveys see Baldwin and Venables (1995), Brown (1993), Burfisher and Jones (1998), Francois and Shiells (1994), Hertel *et al.* (1997), US International Trade Commission (1992, 1998).
2 Slaughter and Swagel (1997) cite evidence for Mexico, Meller and Tokman (1996) study the Chilean case, and Sanchez and Nuñez (1998) examine the Colombian case. See Davis (1992) and Wood (1997) for multi-country studies covering this issue.
3 For empirical evidence on the US see Lawrence and Slaughter (1993), Krugman and Lawrence (1993), Leamer (1998), Baldwin and Cain (1997). See Abrego and Whalley (2000) for a survey of this debate and their original contribution.
4 For a recent survey see Williamson (2000).
5 See Debreu (1959).
6 Kurz (1974), Hahn (1971), Foley (1970).

7 See also Antle (1983) and Fan, Hazel and Thorat (1999).
8 Recent literature labels these technologies as 'General Purpose Technologies'. See Helpman (1998) and Bresnahan and Tratjenberg (1995).
9 In fact one can think of two alternatives to this assumption: in the first, if it were known that producers of transaction services are found exclusively in the importables sector, then transaction cost revenues could be allocated entirely to buying output from the importables sector. Alternatively, it may be possible to estimate a transaction cost production function that uses a mix of primary factors. In this case producers of transaction services would minimise their cost of production subject to a budget constraint that equals transaction costs revenues.
10 See de Melo and Robinson (1989) or more recently Bhattarai *et al.* (1999).

References

Abrego, L. and J. Whalley (2000) 'The Choice of Structural Model in Trade-Wages Decompositions', *Review of International Economics*, 8(3) (August): 462–477.

Anderson, J. E. (2000) 'Why Do Nations Trade (So Little)?' *Pacific Economic Review*, 5: 115–134.

Antle, J. M. (1983) 'Infrastructure and Aggregate Agricultural Productivity: International Evidence', *Economic Development and Cultural Change*, 31(3): 609–619.

Baldwin, R. E. and G. G. Cain (1997) 'Shifts in US Relative and Absolute Wages: The Role Of Trade, Technology and Factor Endowments', NBER Working Paper 5934.

Baldwin, R. E. and A. J. Venables (1995) 'Regional Economic Integration', in G. Grossman and K. Rogoff (eds), *Handbook of International Economics*, Vol. III, Amsterdam: Elsevier.

Bhattarai, K., M. Gosh, and J. Whalley (1999) 'On some Properties of a Trade Closure Widely used in Numerical Modelling', *Economics Letters*, 62: 13–21.

Bresnahan, T. and M. Tratjenberg (1995) 'General Purpose Technologies: Engines of Growth' *Journal of Econometrics*, 65: 83–108.

Brown, D. K. (1993) 'The Impact of a North American Free Trade Area: Applied General Equilibrium Models', in N. Lusting, B. P. Bosworth, and R. Z. Lawrence (eds) *Assessing the Impact, North American Free Trade*, Washington, DC: Brookings Institution.

Burfisher, M. E. and E. A. Jones (eds) (1998) 'Regional Trade Agreements and U.S. Agriculture', Economic Research Service, AER No. 771, Washington, DC: US Department of Agriculture.

Coase, R. (1937) 'The Nature of the Firm', *Economica* 4 (November): 386–405.

Collier, P. (1997) 'Globalization: What should be the African Policy Response?', mimeo, Oxford: Centre for the Study of African Economies, University of Oxford.

Collier, P. (1998) 'Globalization: Implications for African Economic Management', mimeo, Washington, DC: World Bank.

Davis, S. (1992) 'Cross-Country Patterns of Changes in Relative Wages', *NBER Macroeconomics Annual*, Cambridge, MA: National Bureau of Economic Research, 7: 239–291.

Debreu, G. (1959), *Theory of Value: An Axiomatic Analysis of Economic Equilibrium*, New York: Wiley.

De Melo, J. and S. Robinson (1989) 'Product Differentiation and the Treatment of Foreign Trade in Computable General Equilibrium Models of Small Economies', *Journal of International Economics*, 27: 47–67.

Elbadawi, A. I. (1998) 'Can Africa Export Manufactures? The Role of Endowment, Exchange Rates and Transaction Costs', mimeo, Washington, DC: World Bank.

Elbadawi, I., T. Mengistae, and A. Zeufack (2001) 'Geography, Supplier Access, Foreign

Market Potential, and Manufacturing Exports in Africa: An Analysis of Firm Level Data', World Bank Working Paper.

Evans, C. L. (2000) 'The Sources for the Border Effects: Nationality or Location', Manuscript, Federal Reserve Bank of New York.

Fan, S., P. Hazel and S. Thorat (1999) 'Linkages Between Government Spending, Growth and Poverty in Rural India', Research Report 110, Washington, DC: International Food Policy Research Institute

Foley, D. K. (1970) 'Economic Equilibrium with Costly Marketing', *Journal of Economic Theory*, 2: 276–291.

Francois, J. F. and C. R. Shiells (1994) 'AGE Models of North American Free Trade', in J. F. Francois and C. R. Shiells (eds) *Modelling Trade Policy: Applied General Equilibrium Assessments of North American Free Trade*, Cambridge: Cambridge University Press.

Freund, C. and D. Weinhold (2000) 'On the Effect of the Internet on International Trade', Board of Governors of the Federal Reserve System, International Finance Discussion Papers 693.

Goldberg, V. (1985) 'Production Functions, Transaction Costs and the New Institutionalism', in G. R. Feiwel (ed.) *Issues in Contemporary Microeconomics and Welfare*, Albany, NY: SUNY Press.

Guasch, J. Luis, and J. Kogan (2001) 'Inventories in Developing Countries: Levels and Determinants – a Red Flag for Competitiveness and Growth', Working Paper No 2552, Washington, DC: World Bank.

Hahn, F. H. (1971) 'Equilibrium with Transaction Costs', *Econometrica*, 2: 276–291.

Harrison, G., T. Rutherford and D. Tarr (1996) 'Increased Competition and Completion of the Market in the European Union: Static and Steady State Effects', *Journal of Economic Integration*, 11(3): 332–365.

Helpman, E. (ed.) (1998) *General Purpose Technologies and Economic Growth*, Cambridge, MA: MIT Press.

Henderson, V., Z. Shalizi and A. Venables (2001) 'Geography and Development', *Journal of Economic Geography*, 1: 81–106.

Hertel, T. W., W. M. Masters and M. J. Gehlhar (1997) 'Regionalism in World Food Markets: Implications for Trade and Welfare', Plenary paper for the XXIII International Conference of Agricultural Economists, 10–16 August 1997, Sacramento, CA.

Hertel, T. W., T. L. Walmsley and K. Itakura (2001) 'Dynamic Effects of the "New Age", Free Trade Agreement between Japan and Singapore', *Journal of Economic Integration*, December, 16(4): 446–448.

Hummels, D. (2001) 'Time as a Trade Barrier', working paper, Purdue University.

Jalan, J. and M. Ravallion (1998) 'Are there dynamic gains from a poor-area development program?', *Journal of Public Economics*, 67: 65–85.

KPMG (2000) 'The Impact of the New Economy on Poor People and Developing Countries', Draft Final Report to the UK Department for International Development, 7 July.

Krueger, A. (1974) 'The Political Economy of the Rent-Seeking Society', *American Economic Review*, 64(3): 291–303.

Krugman, P. and R. Lawrence (1993) 'Trade, Jobs, and Wages', NBER Working Paper 4478, Washington, DC: National Bureau of Economic Research.

Kurz, M. (1974) 'Equilibrium with Transaction Cost and Money in a Single Market Exchange Economy', *Journal of Economic Theory*, 7: 418–452.

Lawrence, R. Z., and M. Slaughter (1993) 'Trade and U.S. Wages in the 1980s: Giant Sucking Sound or Small Hiccup?', *Brookings Papers on Economic Activity: Microeconomics*, 2: 161–210.

Leamer, E. (1998) 'In Search of Stolper–Samuelson Linkages between International Trade and Lower Wages', in S. M. Collins (ed.) *Imports, Exports, and the American Worker*, Washington, DC: Brookings Institution.

Limao, N. and A. Venables (2001) 'Infrastructure, Geographical Disadvantage, Transport Costs and Trade', *World Bank Economic Review*, 15(3): 451–480.

Meller, P. and A. Tokman (1996) 'Apertura Comercial y Diferencial Salarial en Chile', in P. Meller (ed.), *El Modelo Exportador Chileno*, Santiago, Chile: Economic Research Corporation for Latin America.

Mohammad S and J. Whalley (1984) 'Rent-seeking in India: Its Costs and Policy Significance', *Kyklos*, 37: 387–413.

Obstfeld, M. and K. Rogoff (2000) 'The Six Major Puzzles in International Macroeconomics: Is there a Common Cause?', NBER, Working Paper 7777, Washington, DC: National Bureau of Economic Research.

Pradhan, B. K., A. Sahoo, and M. R. Saluja (1999) 'A Social Accounting Matrix for India, 1994–95', Special Article, *Economic and Political Weekly*, Mumbai, India.

Samuelson, P. A. (1954) 'The Transfer Problem and Transport Costs, II: Analysis of Effects of Trade Impediments', *The Economic Journal*, 64: 264–289.

Sanchez, F. and J. Nuñez (1998) 'Educación y Salarios Relativos en Colombia, 1976–1995: Determinantes, Evolución e Implicaciones para la Distribución del Ingreso', *Archivo de Macroeconomia* 74, Bogota: Colombia: National Planning Department.

Slaughter, M. J., and P. Swagel (1997) 'The Effects of Globalization on Wages in Advanced Economies', Working Paper 97/43, Washington, DC: International Monetary Fund, Research Department.

US International Trade Commission (1992) *Economy-Wide Modelling of the Economic Implications of a FTA with Mexico and a NAFTA with Canada and Mexico*, Publication 2516, May.

US International Trade Commission (1998) *The Economic Implications of Liberalizing APEC Tariff and Non-tariff Barriers to Trade*, Publication 3101, April.

Williamson, O. (2000) 'The New Institutional Economics: Taking Stock, Looking Ahead', *Journal of Economic Literature*, Vol. XXXVIII (September): 595–613.

Wood, A. (1997) 'Openness and Wage Inequality in Developing Countries: The Latin American Challenge to Conventional Wisdom', *World Bank Economic Review* 11(1): 33–57.

Appendix: Policy-related transaction costs in India

This appendix should be considered as a partial updating of the paper by Mohammad and Whalley (1984) on rent-seeking in India. In that paper, the authors estimate the cost of rent seeking in India and quantify its magnitude at between 30 per cent and 45 per cent of GNP per year. They also offer an extensive survey of the numerous economic policies that are likely to cause rent seeking. It should be stressed that rent-seeking activity consists of using productive resources in 'processes generating outputs with no welfare valuation', i.e. consists of wasting resources, and, in this sense, rent-seeking and *iceberg-melting* transaction costs are the same phenomenon.

In what follows,[1] a brief sketch of the recent (1985–2001) evolution of the Indian economic policy controls is reported following the same headings as Mohammad and Whalley's paper.

1 External sector controls

1.1 Import restrictions

1985–1990

The 1980s saw some attempts to simplify the import licensing system in order to provide easier access to intermediate goods imports for domestic production by placing many such items on the readily importable OGL (Open General License) list. To a lesser extent capital goods imports were also eased through flexible operation of the discretionary regime in order to encourage technological upgrading, particularly for export-oriented industries. There was some replacement of quantitative import restrictions by tariffs, primarily in cases where there was no competing domestic production. The import tariff structure was somewhat simplified, however the average tariff rate went up. In October 1986, duty-free imports of capital goods were allowed in selected 'thrust' export industries.

In April 1988, access for exporters to imported capital goods was increased by widening the list of those available on OGL and by making some capital goods available selectively to exporters without going through 'indigenous clearance'

1991–2001

In April 1992, a single negative list consisting of intermediate goods, a few capital goods and most consumer goods replaced import licensing. For most goods other than final consumer goods, the reform in the very first year largely removed QRs (Quantitative Restrictions) on imports. The QRs coverage for manufacturing (defined as the share of value added of the items subject to import licensing to total value added) declined from 90 per cent in the pre-reform period to 51 per cent in the 1994/95. It dropped to 29 per cent for capital goods and 35 per cent for raw materials and intermediates; more de-licensing has followed. Certain petroleum products are the only major raw materials and intermediates whose import remains subject to licensing, and in practice even licenses are not quantitatively restrictive.

Trade liberalisation for consumer goods started in 1992 when large exporters received Special Import Licenses as an incentive, allowing them to import certain consumer goods specified on a positive list. These licenses are freely tradable and their premium accrues to exporters. The positive list has subsequently expanded. Baggage rules on consumer goods imports have also been liberalised. A phased reduction in tariffs thus became a central component of trade policy reform as tariff rates came down in all the budgets presented from 1991 onwards, with the maximum tariff decreased to 50 per cent in March 1995. Systematic reduction in the dispersion of tariff rates produced eight rates of custom duty by April 1995 as opposed to 22 at the beginning of 1991. In 1992, the Tax Reform Committee recommended that, by 1997/98, the tariff structure should have custom duties of 20 per cent on capital goods, 25 to 30 per cent on intermediate goods and 50 per cent on consumer goods. The government accepted the recommendations with an open commitment to lower tariffs further.

Import duties on capital goods have dropped substantially. The composite rate on 'project imports' (imports of various capital goods needed to set up new projects), fell to 25 per cent from 85 per cent. The duty on imports of machinery for electricity generation, petroleum refining, and coal mining came down to 20 per cent; that for fertilisers dropped to zero. The authorities left in place an earlier facility for duty-free imports of capital goods by firms registered under the 100 per cent Export-Oriented Units (EOU) scheme and those in Export Processing Zones (EPZs).

Intermediate goods such as metals and chemicals also obtained substantial tariff reductions. Effective tariff protection for manufacturing has fallen from an estimated 164 per cent in fiscal year 1990/91 to about 72 per cent in 1994/95.

The most recent 2001–02 official trade policy review (Exim policy) considers the following points: a) QRs are totally dismantled; b) standing group to be set up for monitoring import of 300 sensitive items; c) import of new and second-hand automobiles allowed, but subject to conditions; d) import of agricultural products like wheat, rice, maize, other coarse cereals, copra and coconut oil placed in the category of state trading; e) free imports of second-hand capital goods from up to 10 years old.

1.2 Foreign exchange rationing

1985–1990

Since Indian inflation rose faster than that of its trading partners, a devaluation of the nominal effective exchange rate of about 45 per cent was required and achieved. This reflects a considerable change in the official attitude toward exchange rate depreciation, however stringent restrictions still apply to foreign exchange trades.

1991–2001

The rupee was devalued in July 1991 by 24 per cent. Exchange-rate policy went through a series of further changes from 1991 to 1993. In March 1992 a dual exchange-rate system was introduced. Under the new regime, exporters surrendered 40 per cent of their foreign exchange earnings to the Reserve Bank of India at the official exchange rate, retaining the remaining 60 per cent for sale in the free market thus created, which automatically restricted import demand to the available foreign exchange.

In March 1993, the government moved to a unified floating exchange rate. The exchange rate settled at around Rs 31=$1, between the old exchange rate of Rs 24=$1 and the free-market rate of Rs 34=$1. Thus, the nominal exchange rate shifted by 57.5 per cent, from Rs 20=$1 in June 1991 before the devaluation to Rs 31.5=$1 in March 1993.

The rupee is now fully convertible for current-account transactions.

1.3 Export controls and export promotion

1985–1990

Export incentives were substantially increased. Cash assistance and duty draw-backs went up. The value of the incentives net of taxes increased from 2.3 per cent of the value of exports in 1960/61 to 11.1 per cent in 1989/90.

There was a widening of the coverage of products available to exporters against import replenishment and advance licenses. Very substantial income tax concessions were given to business profits attributable to exports. The traditional export subsidies (cash assistance, premium on import replenishment licenses, and duty drawbacks) increased from 9 to 13 per cent of total export.

In 1985 budget, 50 per cent of business profits attributable to exports were made income tax exempt: in the 1988 budget this concession was extended to 100 per cent of the export profits. The interest rate on export credit was reduced from 12 to 9 per cent.

1991–2001

Export subsidies were reduced. With the removal of quantitative restrictions and a shift to a new competitive exchange rate, a large part of the export subsidy regime was dismantled. Cash compensatory support ended very early when the rupee was devalued by 24 per cent in July 1991. Subsequently the International Price Reimbursement Scheme (IPRS), which refunded to the user the difference between the world and domestic prices of major inputs such as steel and rubber, was abolished from 31 March 1994.

The major export incentives still present include duty drawback and the advance licensing scheme to large exporters to import the needed inputs duty free. The EPZs and the scheme of EOUs also continue. The Exim Policy of April 1995 has taken several steps to enhance export incentives, e.g. provision for duty-free importation of capital goods and extension of the EPCG (Export Promotion Capital Goods) scheme to the services sector; improvement in the Advance Licensing Scheme; an introduction of a green channel facility for customs clearance by certain categories of exporters.

2 Capital Markets controls

2.1 Industrial licensing

1985–1990

There was some dilution of external requirements as regards entry and expansion of capacity. The list of industries open to large firms was extended, and the licensing procedure was simplified.

1991–2001

Restrictions on the operation of large industrial houses have been removed. Licensing requirements for investment have been abolished for all except a few strategic and defence industries. Many areas earlier reserved for the public sector are now open to private entrepreneurs. These measures resulted in a strong injection of domestic competition and market orientation in the manufacturing industry.

It should be noticed that considerable resistance to reforms arises from public-sector infrastructure monopolies. Thus, even though doors have been opened for both foreign and domestic private investment into these sectors, actual progress has been slow. The Statement of Industrial Policy 1991 reduced the list reserved for the public sector from 17 to 8. By the end of 1994, the only areas in manufacturing which continued to be reserved to public firms were those related to defence, strategic concerns, and petroleum. Even here the government may invite the private sector to participate, as it has in the case of oil exploration and refining.

2.2 Banks and insurance companies controls

1991–2001

India's economic reforms have extended to both the banking system and the capital markets. To reduce the former dominance of the financial sector by public-sector banks with little commercial discretion in allocating their lending, banking sector reforms have included substantial interest rate deregulation, more liberal licensing of private-sector banks, and more latitude for expansion of the branch networks of foreign banks. The issue of privatisation of the public-sector banks has not yet been addressed.

Capital-market reforms have sought to free the capital market from detailed, direct government controls, replacing them by a system of supervision to ensure better disclosure, greater transparency and thus more investor protection. Efforts are being made to modernise the stock exchanges and improve trading practices and settlement systems. A major current initiative is the introduction of legislation to establish a Central Depository System, which would expedite settlement. There have been no reforms in the insurance sector; an expert committee has recommended opening it to private investment, including foreign investment, but at the time of writing no decision has yet been taken.

2.3 Controls on foreign private investment

1985–1990

In the second half of the 1980s, government began to seek foreign investment in industries deemed to be of the national importance.

1991–2001

Reforms in policy towards foreign investment began with a radically new approach to Foreign Direct Investment (FDI) in the first year of the reforms. The new regime permits FDI in virtually every sector of the economy. Foreign-equity proposals need not be accompanied by technology transfers as required earlier. Royalty payments have been considerably liberalised. In industries reserved for the small-scale sector, foreign equity can go up to 24 per cent. Policy encourages foreign equity up to 100 per cent in export-oriented units, the power sector, electronics and software technology parks. In other industries, foreign equity up to 100 per cent is permitted discretionally. No restrictions hinder the use of foreign brand names/trade marks for internal sale.

Although simplified, controls still remain. A simple fast-track mechanism or 'automatic approval' from the Reserve Bank of India is available for projects of certain kinds, e.g. up to 51 per cent equity in high-priority industries, up to 100 per cent equity in wholly export-oriented units and all foreign-technology agreements, which meet certain economic parameters. For all others, including cases involving foreign-equity participation of over 51 per cent, a high-level Foreign Investment Promotion Board (FIPB) reviews the applications. About 20 per cent of the proposals have gone through the automatic route.

The Foreign Exchange Regulation Act (FERA) has undergone substantial amendment to remove restrictive provisions on the operations of companies with foreign equity of 40 per cent or more (commonly known as FERA companies). All companies incorporated in India are now treated alike irrespective of the level of foreign equity. FERA companies can now acquire and sell immovable property. They can also borrow and accept deposits from the public. Raising equity up to 51 per cent for these companies receives 'automatic approval', if the investment are in any of 35 listed priority industries.

India has joined the Multilateral Investment Guarantee Agency (MIGA) for protecting foreign investment against risks such as war, civil disturbance and ex-propriation. The government specially encourages foreign investment in infrastructure, particularly the power sector. Not only can foreign investors hold 100 per cent equity, but tax holidays are also offered for five years for new power projects.

In the hydrocarbon sector, joint ventures are now permitted in both exploration and development of oil fields and refineries. The telecommunication sector opened up with the announcement in May 1994 of a new telecom policy providing for private investment in basic telephone services as well as value-added services. Air transport, until recently a public-sector monopoly, has opened to the private sector, and new entrants have begun operations. Private toll roads have also been commissioned.

In 1992 the government announced a new policy encouraging *portfolio investment* in Indian industry. The Indian capital markets thus opened to foreign institutional investors such as pension funds and broad-based mutual funds, subject to regulation by the Securities and Exchange Board of India. Indian companies also gained access to capital markets abroad through mechanisms such as Global Depository Receipts or Euro issues. Substantially reduced restrictions on foreign investment produced an inflow of portfolio investment that has grown from practically nil before 1991 to almost $3.5 billion per year since fiscal year 1993/94, while direct investment grew to over $1.3 billion by 1994/95.

Outflows by residents are still forbidden or highly controlled. Inflows and outflows by non-residents have been partially deregulated. Foreign portfolio investment by residents is forbidden.

2.4 Interest rate controls

1991–2001

Interest rate deregulation has been much faster since 1991. The process of liberalisation has gone forward in commercial-bank deposit and loan rates. As recently as 1989/90, the interest rate structure was still very complicated with 50 lending categories and a large number of stipulated interest rates depending on loan size, usage and type of borrower. Starting in April 1992, the structure has become much freer and simpler. By the end of 1993, there were only two restrictions on deposit rates: a fixed rate on savings deposits of 5 per cent and a maximum rate of 10 per cent on term deposits (defined as deposits with maturities above one and a half months). On the lending side, there was a minimum lending rate of 15 per cent for loans above Rs 2 lakhs and a concessional rate of 12 per cent for very small loans. Since then, there has been further deregulation. The lending rate for loans larger than Rs 2 lakhs has been totally freed, though two concessional rates (13.5 per cent and 12 per cent) are now in place for loans of smaller size. The cap on the deposit rate (now 12 per cent) applies only to maturities of one and a half months to two years; the deposit rate for deposits longer than two years is unrestricted.

2.5 Monopoly controls

1985–1990

The asset threshold above which firms are subject to monopoly regulation was raised. Softening of restrictions on monopolies also occurred.

3 Controls in goods markets

3.1 Price controls

1985–1990

Though this form of intervention has been diluted, its scope nevertheless remains intensive. The wholesale price index consists of a total of 360 commodities of which there are 55 major items whose prices are fully administered, partially administered or subjected to different forms of voluntary and other mechanisms of control. Fully administered items include petroleum products, coal, electricity, fertilisers, iron and steel products, non-ferrous metals, drugs and medicines, paper and newsprint.

3.2 Pricing and public enterprises

1991–2001

Budgetary support to public enterprises has been reduced. India's infrastructure has not fared well in the reform process. Market-orientation and domestic deregulation have focused largely on the manufacturing sector, while crucial areas of infrastructure like power generation, telecommunications, roads and ports still function within a maze of regulation.

3.3 Controls on agriculture

1991–2001

The prices of all major agricultural products have been largely determined by the central government's control of foreign trade in them. The prices of cereals (rice, wheat, and coarse grains) and cotton have been held below world prices in most years by controlling exports.

Note

1 The text draws heavily on the three sources cited below

Sources

Vijay, J., and I. M. D. Little (1997) *India's Economic Reforms 1991–2001*, Oxford: Oxford University Press.

Vijay, J., and I. M. D. Little (1994) *India Macroeconomics and Political Economy 1964–1991*, Washington, DC: The World Bank.

Ahluwalia, I. J., R. Mohan and O. Goswami (1996) *Policy Reform in India*, Paris: Development Centre Seminars, OECD.

5 Globalisation–poverty interactions in Bangladesh

Bazlul H. Khondker and
Mustafa K. Mujeri

Introduction and background

Bangladesh began to reverse the initially restricted trade regime it inherited on independence from the mid-1970s. However, from the mid-1980s, a more comprehensive programme of stabilisation and economic reform was implemented within which the creation of a liberal trade regime was emphasised. The belief was that such a strategy would relax some of the constraints of the small domestic market and provide access to foreign direct investment, facilitating technology transfers, creating marketing networks, and providing much-needed managerial and technical skills.

For a country such as Bangladesh, trade liberalisation creates both benefits and costs and whether the benefits outweigh the costs depends on how well the country 'manages' the process towards its own advantage by strengthening the domestic economy, addressing the structural bottlenecks, and improving the policy regimes and institutional capabilities. Although the economic benefits generally flow from trade reforms sooner than from other reforms, how far the benefits have been realised remains a matter of controversy. Some studies suggest that Bangladesh gained relatively little from the trade reforms of the 1990s (Mujeri 2002a, 2002b). However, two consequences of trade liberalisation still remain inadequately addressed: first, the distributional consequences, as reflected in the differential impact on the welfare and poverty status of various socio-economic groups, and second, the impact on the labour market. Both issues are important for Bangladesh in its fight against poverty. If trade liberalisation creates a disproportionate burden and adjustment costs on the poor groups in society, it becomes important to undertake countervailing measures to ensure that the process becomes more equitable. Similarly, with a segmented labour market, the opening up of the economy may bring benefits to a few groups of workers who have specific skills while those at the lower end of the skill profiles might lose out.

The present study seeks to examine these specific issues using simulation techniques in two separate sets of experiments. First, a multi-sector, multi-factor and multi-household computable general equilibrium (CGE) model of the Bangladesh economy is used to examine the impacts of trade liberalisation and inflows of foreign capital on the allocation of resources, income distribution, and the poverty status of different household groups. Second, a double calibration general equilibrium methodology is used to identify the relative contribution of trade and other factors (including technological change) to the change in relative wages of skilled and unskilled labour.

The chapter is organised as follows. Section 2 discusses the extent of liberalisation and the major changes in the external sector due to liberalisation and also provides a brief overview of the economic structure of Bangladesh especially with regard to the labour market and the poverty situation. The poverty and distributional outcomes of two liberalisation policy simulations using a general equilibrium model of the Bangladesh economy are discussed in Section 3. In Section 4, the factors contributing to observed changes in skilled–unskilled wage differentials over the liberalisation period are identified using the double-calibration method. Finally, Section 5 provides some policy implications of the analysis.

Trade policy reforms and global integration

The principal aim of the economic reforms in Bangladesh during the last three decades was to liberalise the external trade and foreign exchange regimes and to rationalise the trade regime by lowering tariff rates, phasing out quantitative restrictions, streamlining import procedures, introducing tax reforms and export promotion measures. The major changes were as follows:

- Both tariff and non-tariff barriers were dismantled: tariff bands were narrowed and import procedures simplified.
- Twenty-four slabs of import duty rates of the 1980s were replaced by only four slabs in 2000.
- The highest customs duty rate was reduced from 350 per cent in 1992 to 37.5 per cent in 2000. The mean tariff declined from 114 per cent in 1989 to 22 per cent in 1999 while the weighted mean tariff declined to 19 per cent.
- The number of commodities under the four-digit code subject to quantitative restrictions declined from 550 in 1987 to 124 under the import policy of 1997–2002. In 1992, about 12 per cent of around 10,000 tariff lines were subject to quantitative restrictions, and this declined to less than 4 per cent by 1999. At present, less than 0.5 per cent of imports, mainly in the textile category, are subject to quantitative restrictions.
- In order to liberalise the foreign exchange market, the multiple exchange rate system was replaced by a unified exchange rate in 1992 and the domestic currency (taka) was pegged to a currency-weighted basket.
- A policy of creeping devaluation has been followed since 1992 to maintain exchange rate flexibility and export competitiveness within a more market-determined exchange rate regime. The taka has also been made convertible for all current account transactions.
- Export promotion measures were also adopted to diversify the export base, improve export quality and stimulate higher value-added exports, and develop backward linkage industries.

- Measures adopted for promoting exports are: special bonded warehouses, export processing zones, duty drawback, rebate on insurance premiums, income tax rebates, export credit guarantees, incentives for the export of non-traditional industrial products, an export promotion fund, value added tax (VAT) refunds, tax holidays, and the ability to retain foreign exchange from export earnings.

As a result of the above policy reforms, Bangladesh's global economic integration increased rapidly during the 1990s as indicated by higher trade to GDP ratio. In support of Bangladesh's greater integration to the global economy, in addition to the increased share of foreign trade in GDP measure, the movements of two additional measures of global integration may also be noted. These are (i) importance of trade and (ii) importance of private capital flows. In the first case, the importance of trade is measured by trade in goods as shares of both PPP GDP and dollar GDP while the dynamism of the trade regime is estimated by the difference in growth in real trade and growth in real GDP. In the second case, the measures used are gross private capital flows and gross foreign direct investment, each expressed as a share of PPP GDP.

The values of these measures for Bangladesh and, for comparison, for three other South Asian countries – India, Pakistan and Sri Lanka – are shown in Table 5.1. From the table: (i) the trade related indicators, in particular, suggest a rapid global economic integration of the Bangladesh economy; (ii) Bangladesh's trade regime showed more dynamism compared with India, Pakistan and Sri Lanka; and (iii) even though the global integration of the Bangladesh economy compares favourably with the South Asian average, it is less than the average for low-income countries.

Some key features of the Bangladesh economy during the last two decades

This section considers some relevant key features of the Bangladesh economy during the last two decades. These include changes in structure of trade, value added, employment and wages, and poverty and inequality. See Table 5.2.

The share of foreign trade (exports and imports) in GDP increased from around 20 per cent in the early 1980s to 33 per cent in 2000. In the case of imports, the rates increased substantially to 21 per cent in terms of volume and 11 per cent in value in the 1990s compared with a decline of 4 per cent in volume and an increase of 4 per cent in value in the 1980s. Exports in volume and value increased by 15 per cent and 11 per cent respectively in the 1990s compared with an average annual growth of around 1 per cent in volume and 8 per cent in value in the 1980s.

During the last decade the structure of economy also witnessed significant changes (see Table 5.3), with the share of agriculture in GDP declining to around a quarter in 2000 from 30 per cent in 1990. The share of manufacturing correspondingly increased from 21 per cent in 1990 to 26 per cent in 2000 due mainly to the impressive performance of manufacturing exports. The share of services remained stable at around 50 per cent.

Table 5.1 Bangladesh's global integration: a South Asian perspective

	Trade related indicators					Capital flow related indicators as % of PPP GDP			
	Trade in goods as % of				Dynamism of trade regime	Gross private capital flows		Gross foreign direct investment	
	PPP GDP		Dollar GDP						
	1988	1998	1988	1998	1988–1998	1988	1998	1988	1998
Bangladesh	4.2	7.0	29.9	56.1	7.2	0.3	0.8	0.0	0.2
India	3.3	3.9	18.2	33.6	4.5	0.2	0.9	0.0	0.1
Pakistan	9.3	8.2	54.8	53.4	0.1	0.7	1.6	0.2	0.3
Sri Lanka	11.5	17.9	88.0	118.8	2.9	2.1	1.8	0.2	0.4
South Asia	4.2	4.8	24.2	40.5	…	0.3	0.9	0.0	0.1
Low-income countries	6.8	8.3	38.6	62.5	…	0.7	2.0	0.2	0.9

Note: The trade in goods as a share of PPP GDP is the sum of merchandise exports and imports measured in current US dollars divided by the value of GDP converted to international dollars (PPP). The trade in goods as a share of goods GDP is the sum of merchandise export and imports divided by the value of GDP less value added in services (all in current US dollars). The growth in real trade less growth in real GDP is the difference between annual growth in trade in goods and services and annual growth in GDP using constant price series. Gross private capital flows are the sum of absolute values of direct, portfolio and other investment inflows and outflows recorded in the balance of payments financial account excluding changes in assets and liabilities of monetary authorities and general government. Gross foreign direct investment is the sum of absolute values of inflows and outflows of foreign direct investment recorded in the balance of payments financial account. It includes equity capital, reinvestment of earnings, other long-term capital and short-term capital.

Source: for details see World Bank (2000).

The average rate of GDP growth was less than 4 per cent during the period 1980–90 while in the period 1995–2000 it increased to more than 5 per cent, suggesting that growth was higher during the period of liberalisation. The growth in per capita GDP also accelerated during the 1990s due to a combination of increased economic growth and reduced population growth.

The labour force increased from 51.2 million in 1991 to 60.3 million in 2000 representing an increase of nearly 18 per cent. Over the same period, the number of employed persons increased by about 16 per cent – from 50.2 million to 58.1 million. Agriculture continues to be the major sector in terms of employment with about 62 per cent of total employed persons in 2000. Estimates of labour force participation and the employed population indicate that the unemployment rate nearly doubled during the period from 1.9 per cent to 3.7 per cent during 1991–2000. A more serious concern, however, is the high rate of underemployment. The problem of underemployment reflects the fact that more than 35 per cent of those employed work less than 35 hours a week, a low level for a developing country such as Bangladesh. At the end of the 1990s, around 39 per cent of the total labour force was either underemployed or unemployed.

Table 5.2 Structural change and growth in merchandise trade in Bangladesh

	Exports			Imports		
	1980	*1990*	*2000*	*1980*	*1990*	*2000*
Total value ($ million)	793	1,671	6,500	2,353	3,618	8,360
Major sectors	*Percentage of total value*					
Food	12	14	7	24	19	15
Agricultural raw materials	19	7	2	6	5	5
Fuels	0	1	0	9	16	7
Ores and metals	0	0	0	3	3	2
Manufactures	68	77	91	58	56	69
Average annual growth (%)	*1980–90*			*1990–99*		
Export volume	1.0			14.9		
Export value	7.8			11.3		
Import volume	−4.3			20.5		
Import value	3.6			10.7		

Source: World Bank (2000, 2002).

Table 5.3 Changes in economic structure during 1980–2000

A. Structure	Share (per cent) in GDP at constant 1995/96 prices			
	1980	*1990*	*1995*	*2000*
Agriculture	33.2	29.5	26.0	25.6
Industry	17.1	20.8	24.3	25.7
Services	49.7	49.7	49.7	48.7
Total	100	100	100	100

B. Growth (per cent) at constant 1995/96 prices				
	1981–1990	*1981–2000*	*1991–1995*	*1995–2000*
Agriculture	2.3	2.8	1.6	4.9
Industry	5.8	6.4	7.5	6.4
Services	3.7	4.8	4.1	4.8
GDP	3.8	4.3	4.4	5.2
Per capita GDP	1.6	2.3	2.4	3.6

Source: BBS (2000, 2001).

Table 5.4 Wage differentials between skilled and unskilled labour

	1984/85	*1989/90*	*1995/96*	*1998/99*
Wage rate (taka per day)				
Skilled manufacturing workers	31.32	58.51	77.60	98.46
Skilled construction workers	53.44	103.85	119.62	147.62
Unskilled agricultural workers	24.45	31.35	37.33	41.88
Ratio: unskilled/skilled wage rates				
Manufacturing	0.78	0.54	0.48	0.43
Construction	0.46	0.31	0.65	0.28

Source: BBS (2002a).

Another important characteristic of the labour market over the last decade was the increasing gap between the wage rates of unskilled agricultural labourers and the skilled manufacturing and construction workers, as shown in Table 5.4. In 1984/85, a skilled worker in the manufacturing and the construction sectors received 1.28 and 2.19 times the daily wage rate of an unskilled agricultural worker respectively. These differentials reached 2.35 and 3.52 respectively by 1998/99. The low level and the slow pace of growth of agricultural wages have been largely due to the relatively high levels of unemployment and underemployment recorded in the agriculture sector.

In Table 5.5, poverty data suggest a salutary effect of per capita real GDP growth on the poverty situation in the 1990s. During this period the annualised rate of poverty reduction was around 1 per cent. Although both urban and rural poverty have declined, the incidence of rural poverty remains higher than that of urban poverty. Over the entire period since the early 1980s, poverty incidence has declined at quite a slow rate, with substantial variations in different sub-periods and between rural and urban areas. National poverty reduced from 58.5 per cent in 1983/84 to 57.1 per cent in 1988/89 envisaging a very slow annual rate of decrease averaging 0.23 per cent. During this period the annual rate of decrease was 1.05 per cent for urban areas and less than 0.1 per cent for rural areas.

As regards inequality, the Gini index of consumption expenditure remained largely unchanged from the early 1980s until 1992 for both rural and urban areas. The urban Gini index rose sharply from 32 per cent in 1992 to 37 per cent in 2000. In rural areas, inequality in consumption expenditure also increased, from 26 per cent to 30 per cent. The trends for income inequality were similar with a sharp increase in the Gini index during the mid-1990s. A similar trend in the deterioration of income distribution may also be noted, both for rural and urban areas. Inequality increased rather sharply during the early 1990s, which coincided with the period of rapid trade liberalisation (Table 5.5).

Table 5.5 Poverty and inequality in Bangladesh

	Poverty line (Tk/person/ month)	Mean consumption (Tk/person/ month)	Head count ratio (%)	Gini index (%)	
				Consumption	Income
Urban					
1983/84	301.72	396.53	50.2	29.8	37.0
1988/89	453.65	695.19	43.9	32.6	38.1
1991/92	534.99	817.12	44.9	31.9	39.8
1995/96	650.45	1,372.47	29.4	37.5	44.4
2000	724.56	1,291.53	36.6	36.6	45.2
Rural					
1983/84	268.92	284.84	59.6	24.6	35.0
1988/89	379.08	435.39	59.2	26.5	36.8
1991/92	469.13	509.67	61.2	25.5	36.4
1995/96	541.77	661.47	55.2	27.5	38.4
2000	634.48	820.20	53.0	29.7	36.6
Memorandum item					
National head count ratio		1983/84 –58.5%		1991/92 –58.8%	
		and 1988/89 –57.1%		and 2000 –49.8%	
		(Annual rate –0.23%)		(Annual rate –1%)	

Note: The figures are based on the Household Expenditure Surveys of the Bangladesh Bureau of Statistics (BBS). The poor have been estimated using the cost of basic needs (CBN) method and are taken as those living below a poverty line, corresponding to an intake of 2,122 kcal/person/day plus a nonfood allowance corresponding to nonfood expenditure among households whose food expenditure equals the food poverty line.

Source: World Bank (1998) and BBS (2002b).

Trade liberalisation and poverty: simulation outcomes within a general equilibrium framework

Against this brief general background of trade reform and structural features of the Bangladesh economy, we now discuss some results of counterfactual simulation experiments, with the aim of understanding more about the effects on poverty attributable to globalisation.[1] In particular, we examine the effects of a reduction in tariff rates and an increase in foreign direct investment (expressed as an increase in the inflow of foreign funds). We use a general equilibrium model of the Bangladesh economy, calibrated to a social accounting matrix for 1995/96 as detailed in Table 5.6. The model is a 'standard' static CGE model whose main features are summarised and set out in Table 5.7.

Table 5.6 Disaggregation and description of factors, institutions and households in the SAM and CGE model

Set	Description of elements
Factors of production	
Labour (6)	• Female: 3 categories according to skill levels (low, medium and high) Low: grades 0–5; medium: grades 6–10; high: grades 11 and above • Male: 3 categories according to skill levels (low, medium and high) Low: grades 0–5; medium: grades 6–10; high: grades 11 and above
Capital (1)	• 1 type of aggregated only
Institutions	
Households (7)	• Rural *agriculture*: 3 categories according to land ownership Labourer household: 0–0.49 hectares; small farmers: 0.5–2.49 hectares; large farmers: >2.5 hectares. • Rural *non-farm*: 1 category according to occupation • Urban: 3 categories according to the level of education of the household's head Low skilled: grades 0–5; medium skilled: grades 6–10; professional: grades 11 and above
Others (2)	• Government • Rest of the world
Activities	
Agriculture (7)	• Crops *non-traded*: rice (Aman and Boro) • Crops *traded*: other grains and commercial crops • Non-crops *non-traded*: forestry • Non-crops *traded*: livestock and fish • Food processing *traded*: rice milling, atta and flour, other food and tobacco
Industries (12)	• Textiles *traded*: clothing, ready-made garments and leather. • Others *traded*: chemicals, fertiliser, petroleum products, machinery and miscellaneous industries
Services (6)	• *Non-traded*: construction, gas, trade services, social services, public administration, financial services and other services

Table 5.7 Summary features of the Bangladesh CGE model

- Labour is mobile across producing activities.[1]
- Capital is immobile and sector-specific.
- Primary factor supplies are exogenous and fixed.
- The world prices of imports and exports are exogenous invoking the small country assumption.
- Current account balance (deficit) is fixed.
- Imports and domestically produced goods are imperfect substitutes.
- Output produced for domestic and export markets reflects differences in quality suggesting imperfect substitutability between them.
- Savings of domestic institution adjust to equate to given investment.
- General price index acts as the numeraire.
- Excess demand conditions are satisfied.

Note
1   An important feature of the labour market is the co-existence of high underemployment but low unemployment. However, the reported four percent unemployment rate is quite low allowing us to envisage a situation of near full employment of labour. Thus, full employment of labour is specified in the model. Moreover, sufficient data on man-hours worked by major sectors is not available to model the underemployment situation.

The two simulations were as follows:

Simulation 1: The base import values and import revenues were taka 254 billion and taka 39 billion respectively and the average tariff rate is 15 per cent. In this simulation, the tariff rates are set equal to zero and the resultant fall in revenue is replaced by raising the rates and expanding the base of direct tax.[2] The base values of all other parameters are retained.

Simulation 2: In the second simulation, the base value of foreign savings is raised (i.e. from 3 per cent of GDP to 5 per cent) to depict a rise in the ratio of foreign investment to GDP. The base values of all other parameters are retained.

Simulation outcomes

Impacts on macro indicators

The impacts on selected macro indicators are summarised in Table 5.8. The real GDP growth in the first simulation is 0.39 per cent compared with the base case. The revenue-neutral tariff elimination (the loss of import revenue is recovered from the direct tax system) led to a drop of demand (mainly domestic) with a consequent repercussion on output and resource allocation. Both agriculture and service sector growth were hampered by deficient domestic demand. As a result, the growth rates of the agricultural and service sectors were 0.15 per cent and 0.10 per cent less than the base case. The manufacturing sector, on the other hand, experienced positive growth (2.2 per cent over the base case) mainly due to a depreciation of the nominal exchange rate and a rise of export prices relative to domestic prices.

Table 5.8 Selected macro effects of the simulations with the model

	Shares (%)	*Growth rates (%)*	
	Base case	*Simulation 1*	*Simulation 2*
Real GDP		*0.39*	*0.26*
Agriculture	0.22	−0.15	−0.30
Manufacturing	0.22	2.19	−1.28
Service	0.56	−0.10	1.10
Traded	0.33	1.74	−1.50
Non-traded	0.67	−0.30	1.15
Consumption		*−1.60*	*0.95*
Imports		4.74	12.89
Exports		17.02	−11.19

Source: authors' calculations.

The observed pattern of manufacturing sector growth is reflected in high growth of the export sector by 17 per cent compared with the base case. The growth of imports by 4.7 per cent is modest considering the full elimination of tariffs. A substantial depreciation of nominal exchange rate counters the large fall in the domestic import prices. These two opposing impacts on the domestic import price explain the moderate increase in imports.

The patterns of growth effects under the second simulation are quite different from the first simulation. In the second simulation, the resources move from both agriculture and manufacturing sectors to generate growth in the service sector. The pattern of resource reallocation also results in a growth in non-traded sectors (1.2 per cent) at the expense of the traded sectors (−1.5 per cent). Also the growth of imports is relatively high (12.9 per cent) in the second simulation. The decline of domestic manufacturing and agricultural outputs results in higher prices of domestic products relative to the import price of their import substitutes. This leads to a substantial growth of imports in this simulation. Similarly, higher prices of domestically supplied products compared with export prices are manifested in a sharp decline of exports (11.2 per cent) compared with the base case.

Welfare effects

The welfare impacts of the simulations are calculated in terms of equivalent variations (EVs). The results are shown in Table 5.9.

The values of EVs are negative for all household groups in the first simulation while, not surprisingly, they are positive in the second simulation as foreign inflows increase resources. The positive EV values are due to positive real consumption growth and the negative EV values are associated with negative growth. In the first simulation, except for the non-farm household group, the observed changes in EV are larger for the high-income household groups (e.g. professionals,

Table 5.9 Welfare impacts: equivalent variations for different household groups

Household groups	Base value Consumption (billion Tk)	Simulation 1 Consumption		Simulation 2 Consumption	
		Growth (%)	EV	Growth (%)	EV
Agricultural labourers	95.59	−1.03	−1.49	0.75	0.71
Small farmers	176.25	−1.21	−3.32	1.06	1.97
Large farmers	188.63	−1.52	−4.38	1.45	3.13
Non-farms	268.77	−1.14	−4.71	0.91	2.65
Worker – low-skilled	168.94	−1.17	−2.77	0.89	1.56
Worker – medium-skilled	151.75	−1.24	−3.36	0.89	1.84
Professionals	329.07	−1.33	−6.32	0.76	3.10
Total	1379.00	...	...	...	...

Source: authors' calculations.

medium-skilled workers, and large farmers) compared with the low-income household groups (e.g. agricultural labourers, and low-skilled workers). This is because these groups have to pay large amounts of their income as additional income taxes to recover the revenue loss from the reduction in tariff revenues. In the case of the second simulation, the welfare gains accrue more to the high-income household groups compared with their poorer counterparts. Among the less well-off household groups, only the non-farm group is observed to benefit. This is due to their higher participation in non-traded and service activities, which benefit from high growth under this simulation. Overall this suggests that the welfare impacts emanating from the increased globalisation measures accrue more to the better-off household groups compared with their less well-off counterparts.

Poverty implications

The implications for changes in poverty do not follow directly from the results of the CGE model. The model generates changes in mean incomes of the representative household groups. The consequent estimates of changes in poverty (based on Foster–Greer–Thorbecke (FGT) measures) have been estimated following a method suggested by Decaluwé *et al.* (1999). Specifically, it involves: (a) an explicit assumption about the distribution of income for each of the seven household groups (Beta distribution) and (b) the postulate of a poverty line fixed in real terms for each household group though varying with endogenously-determined commodity prices. In more detail, the poverty profiles of the representative household groups have been derived using the following methodology.

- The income distribution formulation of each of the seven household groups is depicted by seven household group-specific 'Beta' distribution functions. The specification of the 'Beta' distribution[3] function requires estimates of minimum (min) and maximum (max) incomes together with the values of shape and skewness parameters (e.g. p and q respectively) of the distribution for each of the seven household groups (see Table 5.10). The base year values of these four characteristics by each of the seven household groups are derived from the Household Expenditure Survey 1995/96 (BBS 1998). The derived distribution has been used to assess the implications for poverty within each household group.

- It is assumed that, following a policy change, only the key incomes (i.e. mean, minimum and maximum) of each household group will change and that the shape and skewness parameters of the distributions remain unaffected. The above features suggest that intra-group distributions shift proportionally due to the mean income change, implying the intra-household distributions are constant.
- Specific rural and urban poverty lines have been defined to capture price and other characteristics at these locations. Although the basic needs basket remains invariant under different simulations, changes in commodity prices alter the monetary values of the poverty lines.
- The above estimates (i.e. Beta distributions, incomes and poverty lines) have been used to measure pre- and post-simulation poverty incidence for the seven representative household groups.

The base year poverty profiles of the household groups and in rural and urban locations are shown in Table 5.10, from which the following features may be noted:

- Almost 54 per cent of the rural population is poor while in urban areas the poverty ratio is around 29 per cent. This suggests that the incidence of poverty in rural areas is much higher than in urban areas. Moreover, the poverty gap and severity of poverty observed for rural areas suggest that the rural poverty situation is much worse than urban poverty.
- Among the rural households, the agricultural labour households are the most deprived group. More than 78 per cent of them are poor. In terms of poverty gap and severity index, they are also found to be the most vulnerable group. The small farmer and non-farm household groups follow close behind.
- As might be expected, the incidence of urban poverty is concentrated mainly among the low-skilled worker household group. More than 37 per cent of individuals in this group have incomes below the urban poverty line. High values of the poverty gap and the squared poverty gap ratios (0.14 and 0.07 respectively) reconfirm their vulnerability. The incidence of poverty is quite low for the other two urban household groups.

The poverty estimates based on the simulations are carried out as follows. The incomes of the representative household groups and the commodity prices change in response to the policy changes. The changes in incomes and prices also change the minimum and the maximum incomes within each household group as well as the rural and urban poverty lines in nominal terms.

The resulting post-simulation poverty profiles based on the FGT index are shown in Table 5.11. Due to the negative income growth arising from the first

Table 5.10 Base values of household poverty profiles

| Household | Income (Tk per capita per month) | | | | Population | Beta | | FGT poverty measure[1] | | |
	Min	Max	Mean	Poverty line	share (%)	p	q	Head count	Poverty gap	Squared poverty gap
Rural	18	9,140	697	650	78.65	2.9	37	0.535	0.197	0.099
Agricultural labourers	73	4,245	507	650	29.63	2.9	26	0.781	0.305	0.153
Small farmers	152	6,369	694	650	21.65	2.3	24	0.523	0.164	0.070
Large farmers	18	9,140	981	650	11.32	2.7	22	0.293	0.097	0.047
Non-farms	91	6,935	721	650	37.41	2.3	22	0.486	0.168	0.079
Urban	73	26,533	1,359	725	21.35	1.7	33	0.287	0.109	0.057
Workers – low-skilled	73	16,376	987	725	58.60	2.3	38	0.377	0.136	0.066
Workers – medium-skilled	441	14,833	1884	725	21.92	1.3	11	0.107	0.019	0.005
Professionals	358	26,533	2927	725	19.48	1.4	12	0.062	0.013	0.004

Note

1 The FGT allows us to compare three measures of poverty: head count ratio; poverty gap ratio; and squared poverty gap index. The simplest measure of the *prevalence* of poverty, head count ratio, is the proportion of the population with a per capita income below the poverty line. The *depth* of poverty is measured by the poverty gap index, which estimates the average distance separating the income of the poor from the poverty line as a proportion of the income indicated by the line. The severity measure given by the squared poverty gap index quantifies the aversion of the society towards poverty.

Source: authors' calculations based on BBS (2002a).

Table 5.11 Impacts of policy simulations on poverty profiles (percentage change from base run)

	Simulation 1			Simulation 2		
	Head count	Poverty gap	Severity gap	Head count	Poverty gap	Severity gap
Rural	1.55	1.97	2.52	−0.11	−0.30	−0.53
Agricultural labourers	1.37	2.95	3.14	−0.27	−0.49	−0.61
Small farmers	2.45	3.74	4.25	−0.08	−0.06	−6.53
Large farmers	2.75	3.51	2.41	−0.02	0.00	−0.28
Non-farms	2.13	2.87	3.49	0.052	0.052	0.045
Urban	1.46	1.90	2.03	0.42	0.80	0.95
Workers – low-skilled	2.49	1.25	1.74	0.00	−4.33	−4.37
Workers – medium-skilled	1.57	1.47	2.40	2.49	3.82	5.14
Professionals	3.20	7.92	7.24	1.17	1.68	2.18

Note: The baseline poverty calculations are derived from the 'Beta' distribution to be comparable with the poverty estimates generated using the simulation outcomes. These are usually different from the survey estimates. For example, survey based estimates of rural and urban head count ratios are 53 and 28.1 percent respectively while the corresponding ratios derived from the 'Beta' distribution have found to be 53.5 and 28.7 percent respectively.

Source: authors' calculations.

simulation, the poverty status of all household groups appears to have deteriorated. The decline, however, is marginally higher for the rural households compared with urban households. But the steepest rise in poverty is observed for professional households (3.2 per cent), followed by the large farm households (2.8 per cent), low-skilled workers (2.5 per cent) and the small farmers (2.5 per cent) groups. Thus the poverty impacts are mixed. For high-income households (professional and large farm) relatively high impacts on poverty are overwhelmingly due to higher income tax payments which reduce their consumption expenditure. For the two other less well-off household groups, one reason for higher poverty increases may be due to the fact that the depth and the severity of poverty were initially high for these groups. Therefore, a small loss in real consumption has shifted a significant portion of the population of these household groups into poverty.

In the second simulation, poverty in rural areas appears to improve in contrast to the worsening poverty in the urban areas. The head count index of poverty declined by 0.11 per cent in rural areas, and increased by 0.42 per cent in urban areas. One important observation, however, is that poverty worsened for all relatively well-off household groups except the 'large farmers' group. The rise in the incidence of poverty can be specifically noted for the medium-skilled workers (2.5 per cent), and the professionals (1.2 per cent) households. The relatively steep decline in the manufacturing income in this simulation led to a reduction in the real incomes of these two household groups. The fall has manifested itself by a widening of the poverty gap, a deepening of the severity of poverty and a worsening of the head count index.

What policy conclusions can we draw from the above results? The simulations suggest that, while the globalisation experience in Bangladesh may be mixed, the gains and losses may be relatively small and these may differ across various household groups in the presence of structural bottlenecks and other constraints. In particular, the gains accrue rather more to the relatively well-off households while the extreme poor households benefit less. This indicates that the full potential of globalisation may not be readily translated into poverty reduction in Bangladesh.

Skilled–unskilled wage inequality: an analysis of observed changes

It was observed earlier that since the 1980s the wage increases of skilled workers have been significantly higher than those of unskilled workers. This has led to widening wage inequality between the skilled and the unskilled workers. As extensive trade liberalisation also took place during the same period, this indicates the possible existence of an association between the increase in wage inequality and trade reform. However, trade reform might not be the only factor that contributed to the widening of the wage gap. Indeed the wage and trade literature points to the existence of several other factors which might explain a significant part of the changes in wage inequality.

In this section, a quite different analytical procedure is adopted to analyse this issue. Following Abrego and Whalley (2000), a double-calibration general-equilibrium methodology is used to decompose the observed inequality in wages generated by multiple sources into components associated with each source. The method departs from the traditional applied general equilibrium exercise in two ways. First, it decomposes an observed *ex post* economic outcome into component influences, rather than computing *ex ante* counterfactual equilibria. The approach further recognises the fact that these influences need not, and typically will not, be additive. Second, the analysis is based on a two-period rather than a single-period calibration, since it requires model parameterisations to be as consistent as possible with changes over time, not just with the base year observation. This is termed double calibration. Some salient comparative features of the *ex ante* and *ex post* equilibrium approaches are presented in Table 5.12.

We have applied the technique to a component-by-component decomposition of the increased wage inequality between 1985 and 1996.[4] The model and the techniques presented here suggest that within a general equilibrium setting, other factors such as changes in factor supply and a wider variety of technical changes also enter the picture and play a significant role in explaining the wage differentials between the skilled and the unskilled labour in Bangladesh.

The methodology and model structure

In order to operationalise the double-calibration decomposition analysis, a model of a small, open price-taking economy for Bangladesh has been specified. The model has been calibrated to the data for two years (1985 and 1996) using the Ricardo–Viner (RV) specific-factors specification rather than the more usual

Table 5.12 Salient features of *ex ante* and *ex post* models

Attributes	Ex ante *model*	Ex post *model*
1 Scope	Comprehensive and detailed – usually represented by large number of markets, institutions and variables. Markets for labour, domestic goods and composite goods. Institutions – households, government, rest of the world, capital.	Compact – represented by few key markets and variables such as labour market, production, mobile factor and trade.
2 Technology	Constant returns.	Decreasing returns.
3 Period of calibration	Single.	Multiple.
4 Domestic goods market	Cleared.	Not cleared.
5 Equilibrium condition	Via markets (goods and labour) external sectors and savings and investment balance.	Via labour market.
6 Comparison	Comparative – static across key variables.	Comparative – static between multiple periods on a single variable or indicator.
7 Analysis of simulation	Counterfactual equilibrium outcomes of policy simulation scenario with the base year outcomes.	Decomposition of the observed behaviour of the indicator or variable according to related contributing factors.

Heckscher–Ohlin type (HO) fully mobile factors model specification.[5] To implement the methodology, Bangladesh's economic structure has been assumed to consist of two tradable goods:[6] agriculture and non-agriculture. It is also assumed that agriculture is an importable sector and non-agriculture is exportable (since more than 70 per cent of the exports from Bangladesh are manufacturing textiles of various types). For our purpose, we have assumed that agriculture is intensive in unskilled labour while non-agriculture is intensive in skilled labour. Moreover, the behaviour of the economy is captured through the activities of production, consumption and trade, all of which are solved in each of the two periods. These two periods are denoted as initial and terminal periods. The main features of the double-calibration model follow, and the symbols denoting key important parameters and variables are set out in Table 5.13.

Production and payments to factors

The production of each good (agriculture and non-agriculture) in each period (i.e. initial and terminal) requires the use of two mobile factors: skilled labour and unskilled labour and an unspecified sector-specific fixed factor. The use of an

Table 5.13 Symbols of key parameters and variables

Goods	i	M = imports: agriculture and unskilled labour intensive
		E = exports: non-agriculture and intensive in skilled labour
Periods	t	1 (1985) = initial and 2 (1996) = terminal
Labour	L	U = unskilled labour and S = skilled labour
Factors		
Prices		W = wage rates and P = world prices
Variables		Y = outputs; C = consumption; and T = net trade
Parameters		A_{it} = sector-specific measure of the efficiency of a composite labour factor input; α_{it} is the output elasticity with respect to composite labour
		β_{it} = CES share parameter; $\gamma_{it} = A_{it}B_{it}$
		δ_t^U and δ_t^S = factor-augmenting technical change parameters
		σ_{it} = substitution elasticity = $1/(1-\rho_{it})$

unspecified sector-specific fixed factor suggests that each good in each period is produced according to a decreasing returns to scale technology.

$$Y_{it} = A_{it}L_{it}^{\alpha_{it}} \tag{5.1}$$

The mobile factors – skilled and unskilled labours – are combined via a composite labour input. The composite labour input is specified by a CES function.

$$L_{it} = B_{it} \left[\beta_{it} \left(\delta_{it}^U \cdot U_{it} \right)^{\rho_{it}} + (1 - \beta_{it}) \left(\delta_{it}^S \cdot S_{it} \right)^{\rho_{it}} \right]^{\frac{1}{\rho_{it}}} \tag{5.2}$$

The production function and composite labour input functions (1) and (2) are combined to re-specify the production behaviour for each goods.

$$Y_{it} = \gamma_{it} \left[\beta_{it} \left(\delta_{it}^U \cdot U_{it} \right)^{\rho_{it}} + (1 - \beta_{it}) \left(\delta_{it}^S \cdot S_{it} \right)^{\rho_{it}} \right]^{\frac{\alpha_{it}}{\rho_{it}}} \tag{5.3}$$

The re-specified production function suggests that production of each good in each period depends on: (i) sector-specific (Hicks-neutral) technical changes, represented as γ_{it} is a product of shift parameters of the production and labour input functions; (ii) factor-biased technical changes: δ_{it}^U and δ_{it}^S; and (iii) the endowments of skilled and unskilled labour in each period.

A competitive labour market is assumed so that each type of labour is paid its marginal value product, ensuring full employment of each type of labour in equilibrium in each period. Supplies of labour (i.e. unskilled and skilled), even though they are assumed to be fixed in each time period, do vary between periods. The solution of the first order conditions for each type of labour in each period gives the wage rates of skilled and unskilled labour,[7] W_{st} and W_{ut}

$$W_{ut} = P_{it}\alpha_{it}\beta_{it}(\delta_{it}^{U})^{(\sigma_{it}-1)/\sigma_{it}} Y_{it}^{[\sigma_{it}(\alpha_{it}-1)+1]/\alpha_{it}\sigma_{it}} U_{it}^{-1/\sigma_{it}}\gamma_{it}^{(\sigma_{it}-1)/\alpha_{it}\sigma_{it}}$$
$$W_{st} = P_{it}\alpha_{it}(1-\beta_{it})(\delta_{it}^{s})^{(\sigma_{it}-1)/\sigma_{it}} Y_{it}^{[\sigma_{it}(\alpha_{it}-1)+1]/\alpha_{it}\sigma_{it}} S_{it}^{-1/\sigma_{it}}\gamma_{it}^{(\alpha_{it}-1)/\alpha_{it}\sigma_{it}}$$

$$(5.4)$$

Trade, consumption and equilibrium conditions

Imports and domestically produced goods are homogenous, as is the case with exports. The homogeneity assumption means that trade flow involving any good is one-way only, so that one of the goods is imported and the other exported. Furthermore, when a good is exported, domestic production less consumption is positive and if good i is imported this difference is negative.

In equilibrium a zero trade balance condition holds, i.e.

$$\sum_{i} P_{it}T_{it} = 0 \qquad (5.5)$$

where T_{it} denotes the net trades in each of the two goods. A property of equilibrium in such a model (from Walras' Law) is that the trade balance will be satisfied.

The consumption of each good in equilibrium is given by the difference between production and net trade, i.e.

$$C_{it} = Y_{it} - T_{it} \qquad (5.6)$$

Given the model specification and small open economy assumption, equilibrium in each period is ensured by adjustments to the wage rates of unskilled and skilled labour, which clear the two domestic labour markets. That is

$$\sum_{i} U_{it} = \overline{U_t} \quad \text{and} \quad \sum_{i} S_{it} = \overline{S_t} \qquad (5.7)$$

The above model has been used to obtain estimates of the contributions of factor-biased technical change (δ_t^u and δ_t^s), the change in factor endowments (U and S), and trade shocks, to explain the increases in wage inequality in Bangladesh between 1985 and 1996. The changes in model technology parameters over time have been obtained using two data periods (i.e. 1985 and 1996).

Simulations with trade shocks are modelled in the form of changes in world prices (P_{it}), which in turn results in increased import volumes. In this framework, a shock is considered to be a fall in the relative price of unskilled-intensive to skill-intensive commodities between the initial and terminal years.

In order to assess the contribution of each component of change to overall wage inequality, the equilibrium of period 1, 1985 is considered as the base model solution. Once the base solution is achieved, the model in the first simulation is re-solved by considering only the trade shock, and then in successive simulations each of the technology parameters implied by the calibration procedure are altered to examine their respective contributions to wage inequality. Lastly, the impact of

Table 5.14 Decomposition of wage inequality in Bangladesh: 1985–96

Contributing factors	Experiments		
	First	Second	Third
Increased trade	−2.25	−3.38	−3.60
Factor-biased technical change	−15.80	0	−34.79
Hicks-neutral technical change	0	42.58	−40.39
Factor endowment changes	48.25	34.15	54.13
Changes in β_{it}	−37.39	−40.62	0
Changes in α_{it}	2.48	1.67	1.59

Source: authors' calculations.

changes in factor supply is simulated. The incorporation of all these changes as well as all the other elements observed is consistent with observed wage inequality change between the first and second period equilibrium (i.e. 1985 to 1996). The contribution of each component to total change in wage inequality can then be estimated.

The years 1985 and 1996 have been chosen with regard to observed changes in the key variables. This period witnessed a significant decline in the wage of unskilled workers relative to their skilled counterparts. There was also a significant increase in real GDP, a rise in the trade volume (imports), an opening up of the economy and an increase in the employment of unskilled labour compared with the skilled labour in different sectors.

The results of the decomposition experiments are shown in Table 5.14. Three experiments have been carried out. The assumption underlying the first simulation was that the technical change was factor-biased and hence no Hicks-neutral technical (i.e. sectoral) change occurred in this period (i.e. between 1985 and 1996). Contrary to the first simulation, the assumption of factor-biased technical change was dropped and Hicks-neutral change was incorporated in the second simulation. In both these simulation experiments, the production function parameter that is, the share of unskilled labour in production (β_{it}) in each sector, varied over time. The third simulation allowed for both factor-biased and Hicks-neutral technical change, but β_{it} was held constant over time.

The results suggest that trade made only a small contribution to explaining the rise in wage inequality between 1985 and 1996. The contributions of trade to wage inequality were found to be 2.3 per cent, 3.4 per cent and 3.6 per cent respectively under the first, second and third simulations. However, large contributions have been recorded for factor-biased technical change (e.g. in simulations 1 and 3), which vary significantly depending upon the calibration procedure used. Thus, factor-biased technical change accounts for 16 per cent and 35 per cent of the increase in wage inequality under the first and the third simulations respectively. The finding suggests that when the share parameters, β_{it}, are fixed the factor-biased technical change accounts for more than the observed wage-inequality change.

The change in factor endowments have large negative effects on the rise in wage inequality, but the positive effects of share parameters changes offset these in the first and the second simulations and by the factor-biased technical change in the third simulation.

The general conclusion of the decomposition analysis indicates that skill-biased technical change is the most significant determinant of the increase in wage inequality in Bangladesh between 1985 and 1996. Moreover, changes in factor endowments also played a significant role in determining the net outcome in wage inequality. However, the contribution of trade to the rise in wage inequality appears to be relatively small. The experience of the development process followed in the last decade suggests a higher demand for skilled labour (a relatively scarce factor) rather than (abundant) unskilled labour in Bangladesh. As a result, the wages of skilled labour increased at a faster rate than the unskilled wages, which led to an increased disparity in wages.

The process has significant poverty implications since unskilled workers in the rural areas form the largest majority of the poor in Bangladesh. In view of the relative abundance of unskilled labour and the existence of significant imperfections in the labour market, Bangladesh's pro-poor development agenda needs to focus on providing education and upgrading the skill level of the labour force. This is more likely to reduce the 'wage divide' between the skilled and the unskilled labour with consequent positive income effect on the poor. Policy measures are needed to increase the supply of skilled labour since higher growth and associated technological change may not be sufficient to lead to enhanced supply of skilled labour as previously suggested by Eicher (1996).

Some policy implications

The above analysis highlights the fact that trade reforms have neither readily nor necessarily benefited the poor in Bangladesh. The standard argument that trade liberalisation improves resource allocation, enhances growth, and hence benefits the poor (through the 'trickle-down' channel) does not seem to have worked in the context of Bangladesh. Moreover, it has been observed that tradable goods production does not use unskilled (or less skilled) workers as the most intensively used factor and, indeed, many non-tradable sectors (such as products and services of the informal sector) are more labour intensive than the tradable sector. As a result, with a segmented labour market, the opening up of the economy benefits a few groups who have specific skills while the poor workers at the lower end of the skill profiles remain the losers.

It also needs to be recognised that there is no automatic association between trade liberalisation and growth, and that Bangladesh needs to adopt appropriate phasing and sequencing of trade reforms to liberalise the economy in more strategic ways and to participate in the global economy on its own terms. An open trade regime, on its own, will not necessarily set the economy on a sustained growth path. The reforms are likely to be beneficial when complemented by measures aimed at strengthening the domestic economy, addressing structural bottlenecks, and improving the policy regimes and institutional capabilities. What is important for Bangladesh is the quality, timing, and scope of liberalisation and its success in promoting or facilitating factors such as strengthening of local enterprises, human resource and technological development, and building up export capacity and market access. Specific and sound policies are required in areas such as infrastructure, market facilitation and access, and competitiveness to meet the challenges of the post-MFA (Multi-fibre Agreement) era.

Furthermore, the risks of job and income losses for poor groups in a situation of continuing high unemployment and in a liberalised environment are too high for Bangladesh. This may have a negative effect on growth prospects via deficient demand. Such risks highlight the importance of consistency of the macroeconomic policy regime with trade liberalisation efforts. The liberalisation process thus needs to be far more sensitive to social costs consistent with appropriately targeted social safety nets for the affected poor, and guided by institutional capacity to better manage the transition period of trade liberalisation.

Finally, effective measures are also needed to increase the supply response of poor households and their ability to cope with risk and uncertainty through complementary policies for developing small and medium enterprises and agro-based industries, improving access to the credit market, ensuring better asset distribution, increasing labour market flexibility, disseminating market and technical information, and investing in skill development. At the same time, the international environment needs to be supportive of, and reduce the transition costs of, economic restructuring of the country. On the global front, along with preferential access to Bangladesh's exports in general, this means importing countries reducing tariffs on garments and other labour-intensive exports from Bangladesh where the country may have an increasing comparative advantage.

Acknowledgements

The authors would like to express their deep gratitude to Jeff Round, John Whalley, and Maurizio Bussolo for their guidance in carrying out the study and useful suggestions on earlier drafts of the chapter. Comments received on an earlier draft of the chapter from the participants at the Seminar on 'How Are Globalisation and Poverty Interacting and What Can Governments Do About It?' in the OECD Development Centre, Paris, 9–10 December 2002, are gratefully acknowledged. However, the authors are responsible for the views expressed and for any remaining errors.

Notes

1 The results are drawn from an ESCOR project 'Exploring the Links between Globalization and Poverty in South Asia' under the ESCOR programme on Globalization and Poverty. For details see Khondker and Mujeri (2002).
2 Large farm households, who did not pay any income tax in the base case, have been included in the direct tax net and are assumed to pay income tax at the rate applicable to the professional household group.

3 Other distribution functional forms have also been used to estimate income distribution and poverty impacts using the results of CGE models. Researchers have used lognormal, Pareto, Beta distribution and Kernel non-parametric methods to apply to FGT poverty measures. Boccanfuso *et al.* (2002) provides a detailed review of the choice of these functional forms in the measurements of income distribution and poverty.

4 For details, see Khondker and Mujeri (2002).

5 Abrego and Whalley (2000) argued the advantages of the RV specification in a similar exercise over other specifications on empirical implementation grounds. The HO model with homogeneous goods and constant returns to scale has problems in accommodating relatively large product price changes. It also cannot accommodate wage change for a small open economy arising out of factor-biased technical change. There are two possible ways of dealing with this problem. One is to use an Armington-type structure invoking assumption of heterogeneous goods in preferences. However, they are harder to work analytically and hence general results linking changes in relative prices to relative wages cannot be derived. A second approach consists of moving away from full mobility of all factors and using a specific factors trade model (RV) with decreasing returns to scale. This structure has been more widely used in the analytical international trade literature. Due to above features the second approach was preferred.

6 Since the country is a price-taker, trade will take place at fixed world prices.

7 Given the decreasing returns technology, payments to unskilled and skilled labour do not exhaust the value of production in either sector, and the remaining return accrues to the fixed factor in each sector.

References

Abrego, L. and J. Whalley (2000) 'The Choice of Structural Model in Trade-Wages Decompositions', *Review of International Economics*, 8(3): 462–477.

BBS (1998) *1995/96 Household Expenditure Survey*, Bangladesh Bureau of Statistics, Ministry of Planning, Government of the People's Republic of Bangladesh, Dhaka.

BBS (2000) *1999 Statistical Yearbook of Bangladesh*, Bangladesh Bureau of Statistics, Ministry of Planning, Government of the People's Republic of Bangladesh, Dhaka.

BBS (2001) *National Accounts Statistics*, National Accounting Wing, Bangladesh Bureau of Statistics, Ministry of Planning, Government of the People's Republic of Bangladesh, Dhaka.

BBS (2002a) *Report of Household Income and Expenditure Survey 2000*, Bangladesh Bureau of Statistics, Ministry of Planning, Government of the People's Republic of Bangladesh, Dhaka.

BBS (2002b) *Report of the Labour Force Survey: Bangladesh 1999/2000*, Bangladesh Bureau of Statistics, Ministry of Planning, Government of the People's Republic of Bangladesh, Dhaka.

Boccanfuso, D., B. Decaluwé, and L. Savard (2002) 'Poverty, Income Distribution and CGE Modelling: Does the Functional Form of Distribution Matter?' mimeo, CREFA, Laval University, Quebec City.

Decaluwé, B., A. Patry, L. Savard and E. Thorbecke (1999) 'Poverty Analysis Within A General Equilibrium Framework' mimeo, Laval University, Quebec City and Cornell University, Ithaca, New York.

Eicher, T. S. (1996) 'Interaction between Endogenous Human Capital and Technological Change', *Review of Economic Studies*, 63: 127–144.

Khondker, B. H. and M. K. Mujeri (2002) 'Decomposing Wage Inequality Change in Bangladesh: An Application of Double Calibration Technique', paper prepared for the

ESCOR project, 'Exploring the Links between Globalization and Poverty in South Asia' under the ESCOR programme on 'Globalization and Poverty', University of Warwick, Coventry.

Mujeri, M. K. (2002a) 'Bangladesh: External Sector Performance and Recent Issues', paper presented at the Seminar on Performance of the Bangladesh Economy: Selected Issues, Bangladesh Institute of Development Studies, Dhaka.

Mujeri, M. K. (2002b) 'Globalization–Poverty Links in Bangladesh: Some Broad Observations' in *Bangladesh Facing the Challenge of Globalization: A Review of Bangladesh's Development 2001*, Centre for Policy Dialogue/University Press Limited, Dhaka.

World Bank (1998) *Bangladesh: From Counting the Poor to Making the Poor Count*, Poverty Reduction and Economic Management Network, South Asia Region, World Bank, Washington, DC.

World Bank (2000) *World Development Indicators 2000*, World Bank, Washington, DC.

World Bank (2002) *World Development Indicators 2002*, World Bank, Washington, DC.

6 Poverty and policy in a globalising economy

The case of Ghana

Maurizio Bussolo and Jeffery I. Round

Introduction

In a well-documented attempt to correct severe internal and external imbalances, rampant inflation, and a grossly overvalued exchange rate, at the instigation of the IMF and World Bank, in 1983 Ghana embarked on a major programme of economic reform (Roe and Schneider, 1992; Aryeetey, Harrigan and Nissanke, 2000). The reform package included a liberalisation of the trade and payments regime, initially through a series of devaluations of the exchange rate, but later through the abolition of import licenses and reductions in import tariffs and export tax rates. However, Ghana's attempt to enter a globalising world through market and trade liberalisation has not been smooth or even a one-way process (Aryeetey *et al.*, 2000). In terms of outcomes, the reforms initially seemed to reverse the deteriorating macroeconomic performance that had prevailed previously (although it has faltered during the 1990s). However, policy reform does not appear to have had a uniformly beneficial effect on the poor and vulnerable groups. Poverty incidence has remained persistent and high in spite of the introduction of various social programmes to mitigate the adverse effects of reform. Also, Ghana has struggled to maintain a strict budgetary discipline, especially through the 1990s.

This chapter is set in the general context of examining the potential effects of poverty-alleviating policy measures on the poor. Specifically, we examine the effects of introducing poverty-alleviating income transfers to poor households in a budget-neutral regime. The inclusion of a budget constraint is especially important in view of the history of fiscal indiscipline in Ghana and our desire to minimise the macroeconomic repercussions in our analysis. The general approach we adopt, proposed by Dervis, de Melo and Robinson (1982), is to model distributional mechanisms within a computable general equilibrium (CGE) framework. We use a CGE model in order to conduct a series of counterfactual numerical simulations based on alternative policy shocks. Earlier studies of a similar genre are by Adelman and Robinson (1978); Chia, Wahba and Whalley (1994); Cockburn (2001); and Robilliard, Bourguignon and Robinson (2001). But the scope and range of experiments conducted and technical approaches adopted here differ markedly from these earlier studies. Also, De Maio, Stewart and van der Hoeven (1999) levelled several criticisms at Sahn, Dorosh and Younger (1997) (and others) on their use of CGEs in poverty analysis in Africa.

There are five distinctive features of this chapter. The first is that the model is based on the first detailed social accounting matrix (SAM) for Ghana, estimated for the year 1993, well inside the post-reform era. The second is that, rather than constructing one single (definitive) model several variants are constructed with the aim of seeing how sensitive the results are to variations in the parameterisation, specification and closure rules. In particular we examine sensitivity with respect to the functioning of the factor markets; and we introduce model closures that broadly characterise the long-run and the short-run situations. Thirdly, while the financing rule that supports the income transfers is likely to be country specific, we are able to demonstrate that the ranking in terms of effects on poverty differs in the long run from what it is in the short run. The fourth novelty is that we address one of the main criticisms of these models, namely that they appear to be 'black boxes', thereby limiting their credibility as analytical tools for policy-makers. We introduce more transparency so as to understand the mechanisms underlying the distributional outcomes of the experiments, using a new decomposition procedure. Finally, we address an emerging debate in the modelling literature about the efficacy of parametric versus non-parametric methods to capture income distribution within these models. We report on some comparisons between parametric and non-parametric approaches, relying on detailed results for a large sample of households from the Ghana Living Standards Surveys. But it stops short of introducing a full microsimulation component (Robilliard, Bourguignon and Robinson, 2001).

Section 2 considers aspects of the economic structure of Ghana that underpin the model: specifically, these are features of the SAM framework used, including the household classifications, and a brief discussion of the CGE model. In Section 3 we set up some experiments in order to examine the possible effects of alternative distributive policies on poverty incidence. In Section 4 we examine the sensitivity of these results under alternative model specifications and closures, using parametric and non-parametric approaches, all of which are conducted under revenue-neutral rules. There are significant differences in the poverty responses for different socio-economic groups, and notably, some increases in poverty in the short term if resources are constrained. Finally, Section 5 concludes.

Ghana: the SAM and the CGE model

Ghana SAM for 1993

A social accounting matrix for Ghana for the year 1993 has been prepared in collaboration with the Ghana Statistical Service (Powell and Round, 1998). The SAM includes input–output tables as well as detailed and extensive household survey information obtained from Ghana Living Standards Surveys (GLSS3). The modelling experiments conducted here are based on a variant of the main SAM, referred to here as a 'consolidated SAM', comprising 40 accounts. The consolidated SAM involves straightforward aggregations of the main SAM. As a result, there is some loss of information (for example on certain inter-institutional transfers) but none that imposed major limitations on the particular model structures that have been envisaged. Six 'urban (i.e. non-Accra)' household accounts have been reduced to two, due to the lack of available information from the GLSS on the numbers of households and household sizes at the level necessary for the subsequent poverty analysis. But beyond the main areas of consolidation and of more significance were a series of other adjustments to the original Ghana SAM.[1] For instance, information on taxes on production provided in the original 'full SAM' was too aggregative for the redistributive experiments envisaged. Hence, by drawing on extra information, a few assumptions, and applications of the RAS technique, separate tax revenue accounts were generated for domestic taxes, as well as for import duties and export taxes. Another major adjustment to the SAM was to eliminate the seemingly negative savings that appeared in some household accounts and for the household sector as a whole. Obviously some households may well dissave in the short term but not at the scale and extent of the original negative estimates, and to retain these implausible estimates would have been problematic.

Features of Ghana's initial equilibrium

Some characteristics of the Ghana economy as implied by the structure of the 1993 SAM are set out in the Appendix. Clearly, many of these structural characteristics, representing the initial equilibrium, play a major role in determining the outcomes of the experiments and are therefore worth summarising.

Basic economic structure

The primary (and light manufacturing) sectors account for a large share of gross production, and of value added (both labour and capital). Household demand is also concentrated in these sectors, amounting to over 70 per cent of consumers' expenditure. Hence any increase in households' disposable incomes should initially strongly affect these sectors. Exports are also heavily concentrated in the primary goods sectors – agriculture and minerals – although import intensity is low for agriculture, and quite low for minerals, so any increase in domestic demand for these products has to be satisfied via domestic supply.

Labour intensity

Unincorporated business income, or 'mixed' income (formally a mixture of labour and capital income) is treated here as a category of labour income on the grounds that this may be predominantly informal sector activity. Labour is distinguished by gender, skill and formality. The largest component of labour income is received by the category 'informal/male/unskilled' (37 per cent of total labour value added) and 74 per cent of all labour income is received by unskilled labour. Agriculture is quite intensive in the use of 'informal/male/unskilled' labour so any stimulus in the demand for agricultural goods is likely to increase the generation of income to this factor.

Household groups

Six rural and four urban household groups are distinguished in the SAM; rural according to farm/non-farm and locality, and urban according to Accra/other urban and skill level of the household head. Gross income per capita markedly varies across household groups. Rural households receive a significant share of their labour income from the 'informal/male/unskilled' labour category. Correspondingly, though to a lesser degree, 'informal/female/unskilled' labour features relatively more prominently in the incomes of rural, non-agricultural, and 'urban (not Accra)' households. As expected, skilled labour income constitutes a large majority of income in 'Accra/skilled' households. All capital income is routed through the corporate sector but this sector includes some farms (treated as quasi-corporate enterprises) as well as corporate enterprises, so a high proportion of its income is distributed as transfer income to rural households besides some to urban households. Government transfers to households constitute only a small fraction of household incomes (less than 1 per cent in all except one household category). While the patterns of household income receipts are as expected they are nevertheless complex, and overall there is no clear-cut expectation of how changes in labour remuneration of different types will feed into households and ultimately affect poverty outcomes of the different household groups.

Government accounts

The government accounts implied by the SAM are set out in Table 6.1. The table is divided into two vertical panels. The left-hand panel shows receipts in terms of tax rates, actual amounts (in billion cedis), and the percentage structure. The right-hand panel shows expenditures in terms of both amounts and percentages. Again this table is relevant to examining different transfer-financing schemes in the experiments. Note that in the absence of more detailed evidence, a uniform income tax rate has been assumed across all households (1.3 per cent).

Model structure

The CGE model is a real-side model, appropriate to a small open economy and is purposely simple, having many standard features in common with existing models.[2] The exchange rate is fixed and acts as the numeraire; the balance of payments is always in equilibrium, with foreign savings fixed and equal to the current account deficit. At the same time, it is assumed that the economy is savings-driven, so that the quantity of investment adjusts to the level of savings. The government has a fixed budget for a pre-defined consumption plan. Domestic savings adjust through changes in institutional income. For example household income changes endogenously due to changes in factor income (via employment, wage rates, mixed income and returns to capital) and government income depends endogenously on direct and indirect tax receipts. Investment must equal the sum of domestic and foreign savings. Domestic and imported commodities are combined to produce

Table 6.1 Government accounts

| | Rates | | | | Receipts: structure | | | | | | | | | | Expenditures: structure | | | | | |
| | | | | | Revenues (billion cedis) | | | | | Receipts (%) | | | | | Exp (billion cedis) | | | Expenditures (%) | | |
	Tariffs	Exp. taxes	Ind. taxes	Y taxes	Tariffs	Exp. taxes	Ind. taxes	Y taxes	Other	Tariffs	Exp. taxes	Ind. taxes	Y taxes	Other	Cons.	Transfers	Other	Cons.	Transfers	Other
Agri. forest and fishery products	0.9	17.9	1.4	0.0	1	34	21			0	5	3		00	0		00	0		00
Ores, min., elect., gas, water	0.0	0.0	0.1		0	0	0			0	0	0			0			0		
Food, bev., textiles, leath.	13.5	0.0	9.4		25	0	86			4	0	13			0			0		
Other non metal prod.	32.4	0.0	28.6		35	0	125			5	0	19			0			0		
Metal prod., machinery	9.5	0.0	3.5		61	0	7			9	0	1			0			0		
Construction work	0.0	0.0	0.3		0	0	1			0	0	0			0			0		
Transp., comm. trade serv.	0.0	0.0	0.5		0	0	2			0	0	0			0			0		
Business services	0.0	0.0	0.1		0	0	0			0	0	0			13			2		
Personal and other services	0.0	0.0	0.0		0	0	0			0	0	0			546			81		
All Ghana	8.6				121	34	242			18	5	36			559			83		
Rural farmer head savannah				1.3				4					1			1			0	
Rural farmer head forest				1.3				7					1			2			0	
Rural farmer head coast				1.3				2					0			1			0	
Rural non-agric. head savannah				1.3				2					0			0			0	
Rural non-agric. head forest				1.3				6					1			3			0	
Rural non-agric. head coast				1.3				4					1			1			0	
Urban unskilled				1.3				7					1			4			1	
Urban skilled				1.3				5					1			4			1	
Accra skilled head				1.3				3					0			3			0	
Accra unskilled head				1.3				3					0			1			0	
All households								44					7			21			3	
Corporations				6.9				66					10							
Total direct taxes								110					16	0						
Transfers with corporations									0							45			7	
Transfers with ROW									166					25						
Savings																	49			7
All Accounts									674					100			674			100

composite goods in accordance with the Armington specification, equivalent to assuming a degree of imperfect substitution between domestically-produced and imported goods.

The labour and factor markets are an important aspect of the model structure, and deserve special mention in view of their direct link with the distribution of income across household groups. The factor market specification is simple and a precursor of a more sophisticated treatment of the informal sector and its interaction with the formal sector. In the Ghana SAM there are separate accounts for 'compensation of employees' and 'mixed income' further distinguished by location and skill. The category 'mixed income' represents the income of the self-employed and employers in household enterprises and therefore represents returns to both labour and capital. Household enterprises therefore include formal as well as informal activities. However, we broadly characterise the compensation of employees as the income from the formal sector labour market and mixed income as the return from the informal labour market.

De Maio *et al.* (1999) criticised Sahn *et al.* (1999) in particular and others in the use of CGEs in poverty analysis on the grounds that the results may be sensitive to the model closures, and to broader concerns about distinguishing the short-run consequences from those of the long run. This led us to a central aspect of our simulations, where we construct alternative closures for the factor markets to broadly characterise and distinguish between the long run and short run. In the long-run closure, capital and labour are perfectly mobile across sectors and they are also in excess supply (i.e. their returns are fixed), although it is not truly 'long run' in that there are no long-run accumulation of factors, changes in productivity, or other dynamic trends. In other words, this closure forces the flexible price model to behave as if it were an input–output model, in the sense that everything is demand-driven and there are no supply constraints. On the other hand, we specify that in the short run capital and labour supply are fixed and fully employed (i.e. there is no slack capacity in the economy); additionally capital is sector specific and only labour remains perfectly mobile across sectors. Other smaller differences between the long- and short-run closures include higher elasticities of substitution in the long-run closure, although this is not significant given that factor returns are fixed.

Alongside the model specification and closures are some issues concerning calibration and parameter estimation. The calibration is governed by the benchmark data set, comprising the base year SAM and other ancillary parameter values. The principal sets of parameters in the latter category are the trade substitution (Armington) elasticities which have to be determined exogenously. There are no known estimates available for Ghana and it is necessary to follow some guiding principles, which might lead to plausible values. For most developing countries, the expectation is that elasticities of agricultural products are higher than for industrial goods and services. Also, a high level of two-way trade can be considered to be consistent with a low substitutability between domestic and imported goods. Finally, export price elasticities are expected to be generally higher than import elasticities of substitution.[3] Clearly, the trade elasticity assumptions are unlikely to be as important in redistributive experiments as they would be in experiments concerning trade liberalisation or economic reform.

Policy experiments

The aims of the policy experiments are threefold. First, while in previous studies (e.g. Chia *et al.*, 1994) the targeting programme was financed only by increases in the taxes on household income, here we consider the consequences of alternative financing schemes. Our second aim is to examine the sensitivity of the results to alternative short-run and long-run closures, as described earlier. Thirdly, we consider how the results might vary with respect to alternative ways of performing the poverty calculations (i.e. parametric and non-parametric approaches).

Basic methodology

The basic experimental design is straightforward. An exogenous shock is applied within the CGE model via poverty-reducing lump-sum transfers to households. The shock is assumed not to affect the initial government budget position (i.e. government real savings are fixed) hence the transfers have to be financed either by increasing tax revenues or by reducing expenditures. Here we limit ourselves to the former and consider just two alternative revenue instruments: an increase in (a) corporate direct taxes and (b) direct personal income taxes. Also, the experiments are performed under alternative factor market closures, approximating to the short run and the long run. So just four experiments are carried out, as described in Table 6.2.

In order to examine the impacts of exogenous shocks (in this case income transfers) at the micro level (i.e. on poverty) two broad approaches have usually been adopted. One approach, initially suggested by Adelman and Robinson (1978) and later discussed by Dervis, de Melo and Robinson (1982), is to first assess the impacts on the mean incomes of household groups. From this, and assuming an analytical representation of income distribution for each group (lognormal, beta, etc), the shift in the group mean income can be translated into a shift in the distribution. This may or may not be a parallel shift, depending on the relationship of the group mean income to the mean and variance of the analytical distribution. Usually, intra-group variances, or log-variances are assumed to remain constant. But from this analytical distribution, suitably fitted parametrically to the base data, headcount ratios can be computed as the cumulative density below the poverty line. We refer to this as the parametric approach. A second approach, explored more recently (e.g. Cockburn, 2001, and Robilliard, Bourguignon and Robinson, 2001),

Table 6.2 Model experiments

Closure	Experiment	Revenue-neutral replacement tax
Long run	Exp1L	Corporate taxes
	Exp2L	Households direct taxes
Short run	Exp1S	Corporate taxes
	Exp2S	Households direct taxes

is to ascertain the effects on the income distribution non-parametrically. This assumes the sample of households in the household survey is representative of the population of households. Again, there are variants, such as 'top-down' or fully integrated 'top-down/bottom-up' (Savard, 2003), but the main feature is that the intra-group variance is now endogenously determined. In this study we use a simplified version of the non-parametric approach in which the intra-group variance of incomes remains fixed: incomes (consumption) of all households within each group are assumed to increase in line with the group mean income. Again, this is sufficient to compute headcount ratios, and is referred to here as the non-parametric approach.

The first step of the analysis is to determine the total transfers necessary to eliminate poverty. In a perfect targeting scheme only those individuals who are poor would be targeted and they would receive a transfer equal to the amount required to raise them above the poverty line. In practice this scheme involves identifying the poor and is costly to administer. A polar alternative to this is to administer a universalistic scheme in which *all* individuals receive z (the poverty line), therefore sufficient amount to eliminate poverty. Thus the total transfers T_h to household group h with n_h individuals are $n_h z$. However, simulating the effects of these (essentially micro) transfer payments in a standard CGE model under the parametric approach is problematic. Ideally, the effect of transferring z to each individual should be to shift the income distribution to rightwards by z. But this is usually achieved by transferring income of T_h to each household group. Thus, while the mean shifts from $(\overline{Y}_h)$ to $(\overline{Y}_h + z)$ individual households receive transfers proportional to their income and not therefore equal amounts z. We assume income within groups is lognormally distributed, so income transfers T_h are effectively also lognormally distributed within groups.

Some initial results

In this study we follow local practice and fix an expenditure-based poverty line of one third of the mean per capita expenditure in 1993; and the poverty measure is based on P_0 (the headcount ratio). Thus, the choice of the poverty line, though initially arbitrary and based on a relative position, becomes an absolute benchmark in the subsequent simulations. P_0 is sufficient for making broad poverty comparisons providing first order dominance holds. Previous studies on Ghana have highlighted the fact that poverty is highly concentrated in rural areas and the results obtained from an analysis of the 1993 Ghana SAM and GLSS3 for 1991–92 are in line with these findings.

Table 6.3 shows the summary statistics that are used as a basis for our simulations. It reports data relating to poverty and per capita expenditure across socio-economic groups as derived from the GLSS3, as well as the estimated parameter values used in fitting lognormal distributions[4] to separate household categories as a basis for the parametric approach to the poverty analysis.

The observed differences across socio-economic groups shown in Table 6.3 are quite marked. For example, while only 11.7 per cent of the population belong to

Table 6.3 Ghana poverty statistics 1991–92

	Number of individuals ('000)	Total consumption (billion cedis)	Per capita consumption ('000 cedis)	μ	σ²	Lognormal		GLSS3	
						Poverty ratio	% of national poverty	Poverty ratio	% of national poverty
Base year – no shock									
Rural farmer head savannah	2,584	338.6	131.0	4.6	0.6	59.4	31.6	72.4	28.6
Rural farmer head forest	2,740	464.8	169.7	5.0	0.4	36.9	20.8	56.8	23.8
Rural farmer head coast	1,006	188.5	187.4	5.1	0.3	29.5	6.1	43.8	6.7
Rural non-agric. head savannah	864	140.5	162.5	4.8	0.6	48.0	8.5	58.8	7.8
Rural non-agric. head forest	1,649	396.8	240.6	5.2	0.5	24.4	8.3	38.7	9.8
Rural non-agric. head coast	1,091	265.7	243.6	5.2	0.5	24.6	5.5	31.9	5.3
Urban unskilled	2,266	530.5	234.1	5.2	0.5	27.9	13.0	32.3	11.2
Urban skilled	1,234	357.3	289.6	5.4	0.5	15.5	3.9	22.7	4.3
Accra skilled head	467	214.0	458.9	5.9	0.5	4.7	0.5	9.0	0.6
Accra unskilled head	626	181.4	290.0	5.5	0.4	14.0	1.8	20.1	1.9
Ghana	14,526	3078.0	211.9			33.5	100.0	43.2	100.0
Rural	9,934	1794.8	180.7			39.5	80.8	52.1	82.0
Urban	4,592	1283.2	279.5			20.3	19.2	24.9	18.0

Source: GLSS3 and authors' calculations. Poverty line z = 116,500 cedis.

households in the 'Accra/urban skilled' category, this household group accounts for 18.5 per cent of total household consumption. On the other hand 17.8 per cent of the population belong to 'rural/savannah/farm' households whereas this group accounts for only 11.0 per cent of total household consumption. The comparisons across urban and rural households as a whole are also borne out by the figures: 68.4 per cent of the population belongs to rural households, whereas only 58.3 per cent of total consumption expenditure is incurred by rural households.[5] The column for per capita consumption also confirms significant disparities between groups.

The same (national) poverty line is used for each group. It is set at approximately 116,500 cedis (one third of the mean per capita expenditure across Ghana) in 1991–2. On this basis, and using the lognormal assumption, poverty profiles can easily be calculated. The results are shown in the penultimate columns of Table 6.3. Comparisons can also be made with the actual poverty profiles based on the GLSS3 results. While there are marked differences between actual and lognormal-based estimates, a significant general feature of both sets of results is that poverty is clearly more prevalent in the rural population. Rural areas include about 80 per cent of the poor; and those living in the savannah regions record the highest poverty ratios. Also, in general, farmers are poorer than non-agricultural rural workers, in spite of considerable imputation of own account production. According to this evidence, households living in Accra are considerably less poor than other urban groups. Overall the between-group disparities are very high indeed, suggesting that targeted policies might be quite effective in reducing poverty overall.

Applying the shocks under the various experiments set out in Table 6.2, and combining the outcomes on changes in prices and mean incomes with the parametric approach (lognormal assumptions) as outlined in above, we generate a series of implications for the headcount ratios. Percentage changes in the resulting headcount ratios (P_0) with respect to the initial situation are summarised in Table 6.4.

The first (and not too surprising) feature of these results is that, when resources are constraining the economy (i.e. the short-run closure) – shown in the right-hand panel – poverty alleviation via budget-neutral government transfers is not particularly effective. The aggregate (all Ghana) poverty index is, at best, reduced by 6.1 per cent (experiment 2S), and if corporate tax is chosen as the replacement tax then poverty actually increases (experiments 1S). In the long run, when resource constraints are relaxed (shown in the left-hand panel), poverty reductions are generally much more widespread. Note that there is a potential effect on the poverty line as a result of the policy shocks: under experiments 1L and 2L (the long-run closure) prices do not change, so the poverty line does not change. But it does shift under the short-run closure due to relative price changes, and this is accommodated in the results.

In experiment 1L (first column), when government transfers are financed by increased corporate income direct taxes and there are no supply constraints (the long-run closure), poverty is reduced for the whole of Ghana by 32.1 per cent, and on average urban poverty is reduced more than rural poverty. But although

Table 6.4 Redistribution policy – poverty effects

	Benchmark P_0	Long run		Short run	
		Corp tax Exp 1L	H'hold tax Exp 2L	Corp tax Exp 1S	H'hold tax Exp 2S
Poverty ratios P_0		Percentage change with respect to benchmark			
Rural farmer head savannah	59.4	−20.4	−23.3	9.4	−20.1
Rural farmer head forest	36.9	−7.8	−13.8	64.0	−7.0
Rural farmer head coast	29.5	−42.1	−23.4	15.3	−16.0
Rural non-agric. head savannah	48.0	−48.3	−13.4	−30.6	−9.2
Rural non-agric. head forest	24.4	−38.7	5.7	4.9	14.2
Rural non-agric. head coast	24.6	−63.3	2.7	−39.6	11.5
Urban skilled	15.5	−55.3	8.7	−22.8	19.2
Urban unskilled	27.9	−53.0	−7.1	−24.9	−0.1
Accra skilled head	4.7	−49.6	63.6	−9.8	82.8
Accra unskilled head	14.0	−75.1	15.9	−53.9	29.5
Rural	39.5	−26.5	−15.1	15.9	−9.6
Urban	20.3	−55.5	0.0	−26.8	8.6
Ghana	33.5	−32.1	−12.2	7.7	−6.1

Note: shaded cells are those for which poverty index worsens.

all household groups appear to benefit and show poverty reductions, these reductions are unevenly spread across groups. In particular – among the three groups that account for the largest shares of poverty[6] – 'rural/farmers/forest' shows only a small poverty reduction whereas 'Urban/unskilled' households benefit from a considerable reduction (53.0 per cent). The same financing method employed under tight factor markets (experiment 1S) produces quite different aggregate results: all Ghana poverty worsens by 7.7 per cent, with rural population seeing its poor increasing (15.9 per cent) and urban population decreasing (−26.8 per cent). Notice that, in this short-run scenario, the across household-group ranking of poverty variations is similar to that of the long-run case, although rural groups experience a worsening of poverty and urban groups show a gain. Interestingly, under the short-run simulations especially, the two financing rules lead to marked differences between gainers and losers in the poverty stakes. In the former, urban (and some rural non-agricultural) households experience poverty reductions, whereas in the latter it is rural households who gain. This is of course not surprising in view of the patterns of labour income payments across households, and given also that in the SAM some profits from farm enterprises are treated as corporate income.

Seeking more transparency from the results

CGE models are often criticised as being 'black boxes'. Moreover, Devarajan and Robinson (2002) recently commented: 'A CGE model can, and often does, generate empirical surprises, but it cannot generate theoretical surprises.' It is therefore desirable to seek more transparency about the nature of the transmission mechanisms following the initial shock. A decomposition analysis based on the total differentials of the subset of the model's equations that generate aggregate household consumption provides insights. Note also that applying marginal changes in combination with non-marginal shocks yields linear approximations of the individual effects contributing to the outcomes, leading to some discrepancies.

Decomposition algebra

Six equations in the model are relevant to the decomposition. In all cases subscript h refers to household group h.

The *poverty index* (P_α) is a function of the consumption in value (CT) and the poverty line expressed in nominal terms $(z(P^C))$:

$$P_{\alpha,h} = f(CT_h, z(P^C)) \tag{6.1}$$

The *consumption in value* is the sum of commodities prices (P_i^C) times the quantities demanded (C_i):

$$CT_h = \sum_i P_i^C \cdot C_{ih} \tag{6.2}$$

Quantities demanded are determined from extended linear expenditure system (ELES) equations, expressed as functions of prices (P_i^C) and disposable income (Y^D), and where θ_i and μ_i are the committed quantities and supernumerary shares respectively:

$$C_{ih} = \theta_i + \frac{\mu_i}{P_i^C}\left(Y^D - \sum_k P_k^C \cdot \theta_k\right) \tag{6.3}$$

Commodities prices (P_i^C) are Armington CES functions of domestic prices (P_i^d) and imported prices (P_i^m):

$$P_i^C = \text{CES}\,(P_i^d, P_i^m) \tag{6.4}$$

Disposable income for household group h is adjusted for taxes (tax rate τ_h) and private transfers (TR) in nominal prices (price index P^I):

$$Y_h^D = (1 - \tau_h)Y_h^H + P^I \cdot TR_h^{NG} \tag{6.5}$$

Total pre-tax income represents factor income (labour and capital) and transfer income from corporate sector, government and the rest of the world (the exchange rate is the numeraire):

$$Y_h^H = \sum_l \phi_{h,l}^L Y_l^L + \phi_h^K (1-k) Y^K + \phi_h^C (1-\kappa) Y^C + P^I \cdot TR_h^G + TR_h^R \qquad (6.6)$$

where k represents the proportion of retained capital earnings, κ is the corporate tax rate, and $\phi_h^C, \phi_h^K, \phi_h^L$ represent distribution matrices derived from the initial SAM and used to allocate corporate, capital and labour incomes respectively to households.

With the exception of the poverty index, now we consider the expressions for the total differentials in detail. Note that they represent approximate (linear) changes from the benchmark, subscript 0, through to the post-shock equilibrium, t. *Changes in nominal consumption:*

$$\Delta CT_h = CT_{h,t} - CT_{h,0} = \Delta QC_h + \Delta PC_h \qquad (6.7)$$

where

$$\Delta QC_h = \sum_i P_{i,0}^C (C_{ih,t} - C_{ih,0}) \qquad (6.8)$$

$$\Delta PC_h = \sum_i C_{ih,t} (P_{i,t}^C - P_{i,0}^C) \qquad (6.9)$$

Equation (6.7) simply states that the total difference in the nominal value of consumption (ΔCT_h) between the benchmark (0) and the new equilibrium (t) is equal to a consumption quantity difference (ΔQC) and a consumption price difference (ΔPC). Equations (6.8) and (6.9) define the total quantity and price differences in nominal terms.

From equation (6.3) the change in (nominal) consumption quantities (ΔQC_h) can be decomposed into an increment due to a change in disposable income ($\Delta C_i^{Y^D}$) and to a change in prices ($\Delta C_i^{P^C}$), both in nominal terms.
Change in consumption quantities due to change in disposable income (ΔY^D):

$$\Delta C_i^{Y^D} = \mu_i \left(Y_t^D - Y_0^D \right) \qquad (6.8a)$$

Change in consumption quantities due to change in prices (ΔP^C):

$$\Delta C_i^{P^C} \cong -\frac{\mu_i}{P_{i,t}^C} \left(Y_t^D - \sum_j P_{j,t}^C \cdot \theta_j \right) \left(P_{i,t}^C - P_{i,0}^C \right) \qquad (6.8b)$$

Equations (6.8a) and (6.8b) are aggregated across all goods to determine the change in total real consumption for each household group. Aggregating these equations across goods:

$$\Delta C_h^{Y^D} = \sum_i \Delta C_{ih}^{Y^D} \qquad (6.10)$$

$$\Delta C_h^{P^C} = \sum_i \Delta C_{ih}^{P^C} \qquad (6.11)$$

Note that the sum of $\Delta C_h^{Y^D}$ and $\Delta C_h^{P^C}$ from equations (6.10) and (6.11) represent approximately the same variation as in equation (6.8).

Change in disposable income (ΔY^D): The total change in disposable income can be decomposed into three component changes which are due to changes in taxable income, taxes, and the price index (h is suppressed here for clarity).

$$\Delta Y^D = \Delta Y^{D\text{-}YH} + \Delta Y^{D\text{-}Tax} + \Delta Y^{D\text{-}PI} \tag{6.12}$$

where the change in:
Y^D due to a change in taxable income is

$$\Delta Y^{D\text{-}YH} = (1 - \tau_0)\left(Y_t^H - Y_0^H\right) \tag{6.13}$$

Y^D due to a change in tax rates is

$$\Delta Y^{D\text{-}tax} = -(\tau_t - \tau_0)Y_t^H \tag{6.14}$$

Y^D due to a change in the price index is

$$\Delta Y^{D\text{-}PI} = -TR^{NG}\left(P_t^I - P_0^I\right) \tag{6.15}$$

Change in taxable income (ΔY^H): This mainly arises from factor income changes but more generally it can be decomposed into changes due to variations in the components of total household taxable income (equation (8.6)): labour income, capital income, distributed corporate profits, corporate taxes, the price index and transfers, as follows:

$$\Delta Y_h^H = \Delta Y_h^{H\text{-}YL} + \Delta Y_h^{H\text{-}YK} + \Delta Y_h^{H\text{-}YC} + \Delta Y_h^{H\text{-}TaxC} + \Delta Y_h^{H\text{-}PI} + \Delta Y_h^{H\text{-}TR} \tag{6.16}$$

where the change in:
y^H due to change in labour income is:

$$\Delta Y_h^{H\text{-}YL} = \sum_l \phi_{h,l}^L \left(Y_{l,t}^L - Y_{l,0}^L\right) \tag{6.17}$$

Y^H due to a change in capital income is:

$$\Delta Y_h^{H\text{-}YK} = \phi_h^K (1 - k)\left(Y_t^K - Y_0^K\right) \tag{6.18}$$

Y^H due to a change in distributed corporate profits is:

$$\Delta Y_h^{H\text{-}YC} = \phi_h^C (1 - \kappa)\left(Y_t^C - Y_0^C\right) \tag{6.19}$$

Y^H due to a change in the corporate tax rate is:

$$\Delta Y_h^{H\text{-}TaxC} = -\phi_H^C Y_t^C (\kappa_t - \kappa_0) \tag{6.20}$$

Y^{H} due to a change in the price index is:

$$\Delta Y_h^{\mathrm{H\_PI}} = TR_t^{\mathrm{G}} \left(P_t^{\mathrm{I}} - P_0^{\mathrm{I}} \right) \tag{6.21}$$

Y^{H} due to a change in government transfers is:

$$\Delta Y_h^{\mathrm{H\_TR}} = P_t^{\mathrm{I}} \left(TR_t^{\mathrm{G}} - TR_0^{\mathrm{G}} \right) \tag{6.22}$$

Decomposition results

Table 6.5 sets out an analysis of the differential effects that make up the aggregate effects on total nominal consumption in the first experiment. The poverty ratios are based on nominal consumption. These results refer to comparisons of long- and short-run closures for the case where the income transfers to households are financed by increases in corporate taxes. The table shows results for the ten household groups separately as well as for 'all Ghana'. For illustration, consider the first row, relating to 'rural/farmer/savannah' households under experiment 1L. The sixteen columns correspond directly to equations (6.7) to (6.22). Reading from the right, column 16 records the initial income transfer from government to this household group, amounting to 301 (billion cedis), determined by equation (6.22). This constitutes the first component of the change in taxable income (ΔY^{H}). Continuing to work from the right, note that with no supply constraints prices do not change, so there is zero effect on Y_{H} from equation (6.21) hence column 15 is zero. Given that corporate taxes have to increase to finance the transfers, column 14 records a large reduction in Y_{H} (293). Note however that corporate incomes increase and this has an offsetting positive increase in distributed income to households (column 13) amounting to 37. The change in labour income accruing to this household group is 48, shown in column 11, arising from equation (6.17).

The overall effect on taxable income is an increase of 92, shown in column 10. This is then translated into a direct effect on disposable income (ΔY^{D}) via column 7, by deducting income taxes, which amounts to an increase of 91. This is the only change in disposable income (column 6, equation (12) as there are no changes in household taxes (column 8) or changes in the price index (column 9), these being the only other possible contributory effects. The resulting increase in disposable income then impacts on consumption quantities (column 4). The former is the only impact on the change in consumption quantities, 91 (column 2), as price effects are zero in this case. For the same reason, the effect on consumption in value (column 1) is due entirely to the change in consumption quantities. Overall, with no change in prices and hence no change in the nominal poverty line, the increase in nominal consumption will lead to a reduction in the poverty ratio, as confirmed in Table 6.4.

The effects are quite different when experiment 1S is considered. These are shown in the lower panel of Table 6.5. Considering the same initial shock (an income transfer to 'rural/farmer/savannah' households) of 296 billion cedis[7], the final reduction in nominal consumption is 34 billion cedis. Notably it is now both

Table 6.5 Redistribution policy: transmission mechanism for experiments 1L and 1S

	(1) ΔCT_h	(2) ΔQC_h	(3) ΔPC_h	(4) ΔC_Ydh	(5) ΔC_Pch	(6) ΔYd	(7) ΔYd_Yhh	(8) ΔYd_Tax	(9) ΔYd_Pl	(10) ΔYhh	(11) ΔYhh_YL	(12) ΔYhh_YK	(13) ΔYhh_YC	(14) ΔYhh_TaxC	(15) ΔYhh_Pl	(16) ΔYhh_TR
Experiment 1L (corporate taxes, long run)																
Rural farmer head savannah	91	91		91		91	91			92	48		37	−293		301
Rural farmer head forest	22	22		22		27	27			27	83		54	−429		319
Rural farmer head coast	50	50		50		51	51			51	33		14	−113		117
Rural non-agric. head savannah	88	88		88		101	101			102	34		5	−37		101
Rural non-agric. head forest	108	108		108		132	132			134	95		22	−176		192
Rural non-agric. head coast	156	156		156		173	173			175	77		4	−33		127
Urban skilled	131	131		131		139	139			141	73		11	−87		144
Urban unskilled	255	255		255		260	260			263	121		17	−139		264
Accra skilled head	50	50		50		61	61			61	43		5	−41		54
Accra unskilled head	111	111		111		119	119			120	51			−4		73
Ghana	1061	1061	0	1061	0	1152	1152	0	0	1166	657	0	169	−1352	0	1692
Experiment 1S (corporate taxes, short run)																
Rural farmer head savannah	−34	−37	3	−34	−2	−34	−34			−40	2		−16	−316	−5	296
Rural farmer head forest	−137	−140	3	−136	−2	−167	−167			−175	3		−23	−463	−6	313
Rural farmer head coast	−12	−14	2	−12	−2	−12	−12			−14	1		−6	−122	−2	115
Rural non-agric. head savanah	49	47	2	49	−1	57	57			56	1		−2	−40	−2	99
Rural non-agric. head forest	−7	−11	4	−7	−3	−9	−9			−12	2		−10	−190	−4	189
Rural non-agric. head coast	79	77	2	79	0	87	87			86	1		−2	−36	−2	125
Urban skilled	44	43	1	44	1	47	47			45	4		−5	−93	−3	141
Urban unskilled	99	93	6	98	−4	101	101			97	1		−8	−150	−5	259
Accra skilled head	9	7	2	9	−2	11	11			10	4		−2	−44	−1	53
Accra unskilled head	61	60	2	61	−1	66	66			65	0		0	−4	−1	72
Ghana	151	126	25	151	−17	146	146	0	0	117	19	0	−74	−1459	−31	1661

resource constraints and price effects that determine this result. In experiment 1S, the total change in taxable income is negative due to: reduced corporate incomes (column 14), a negative price index effect (column 15), and a much smaller off-setting labour income effect (column 11). Indeed, it can be observed that, in both experiments, the negative changes due to increased corporate taxes almost entirely offset the initial positive transfer shock. And we observe that differences between the two experiments are due entirely to different factor market responses, which, in turn, are the result of different factor market closures.

In summary, it seems that if the transfer policy is financed by an increase in corporate direct taxes then the impact on the poverty ratios will strongly depend on the adjustment mechanism in factor markets. Also, given the pattern of allocation of corporate incomes (shown in Table 6A.4 p. 170), urban poverty will necessarily be reduced more sharply than rural poverty.[8]

The differential general equilibrium effects of experiments 1L and 1S can also be observed in terms of the sectoral variations of final consumption and real output as shown in Table 6.6. The main points here are that, while in experiment 1L consumption varies in fairly similar proportion across all sectors, in experiment 1S certain sectors, notably agriculture, record a smaller variation relative to the others. This is due to the fact that, in the short-run case, rural household consumption is generally reduced in contrast with the increasing consumption of urban households, coupled with the differentials between rural and urban consumption patterns (rural households consume a much larger share of agricultural commodities than urban households).

Finally, the second panel of Table 6.6 again shows the strong dependency of changes in sectoral real outputs on the factor market closure. In particular, with resource constraints (i.e. short-run closure), there is very little economy-wide real output variation and only a small sectoral reallocation is observed. Construction output goes down due to the reduction in savings, which affects total investment and this is mainly concentrated in the construction sector.

Now consider experiments 2L and 2S, in which the replacement tax is switched from corporate taxes to household income taxes. Overall, Table 6.4 showed that Ghana-wide poverty reduction is lower in experiment 2 than in experiment 1. Also, in experiment 2, rural poverty is reduced more than urban poverty, which generally shows an increase in most urban household groups in both the long and short run. The explanation for this differential rural–urban effect is due to the fact that, according to the SAM estimates, rural households receive a higher proportion of transfers (that is, combined government and corporate income transfers) than they pay in taxes – relative, that is, to the situation for urban households. Thus, when household direct taxes are increased to finance the poverty-alleviating transfers, urban households pay more in taxes than they would have paid out in experiment 1 via reductions in transfers. So the burden falls relatively more heavily on urban households.

A comparison of Tables 6.5 and 6.7 shows these mechanisms more clearly. As before, Table 6.7 shows the initial effect of household income transfers in column 16. Again consider experiment 2L and 'rural/farm/savannah' households as

Table 6.6 Total final consumption and real output

	Benchmark	Long run		Short run	
		Corp tax Exp 1L	H'hold tax Exp 2L	Corp tax Exp 1S	H'hold tax Exp 2S
	(billion cedis)	*(percentage change with respect to benchmark)*			
Total nominal consumption					
Agri. forest and fishery products	1190	32	7	2	3
Ores, min., elect., gas, water	162	38	2	10	−1
Food, bev., textiles, leath.	798	35	4	6	0
Other non metal prod.	237	34	4	5	0
Metal prod, machinery	112	37	0	9	−4
Construction work	52	35	4	6	0
Transp., comm. trade serv.	150	36	2	7	−2
Business services	238	37	2	9	−2
Personal and other services	138	35	2	7	−2
Economy-wide	3077	34	5	5	1
Real output					
Agri. forest and fishery products	1531	36	7	1	1
Ores, min., elect., gas, water	565	29	2	0	0
Food, bev., textiles, leath.	999	27	3	0	0
Other non metal prod.	562	36	4	1	0
Metal prod., machinery	194	2	1	−2	0
Construction work	438	−3	1	−9	0
Transp., comm. trade serv.	423	28	3	0	0
Business services	381	26	2	0	0
Personal and other services	693	7	0	1	0
Economy-wide	5786	25	4	0	0

Source: authors' calculations.

an example. The initial transfer is 301; and this is boosted marginally to 314 by increased activity (labour income, column 11 and corporate transfer income, column 13). Increased household direct taxes (column 8) reduce the increase in disposable income to 106 (column 6), which convert into an increase in nominal consumption of the same amount (column 1). The same calculations for urban households lead to a quite different outcome. The household categories 'urban-skilled' and 'Accra' households each show a reduction in disposable income (column 6) and nominal consumption (column 1). In this case (i.e. experiment 2) the outcome appears to be similar in the short run (2S) and the long run (2L). Household factor incomes increase slightly more in the long run than in the short run (columns 12 to 14) but not significantly. Table 6.6 confirms a positive change in total real output in experiment 2L. However the increase is smaller than in experiment 1L because the consumer demand boost due to the net increase in household incomes is so much lower.

Finally, and significantly, note from Table 6.4 that the resulting effects on aggregate poverty according to the alternative financing rules differ as between the

Table 6.7 Redistribution policy – transmission mechanism for experiments 2L and 2S

	(1) ΔCT_h	(2) ΔQC_h	(3) ΔPC_h	(4) ΔC_Ydh	(5) ΔC_Pch	(6) ΔYd	(7) ΔYd_Yhh	(8) ΔYd_Tax	(9) ΔYd_Pl	(10) ΔYhh	(11) ΔYhh_YL	(12) ΔYhh_YK	(13) ΔYhh_YC	(14) ΔYhh_TaxC	(15) ΔYhh_Pl	(16) ΔYhh_TR
Experiment 2L (direct taxes, long run)																
Rural farmer head sav.	106	106		106		106	310	−204		314	8		4			301
Rural farmer head forest	40	40		40		49	336	−287		340	14		6			319
Rural farmer head coast	25	25		25		25	123	−98		124	6		2			117
Rural non-agric. head savannah	19	19		19		22	105	−84		107	5		1			101
Rural non-agric. head forest	−12	−12		−12		−14	207	−222		210	15		3			192
Rural non-agric. head coast	−4	−4		−4		−4	138	−142		140	12		1			127
Urban skilled	−13	−13		−13		−14	153	−167		155	10		1			144
Urban unskilled	24	24		24		24	282	−258		286	20		2			264
Accra skilled head	−33	−33		−33		−40	60	−100		60	5		1			54
Accra unskilled head	−11	−11		−11		−12	80	−92		81	8		0			73
Ghana	140	140	0	140	0	141	1793	−1653	0	1816	104	0	20	0	0	1692
Experiment 2S (direct taxes, short run)																
Rural farmer head sav.	91	88	3	91	−3	92	299	−207		303	2		−1		1	301
Rural farmer head forest	22	19	3	22	−3	27	317	−290		322	3		−1		1	320
Rural farmer head coast	17	16	1	17	−1	17	117	−99		118	1		0		0	117
Rural non-agric. head sav.	13	12	1	13	−1	15	100	−85		102	1		0		0	101
Rural non-agric. head forest	−27	−28	2	−26	−2	−33	191	−224		194	2		−1		0	192
Rural non-agric. head coast	−15	−16	1	−15	−1	−16	127	−143		129	1		0		0	127
Urban skilled	−26	−27	1	−25	−1	−27	142	−169		144	0		0		0	144
Urban unskilled	3	1	2	3	−2	3	264	−260		267	3		0		0	264
Accra skilled head	−40	−40	0	−40	0	−48	53	−101		54	−1		0		0	54
Accra unskilled head	−18	−19	0	−18	0	−19	73	−92		74	1		0		0	73
Ghana	23	7	16	22	−16	11	1682	−1671	0	1706	14	0	−4	0	2	1694

Source: authors' calculations.

short run and the long run. In the short run, financing via household taxes leads to an overall reduction, whereas with corporate taxes poverty actually increases. Compare this with the long run, when the ranking is reversed: here, corporate tax financing reduces aggregate poverty by more than it would with household taxes. So the combination of the financing instrument and the closure can have materially different effects on the outcome. More particularly, the choice of the financing rule will depend on whether the policy aim is to seek poverty reduction in the long run or the short run. These are significant insights emerging from these simulations.

Parametric versus non-parametric approaches

A final simulation exercise has been carried out in order to compare the parametric approach (i.e. using the lognormal distribution) for the poverty calculations as opposed to applying a non-parametric approach using the household survey results (GLSS3) directly. This exercise has been prompted by the work of Cockburn (2001) who applied the non-parametric approach in a model of Nepal. But first it should be noted that there are significant conceptual and technical difficulties involved in matching household survey data and the macroeconomic accounts, due partly to definitional difficulties and partly to under-recording/mis-recording of incomes and expenditures by households. These data issues are not discussed further here, where we simply present a comparison of the outcomes for the parametric and non-parametric approaches, but they are significant issues nonetheless making the implementation of the non-parametric approach a non-trivial exercise.

A comparison of poverty statistics obtained directly from GLSS3 with those from a fitted lognormal distribution has already been shown in Table 6.2. It can be seen that the estimates of poverty ratios across socio-economic groups of households are some distance apart, although not in terms of their implications for poverty shares. This immediately suggests that the lognormal might not be an adequate approximation to the income distribution for all Ghana household groups, although in terms of changes in poverty ratios some further comments follow.

Recall that the results of the CGE experiments generate changes in the group-specific consumption expenditures, as well as prices, for the purpose of computing the corresponding impacts on the poverty ratios. The information can be used to calculate revised poverty ratios under the GLSS-based (non-parametric) as well as the parametric situations. In the former case, expenditures of all households in each household group are scaled according to the aggregate change in expenditures for that group, thereby enabling us to recalculate the percentage of individuals falling below the poverty line. A more sensitive procedure might be to re-compute the nominal consumption of each household in accordance with the changes for each commodity it purchases, reflecting the changes in each household's commodity bundle. However this has not been pursued here as it is unlikely to change the results significantly.

Table 6.8 presents summary results for four sets of experiments in the same format as previously. The upper panel reproduces the results previously reported in Table 6.4, whereas the lower panel records a new set of results based on the

Table 6.8 Redistribution policy: poverty effects – parametric vs. non-parametric

	Benchmark	Long run		Short run	
	P_0	Corp tax H'hold tax		Corp tax H'hold tax	
		Exp 1L	Exp 2L	Exp 1S	Exp 2S
		(Percentage change with respect to benchmark)			
Poverty ratios P_0 (parametric: lognormal distribution)					
Rural farmer head savannah	59.4	−20.4	−23.3	9.4	−20.1
Rural farmer head forest	36.9	−7.8	−13.8	64.0	−7.0
Rural farmer head coast	29.5	−42.1	−23.4	15.3	−16.0
Rural non-agric. head savannah	48.0	−48.3	−13.4	−30.6	−9.2
Rural non-agric. head forest	24.4	−38.7	5.7	4.9	14.2
Rural non-agric. head coast	24.6	−63.3	2.7	−39.6	11.5
Urban skilled	15.5	−55.3	8.7	−22.8	19.2
Urban unskilled	27.9	−53.0	−7.1	−24.9	−0.1
Accra skilled head	4.7	−49.6	63.6	−9.8	82.8
Accra unskilled head	14.0	−75.1	15.9	−53.9	29.5
Rural	39.5	−26.5	−15.1	15.9	−9.6
Urban	20.3	−55.5	0.0	−26.8	8.6
Ghana	33.5	−32.1	−12.2	7.7	−6.1
Poverty ratios P_0 (non-parametric distribution)					
Rural farmer head savannah	72.4	−22.0	−24.9	5.5	−21.1
Rural farmer head forest	56.8	−5.5	−11.2	34.4	−5.3
Rural farmer head coast	43.8	−38.8	−25.2	14.3	−14.3
Rural non-agric. head savannah	58.8	−46.8	−9.9	−30.5	−7.1
Rural non-agric. head forest	38.7	−33.2	6.4	5.5	11.8
Rural non-agric. head coast	31.9	−69.7	6.6	−38.5	13.1
Urban skilled	22.7	−57.5	12.6	−25.3	23.0
Urban unskilled	32.3	−55.7	−6.2	−26.7	0.0
Accra skilled head	9.0	−50.0	143.7	−18.7	156.3
Accra unskilled head	20.1	−82.2	11.1	−60.0	22.2
Rural	52.1	−26.3	−12.5	8.1	−7.1
Urban	24.9	−59.2	7.3	−30.2	15.4
Ghana	43.2	−32.5	−8.8	0.9	−2.8

Note: shaded cells are those for which the poverty index worsens.

Source: authors' calculations.

non-parametric approach. The results show some interesting features. First, and reflecting the different initial estimates of the poverty ratios, the benchmarks in the two panels of the table are clearly very different. Second, the percentage changes in the poverty ratios under the alternative experiments differ across household groups, and in some cases quite markedly, in both the upper and lower panels. Third, and most notably, the pattern of poverty increases and poverty decreases is exactly the same in both panels – that is, the pattern of gainers and losers is the same in both the non-parametric and parametric cases. But it must be remembered that in both cases there is no allowance for household response at a micro level, as might be the case in a full microsimulation approach (Robilliard *et al.*, 2001). So overall the parametric and non-parametric approaches suggest differences in magnitude though not in direction, further suggesting that the parametric approach may be sufficient in yielding directional evidence in these kinds of simulations.

Conclusions

This chapter has set out to tackle a range of issues to do with the analysis of the impact of policy shocks in Ghana in a CGE modelling framework. It is set in the context of an era of economic reform and trade liberalisation in Ghana, a persistently high budget deficit, and is partly prompted by a debate between Sahn *et al.* (1999) and De Maio *et al.* (1999) about the general efficacy of CGE modelling for policy analysis. The experiments are conducted under conditions designed to ensure the maximum degree of comparability. In particular, in assessing the effects of poverty-alleviating transfers the model is constrained to perform according to a revenue-neutral regime. This is important, not only to limit the simulation effects and gain transparency in the results, but also because, according to recent evidence, relaxing the government deficit may contribute to exacerbate rather than alleviate poverty policy management in Ghana.

Our results are indicative of two main conclusions. First, the results confirm intuition that the financing rule matters greatly. The poverty outcomes are very different according to which of the two rules (household income taxation or corporate taxation) is chosen. In general, the ranking is most likely going to be country specific, and it will also depend on whether policies are considered over the short run or the long run. In our experiments for Ghana, the long-run results are unambiguous, the ranking of financing rules suggest corporate taxes would be more effective than household direct taxes. Because of the different exogenous shocks the short-run rankings are less clear-cut, except that in this case there appears to be an increase in overall poverty under the corporate tax financing rule. In terms of the effects on different types of households the structure of the SAM provides important clues as to which socio-economic groups may gain relative to the others. Second, the factor market closures (roughly corresponding to the long run and the short run) are seen as being crucially important in determining the outcomes. The results are very different under the two closures and therefore indicative that outcomes might differ in the short and the long run.

Overall the results confirm that while some households do gain from income transfers the general equilibrium effects of these shocks mean that there will be losers too. What is particularly intriguing is the degree of variation in outcomes across different socio-economic household groups. Not surprisingly, in the short run, when resources are more likely to be constrained, poverty actually increases for many households. But this also applies to some households in the face of more factor market flexibility. This serves as a reminder that policy measures to alleviate poverty in a globalising economy do not always lead straightforwardly to the desired outcome.

Notes

1 The derivation of the consolidated SAM is discussed in a note available from the authors.
2 It is similar in structure to other country-specific models developed by the OECD Development Centre.
3 Sadoulet and De Janvry (1995: p.354) state that ' . . . the possible range of substitutability is relatively well represented by four values: 0.3 for very low substitutability, 0.8 for medium-low, 1.2 for medium-high, and 3.0 for very high'.
4 Decaluwé *et al.* (1999) have suggested that a Beta distribution may have more desirable properties. For example, one disadvantage of the lognormal distribution is its poor description of the tails of the income distribution. However this disadvantage is mitigated when the distribution is separately parameterised for different (and diverse) household groups as we do here.
5 The income and expenditure estimates include imputations for subsistence and other non-monetary items.
6 According to Table 6.3, rural farmer head savannah, rural farmer head forest, and urban unskilled household groups account for 65.4 per cent of all poor.
7 It is the same transfer in real terms, but now valued at the post-shock price index.
8 More after tax corporate income is distributed to rural households than to urban households, so if corporate taxes increase and distributed income falls then rural households will fare worse than urban households.

Acknowledgements

Earlier versions of this chapter were presented at an ESRC Development Economics Study Group conference at Nottingham; PEP-MIMAP workshops in Singapore and Senegal, and an OECD Development Centre seminar, Paris (subsequently appearing as working paper WP 220), and to the 'Ghana at the Half Century' conference in Ghana, July 2004. We thank participants of these meetings, especially Luc Savard, for helpful comments, and also Diego Colatei for his earlier contribution to an earlier study. However, any remaining errors are our responsibility.

References

Adelman, I. and S. Robinson (1978) *Income Distribution Policies in Developing Countries*, Stanford University Press: California.
Aryeetey, E., J. Harrigan and M. Nissanke (2000) *Economic Reforms in Ghana: The Miracle and the Mirage*, James Currey: Oxford.
Chia, N.-C., S. M. Wahba and J. Whalley (1994) 'Assessing Poverty-reducing Programmes: a General Equilibrium Approach', *Journal of African Economies*, 3(2): 309–338.
Cockburn, J. (2001) 'Trade Liberalisation and Poverty in Nepal: A Computable General Equilibrium Micro Simulation Analysis', Discussion Paper 01-18, CRIFA, Universit, of Laval. (Chapter 7 of this volume.)
Decaluwé, B. A. Praty, L. Savard and E. Thorbecke (1999) 'Poverty Analysis Within a General Equilibrium Framework', CRÉFA, Département d'economique, Université of Laval, Working Paper 9909. http://www.ecn.ulaval.ca/w3/recherche/cahiers/1999/9909.pdf (accessed 22 December 2004).
De Maio, L., F. Stewart, S. van der Hoeven (1999) 'Computable General Equilibrium Models, Adjustment and the Poor in Africa', *World Development*, 27(3): 453–470.

Dervis, K., J. de Melo and S. Robinson (1982) *General Equilibrium Models for Development Policy*, Cambridge University Press and the World Bank: Washington, DC.

Devarajan, S. and S. Robinson (2002) 'The Impact of Computable General Equilibrium Models on Policy', paper presented to the conference 'Frontiers in Applied General Equilibrium Modelling', Cowles Foundation, Yale University (April). http://132.203.59.36/PEP/Group/mpia-read/PDFs/Devarajan%20&%20Robinson.pdf (accessed 22 December 2004).

Powell, M. and J. I. Round (1998) 'A Social Accounting Matrix for Ghana: 1993', Ghana Statistical Service, Accra.

Robilliard, A.-S., F. Bourguignon and S. Robinson (2001) 'Crisis and Income Distribution: A Micro-Macro Model for Indonesia', mimeo, World Bank, DIAL, and IFPRI. http://www.worldbank.org/wbi/macroeconomics/modeling/Robilliard- Crisis.pdf (accessed 22 December 2004).

Roe, A. R., and H. Schneider (1992) *Adjustment and Equity in Ghana*, OECD Development Centre: Paris.

Sadoulet, E. and A. de Janvry (1995) *Quantitative Development Policy Analysis*, Johns Hopkins University Press, Baltimore, MD.

Sahn, D., P. A. Dorosh and S. D. Younger (1997) *Economic Policy and Poverty: Structural Adjustment in Africa Reconsidered*, Cambridge University Press, Cambridge.

Sahn D., P. A. Dorosh and S. D. Younger (1999) 'A Reply to De Maio, Stewart and van der Hoeven', *World Development*, 27(3): 471–475.

Savard L, (2003) 'Poverty and Inequality Analysis within a CGE Framework: a Comparative Analysis of the Representative Agent and Microsimulation Approaches', Cahiers de Recherch, 0412, CIRPEE, Dakar, Senegal. http://132.203.59.36/PEP/Group/mpia-read/PDFs/savard- Poverty_Inequality_CGE.pdf (accessed 22 December 2004).

Appendix: Structural features based on the Ghana SAM, 1993

Table 6A.1 Ghana's economic structure (percentage)

	Gross product XP	Labour income	Capital income	K / L	Household demand	Govern- ment demand	Investment demand	Export supply X	Import demand M	Export intensity X/XP	Import intensity M/D
Agriculture, forestry, fishery products	26	39	14	13	39	0	−17	25	6	12	6
Ores, minerals, electricity, gas, water	10	4	29	252	5	0	1	41	6	55	24
Food, beverages, textiles, leather	17	17	8	16	26	0	22	0	13	0	16
Other non-metal products	10	5	5	37	8	0	−17	15	8	20	19
Metal product machinery	3	3	1	17	4	0	68	5	45	20	80
Construction work	8	5	16	106	2	0	43	0	0	0	0
Transport, commercial trade services	7	5	7	54	5	0	0	12	8	21	25
Business services	7	5	12	83	8	2	0	0	14	0	34
Personal and other services	12	16	7	16	4	98	0	1	0	1	0
Economy-wide	100	100	100	36	100	100	100	100	100	13	24

Source: authors' calculations based on the revised Ghana SAM for 1993.

Table 6A.2 Labour sectoral intensity

	Skilled male	Unskilled male	Skilled female	Unskilled female female	Informal skilled male	Informal unskilled male	Informal skilled female	Informal unskilled female	All skills
Value added structure by sector									
Agriculture, forestry, fishery products	2	18	0	8	12	64	3	42	37
Ores, minerals, electricity, gas, water	4	7	6	3	16	1	22	4	6
Food, beverages, textiles, leather	2	9	2	13	13	22	10	29	18
Other non-metal products	3	6	3	8	13	4	17	12	8
Metal products, machinery	2	2	3	4	15	1	20	5	6
Construction work	2	9	0	4	0	1	0	0	2
Transport, commercial trade services	8	20	3	3	8	2	8	1	5
Business services	12	6	11	12	15	1	19	3	6
Personal and other services	65	24	71	45	8	4	1	3	11
Economy-wide	100	100	100	100	100	100	100	100	100
Value added structure by skill									
Agriculture, forestry, fishery products	0	5	0	0	1	64	1	27	100
Ores, minerals, electricity, gas, water	3	11	3	1	7	5	57	13	100
Food, beverages, textiles, leather	1	5	0	1	2	44	9	38	100
Other non-metal products	1	7	1	2	4	16	32	35	100
Metal products, machinery	2	4	1	1	7	8	55	22	100
Construction work	6	58	0	4	1	28	2	1	100
Transport, commercial trade services	6	43	1	1	4	14	24	5	100
Business services	8	11	5	4	7	4	50	11	100
Personal and other services	28	25	17	9	2	12	1	7	100
Economy-wide	5	11	3	2	3	37	16	24	100

Source: authors' calculations based on the revised Ghana SAM FOR 1993.

Table 6A.3 Households – basic statistics

Household groups	Population (%)	Income (%)	Per capita Y (10^9 cedis)
Rural farmer head savannah	18	10	0.13
Rural farmer head forest	19	17	0.21
Rural farmer head coast	7	5	0.19
Rural non-agric. head savannah	6	5	0.19
Rural non-agric. head forest	11	14	0.31
Rural non-agric. head coast	8	9	0.29
Urban unskilled	16	16	0.24
Urban skilled	8	11	0.31
Accra skilled head	3	7	0.56
Accra unskilled head	4	6	0.34
All population	100	100	0.24

Source: authors' calculations based on the revised Ghana SAM for 1993.

Table 6A.4 Households – income distribution

Across households percentages	Skilled male	Unskilled male	Skilled female	Unskilled female	Informal skilled male	Informal unskilled male	Informal skilled female	Informal unskilled female	All skills	Capital	Factor income income	Corporate distributed income	Govern-ment transfers	ROW transfers
Rural farmer head savannah	0	0	1	0	0	17	2	8	6	0	6	22	4	11
Rural farmer head forest	0	2	3	4	0	26	4	18	11	0	11	32	11	36
Rural farmer head coast	0	1	0	0	0	7	2	11	4	0	4	8	4	11
Rural non-agric. head savannah	8	6	4	0	7	5	4	5	5	0	5	3	2	4
Rural non-agric. head forest	16	22	9	12	15	13	11	15	15	0	15	13	15	18
Rural non-agric. head coast	8	13	4	3	5	5	20	15	11	0	11	2	7	3
Urban unskilled	2	33	8	31	1	20	18	15	18	0	18	10	20	7
Urban skilled	33	0	28	5	53	0	25	1	13	0	13	6	17	1
Accra skilled head	32	0	38	9	20	0	9	3	9	0	9	3	14	4
Accra unskilled head	0	20	5	36	0	5	4	9	8	0	8	0	7	6

Across income sources percentages (Labour categories income as percentage of total labour income)	Labour (% factor Y)	Capital (% factor Y)	Factor Y (% total Y)	Corporate (% total Y)	Govern-ment transfers (% total Y)	ROW transfers (% total Y)
Rural farmer head savannah	100	0	45	49	0.3	5
Rural farmer head forest	100	0	47	42	0.4	10
Rural farmer head coast	100	0	56	34	0.4	9
Rural non-agric. head savannah	100	0	83	13	0.3	4
Rural non-agric. head forest	100	0	74	20	0.6	6
Rural non-agric. head coast	100	0	92	6	0.5	1
Urban unskilled	100	0	82	15	0.8	2
Urban skilled	100	0	86	13	0.9	1
Accra skilled head	100	0	87	9	1.1	3
Accra unskilled head	100	0	94	1	0.6	5
All households	100	0	72	22	0.6	5

Source: authors' calculations based on the revised Ghana SAM for 1993.

7 Trade liberalisation and poverty in Nepal

A computable general equilibrium micro-simulation analysis

John Cockburn

Introduction

In recent years, the impacts of macroeconomic shocks, such as fiscal reform and trade liberalisation, on income distribution and poverty have become the subject of intense debate. Which tax regime is most equitable? Do the poor share in the gains from freer trade? What alternative or accompanying policies could be used to ensure a more equitable distribution? What are the mechanisms involved?

From a research perspective, the analysis of macroeconomic shocks and the analysis of income distribution and poverty use very different techniques and sources of data. Given its economy-wide nature and the strong general equilibrium effects they imply, the impacts of macroeconomic shocks are ideally examined in the context of a computable general equilibrium (CGE) model based on national accounting data. In contrast, income distribution and poverty issues are generally analysed on the basis of household or individual data in recognition of the heterogeneity of these agents and the importance of capturing their full distribution. A variety of income and, more recently, multidimensional indicators are used in this poverty analysis.

In this study we attempt to meld these two currents. By explicitly integrating into a CGE model all households from a national household survey, we are able to simulate how each individual household is affected by trade liberalisation. Each household is characterised primarily by its sources of income and consumption patterns. Conceptually speaking, we replace the representative household(s) of a conventional CGE by a nationally representative sample of actual households to construct a CGE micro-simulation model. In this way, we are able to simulate the impact of macroeconomic shocks on conventional poverty and distributional indicators. Indeed, we generate all the individual household income and consumption data required to calculate and compare these indicators under alternative policy scenarios. Furthermore, we demonstrate that the technique is easy to implement and requires only a standard CGE model and a nationally representative household survey with information on household income and consumption. The technique is illustrated through the analysis of the elimination of all import tariffs in Nepal.

Survey of the literature

There have been numerous attempts to adapt CGE models to the analysis of income distribution and poverty issues. The simplest approach is to increase the number of categories of households. In this context, it is possible to examine how different types of households (rural vs. urban, landholders vs. sharecroppers, region A vs. region B, etc.) are affected by a given shock. However, nothing can be said about the relative impacts on households within any given category as the model only generates information on the representative (or "average") household. There is increasing evidence that households within a given category may be affected quite differently according to their asset profiles, location, household composition, education, etc. Of course, this problem of intra-category variation decreases with the degree of disaggregation of household categories. Yet even in the most disaggregated versions – Piggott and Whalley (1985) have over 100 household categories – substantial intra-category heterogeneity in the impacts of a given shock are likely to subsist.

A popular alternative is to assume a lognormal distribution of income within each category where the variance is estimated using base year data (see De Janvry, Sadoulet and Fargeix, 1991). In this approach, the CGE model is used to estimate the change in the average income for each household category, while the variance of this income is assumed to be fixed. Boccanfuso, Decaluwé and Savard (2004) compare different functional forms, including non-parametric techniques, for within-category income distributions, which they argue can better represent the different types of intra-category income distributions commonly observed.

Regardless of the distribution chosen, one must assume that all but the first moment is fixed and unaffected by the shock analysed. This assumption is hard to defend given the heterogeneity of income sources and consumption patterns of households even within very disaggregate categories. Indeed, it is often found that intra-category income variance amounts to more than half of total income variance.

The alternative, of course, is to model each household individually. As we explain below, this poses no particular technical difficulties as it simply implies constructing a model with as many household categories as there are households in the household survey providing the base data. An independent strand of literature performs such individual-level analysis, commonly referred to as microsimulations, of macro shocks. This literature traces its origins to research by Orcutt (1957) and Orcutt *et al.* (1961). More recently, some authors have developed microsimulation models using household surveys to study issues of income distribution (Bourguignon, Fournier and Gurgand, 2000). However, these models are not part of a general equilibrium framework.

Decaluwé, Dumont and Savard (1999) present a CGE micro-simulation model for 150 households based on fictional archetypal data. They construct the model so as to allow comparisons with the earlier approaches with multiple household categories and fixed intra-category income distributions. They show that intra-category variations are important, at least in this fictional context.

The only general equilibrium micro-simulations with true data are Tongeren (1994), Cogneau (1999) and Cogneau and Robillard (2001). Tongeren models individual firms rather than individual households. Cogneau's study concerns a city, Antananarivo, rather than a nation and is primarily concerned with labour market issues. Cogneau and Robillard examine the impact of various growth shocks, such as increases in total factor productivity, on poverty and income distribution in the context of a national model of Madagascar. They find that "although mean income and price changes are significant, the impact of the various growth shocks on the total indicators of poverty and inequality appears relatively small". They show that the neglect of general equilibrium effects, as in standard micro-simulations, and the assumption of a fixed intra-group income distribution, as in standard CGE models, both strongly bias results. However, their model's disaggregation of the household account is obtained at the cost of sectoral disaggregation as the model distinguishes only three branches and four goods. As the poverty and income distribution effects of macroeconomic shocks are mediated primarily by differences in household income and consumption patterns, this level of aggregation fails to capture many of the intra-household differences.

In this chapter, we develop a CGE micro-simulation model that is simple in structure – maintaining the characteristics of an archetypal CGE model – while allowing full integration of 3,373 households. Furthermore, this household disaggregation is obtained without sacrificing the disaggregation of factors, branches and products required to capture the links between trade liberalisation and household-level welfare. Indeed, we trace the impacts of trade liberalisation as it affects production in 45 separate branches (15 branches, 3 regions), with quite different initial tariff rates. These sectoral effects in turn influence the remuneration of 15 separate factors of production (skilled and unskilled labour, agricultural and non-agricultural capital, and land; all broken down into three regions). As the household survey data provide information on each household's income from each of these factors and each household's consumption of each of the 15 goods produced by the branches, the links between trade liberalisation and household welfare are complete.

Methodology

The construction of a basic CGE micro-simulation model is technically straight-forward although, obviously, more sophisticated approaches can be envisaged. The objective is to integrate every household from a nationally representative house-hold survey directly into an existing CGE model. In the case of Nepal, we use an existing CGE model constructed in collaboration with Prakash Sapkota of the Himalayan Institute of Development in Kathmandu. This model is itself based on an archetypal CGE training model developed by Decaluwé, Martin, and Souissi (1995). Household income, expenditure and savings data is obtained from the Nepalese 1995 Living Standards Survey (NLSS), based on a nationally represen-tative sample of 3,373 households.

The Nepalese CGE model is based on a 1986 social accounting matrix (SAM) of Nepal (Sapkota, 2001) that includes the following 50 accounts.

- *Factors*: skilled and unskilled labour, land, agricultural and non-agricultural capital in each of the three regions.
- *Agents*: households (urban; small, large and non-farm Terai (fertile plains); small, large and non-farm hills and mountains), firms, government, savings and the rest of the world.
- *Branches* of production: paddy; other food crops; cash crops; livestock and fisheries; forestry; mining and quarrying; manufacturing; construction; gas, electricity and water; hotel and restaurant; transportation and communication; wholesale and retail trade; banking, real estate and housing; government services; and other services.
- *Goods for domestic consumption*: same as above, plus non-competing imports.
- *Export goods*: other food crops; cash crops; livestock and fisheries; forestry; manufacturing; hotel and restaurant; transportation and communication; wholesale and retail trade; and other services.

The household categories in the existing CGE model were first aggregated to three categories (urban, Terai, and hills/mountains) to facilitate reconciliation with the NLSS data.[1] The household income and expenditure vectors in the aggregate SAM were then recalculated using the NLSS data. This involved first establishing links between each of the 15 domestic final consumer goods in the SAM and the consumption categories used in the NLSS. In the same way, links were established between the household income sources in the SAM (remuneration of the five factors; dividends; net transfers from government and from the rest of the world) and the sources of income identified in the NLSS. Once these links were established, we calculated aggregate values for the three household categories by multiplying individual household values by their respective NLSS sampling weights and summing over all households in each region.[2]

With the introduction of the NLSS data, the SAM inevitably becomes unbalanced. We assume that the NLSS data, which is based on a large-scale nationally representative household survey, is correct and that the adjustment must be made through the other SAM accounts. We thus fixed the NLSS-based household income and expenditure vectors, and modified all other values in the SAM until the row and column sums were all equal. For this purpose, we prepared a simple program that seeks to establish equilibrium while minimising the variations in all SAM cells. Several optimisation criteria could be imagined. We chose to minimise the sum of the square of the rates of variation between the original $(A0_{ij})$ and new (A_{ij}) SAM values: $\min \sum_i \sum_j ((A_{ij} - A0_{ij})/A0_{ij})^2$ subject to $\sum_i A_{ij} = \sum_j A_{ij}$ and $A_{hj} = A0_{hj}$ where h represents the household account in the SAM.

When the aggregate SAM was balanced and coherent with the household survey data, we increased the number of household categories in the CGE to 3,373, the number of households in the NLSS survey, and introduced individual household income, consumption and savings data. Income and expenditure vectors for each household were first multiplied by their sample weights before introduction into the model. The rest of the model calibration and resolution remains unchanged with respect to a standard CGE.[3]

Household consumption is modelled using a LES (linear expenditure system) expenditure function:

$$CH_{h,i} = MINI_{h,i} + \beta_{h,i}^C \left(CTH_h - \sum_j PC_j MINI_{h,j} \right) /PC_i$$

where, for household h, $CH_{h,i}$ is its consumption of good i, $MINI_{h,i}$ is its minimum subsistence requirement of commodity i, $\beta_{h,i}^C$ is the marginal share of good i in its consumption, CTH_h is its total consumption and PC_j is the composite price of good j. Calibration of this function is obtained using estimates of income elasticities and Frisch parameters from the literature.[4] This specification captures differential impacts on households of trade liberalisation-induced changes in relative consumer prices.

Household income comes from factor remuneration and from transfers by firms (dividends), government (transfers minus income tax) and the rest of the world. Factor payments to households are a fixed share of the total remuneration of each factor, where the shares for each household are calibrated from the household survey data.[5] As macro shocks modify the relative returns to these factors, households are affected according to their factor endowments. Transfers from the government and the rest of the world are assumed fixed. Income tax is a small fixed share (1.5 to 5.0 per cent, depending on the household's region of residence) of income. Dividends are a fixed share of firm capital income.

In order to better capture the channels through which trade liberalisation affects households, all sectors and factors of production are separated into the same three regions as households: urban, Terai, and hills/mountains.[6] Factors are mobile between sectors within each region but not between regions.[7] Agricultural capital is only mobile among agricultural sectors,[8] just as non-agricultural capital is mobile between all other sectors. National production in each sector is a CET (constant elasticity of transformation) combination of regional productions. As they are expected to be close substitutes, we use high elasticities of substitution (=10). Investment volume is fixed to avoid intertemporal welfare effects and foreign savings are also fixed. The numeraire is the "nominal exchange rate". Government consumption volume is fixed as welfare analysis is based on household consumption alone. Imported and domestic goods are imperfect substitutes in domestic consumption (Armington hypothesis), and exports and local sales are imperfect substitutes from the viewpoint of local producers. World prices for Nepal's imports and exports are fixed (small country hypothesis). The rest of the model is standard. Poverty and income distribution analysis is performed using DAD software.[9]

Simulation results

To illustrate the analysis that can be performed with this type of model, we study the impact of the elimination of all import tariffs with a compensatory uniform consumption tax designed to maintain government revenue constant. Of course, this is just one example of the numerous policies that could be studied using this model.

Generally speaking, we might expect that the elimination of import tariffs would be pro-poor if the tariffs initially protect sectors that use factors (capital, etc.) that provide a small share of income for the poor. On the other hand, the poor may consume proportionately less of import (or import-competing) goods and thus benefit less from the resulting reduction in the prices of these goods.[10] In this general equilibrium framework, the resulting income and consumption effects will, in turn, feed back into the model and influence the overall results.

We begin with the initial tariff rates and trace the impacts of their elimination through the model, from sectoral supply and demand to factor remuneration and, finally, household income and consumption, bearing in mind that in a CGE model all variables interact and are determined simultaneously. We examine the case where the elimination of import tariffs is compensated by the introduction of a uniform 1.1 per cent consumption tax, endogenously determined so as to maintain revenue neutrality. As the consumption tax is applied uniformly to all goods, it does not create any distortions in the relative consumption prices allowing us to focus on the impacts of the elimination of all tariffs.

Table 7.1 presents sectoral supply and demand effects. Initial tariff rates (tm) are highest in the paddy, other food crop, mining and gas/electricity/water sectors and it is these sectors that experience the greatest increase in import volumes (δM) following the elimination of tariffs. However, imports represent a small share of local consumption (M/Q) in all but the manufacturing sector and, to a lesser degree, the transport/communication, mining and trade sectors. Thus, despite high Armington elasticities of substitution between imported and local goods (=5), the impact on local demand for domestic production (δD) is small for all but the mining and manufacturing sectors, and the decline in producer prices for local sales (PD) is moderate.

Faced with a moderate reduction in local prices and fixed export prices, and with a CET elasticity of 5, producers of exportable goods divert a portion of their sales to the export market. In sectors where a large share of local production is initially exported (EX/XS) – hotel and restaurant, transport/communication, trade and manufacturing – this export response leads to an increase in sectoral production (δXS) or, in the case of manufacturing, partially offsets the decline in local sales. In the other sectors, the change in sectoral production is roughly equal to the change in local sales (δD). Sectors with high export shares also experience a reduction in their output price (δP) that is inferior to that of their local sales given that export prices are fixed. As elasticities of substitution between regions in sectoral production are assumed to be high (=10), there is little regional variation in the production response $(\delta XS(=\delta VA))$ or producer price changes (not shown) within any given sector.

Table 7.1 Effects of trade liberalisation on sectoral production (%)

	Imports/local sales					Exports/production				δXS=δVA		
	tm	δM	M/Q	δD	δPD	δEX	EX/XS	δXS	δPT	Urban	Terai	Hills
AGRICULTURE												
Paddy	13.5	52.4	0.2	-0.8	-4.0	21.6	0.1	-0.7	-4.0	-0.7	-0.5	-1.4
Other food crops	12.2	43.4	0.6	-0.8	-4.0	21.9	0.2	-0.8	-4.0	0.8	0.4	-1.7
Cash crops	7.0	11.7	3.5	-0.7	-4.3	23.8	2.0	-0.2	-4.2	-1.3	-0.8	0.4
Livestock/fisheries	4.4	-1.5	1.2	-0.9	-4.4	24.0	1.9	-0.4	-4.3	-1.0	-0.9	0.0
Forestry				0.8	-4.2	25.1	0.1	0.9	-4.2	-0.5	0.6	1.6
NON-AGRICULTURE												
Mining	12.3	39.8	8.6	-10.4	-2.6			-10.4	-2.6	-12.2	-11.8	-9.8
Manufacturing	8.1	15.8	47.0	-8.1	-3.1	7.8	16.8	-5.4	-2.6	-6.0	-5.4	-3.5
Construction				-0.9	-2.4			-0.9	-2.4	-1.2	-0.7	-0.6
Gas, electricity, water	10.9	47.7	2.4	-2.3	-2.0			-2.3	-2.0	-2.4	-1.9	-1.9
Hotel and restaurant				1.6	-2.4	14.9	55.9	9.1	-1.0	9.2	10.1	6.6
Transport/communications	6.0	13.8	13.3	-1.4	-2.9	14.4	30.5	3.5	-2.0	3.4	4.0	3.0
Trade	3.4	2.2	6.8	1.5	-3.1	18.9	20.9	5.2	-2.4	3.2	6.4	10.0
Banking and real estate				0.9	-2.1			0.9	-2.1	0.5	1.6	0.5
Government services				-0.1	-2.5			-0.1	-2.5	-0.1	-0.3	0.3
Other services				-0.1	-2.2	11.6	0.8	0.0	-2.2	1.6	0.2	-2.7

Note: tm = initial tariff rate; δ = variation; M = imports; Q = domestic consumption; M/Q = import penetration rate; D = local sales of domestic output; PD = price of local sales of domestic output; EX = exports; XS = domestic output; EX/XS = export intensity ratio; PT = producer price of composite domestic output; VA = value added; base year values except for variations.

Table 7.2 Effects of trade liberalisation on factor remuneration

	Wage rate		Returns to:			Change in other income
	Unskilled	*Skilled*	*Ag. cap.*	*Non-ag. cap.*	*Land*	
Urban	−2.9	−2.3	−5.4	−1.7	−5.4	0.02
Terai	−4.1	−2.3	−5.1	−0.6	−5.1	0.02
Hills and mountains	−4.3	−2.3	−4.4	−0.8	−4.4	0.02

Note: Ag. cap. = agricultural capital; Non-ag. cap. = non-agricultural capital

In summary, trade liberalisation engenders a clear sectoral reallocation of resources from the mining and manufacturing sectors, where initial tariffs and import shares were relatively high, in favour of the hotel/restaurant, trade and transport/communication sectors, with the other sectors remaining relatively unaffected. Prices decline the most in the agricultural sectors, although the differences are small.

Let us now see how these production effects influence factor remuneration (Table 7.2). The general decline in nominal factor remuneration rates should be considered in the framework of a trade liberalisation-induced 3.2 per cent fall in consumer and producer prices. In this context, we are most interested in how the rates of remuneration of factors change relative to one another.

To understand these results, we take into account, for each factor, the share of each sector in its total remuneration (Table 7.3). Unskilled labour is primarily remunerated by agricultural sectors except in urban regions where construction, banking/real estate, transport/communication and manufacturing are important employers. As output prices fall by roughly 4 per cent in the agricultural sector, we see similar declines in the remuneration of unskilled labour.[11] The decline is smaller for urban unskilled labour as it is not so tightly linked to the agricultural sector. Skilled labour is employed primarily by the government services sector and, consequently, the variation in skilled wage rate closely follows that of the government sector output prices. Agricultural capital and land are remunerated primarily by the cash crops, paddy and livestock/fisheries sectors. As agricultural output prices decline the most following trade liberalisation, these purely agricultural factors are the biggest losers, particularly in the urban region where agricultural production experiences the largest declines. Non-agricultural capital is the biggest relative winner.

How do changes in the factor remuneration affect nominal household income? This depends on the share of income the household draws from each factor. In Table 7.4 we decompose the average income changes for households in each region into changes in income from each factor.[12] The latter are equal to the factor's share in the household income multiplied by the change in the factor's remuneration rate (drawn from Table 7.2).

Terai and hill/mountain households derive their income from similar sources, primarily unskilled labour and land. As the remuneration of these two factors undergoes the largest declines, we can understand that households in these two

Table 7.3 Sectoral breakdown in total factor remuneration (%)

	Unskilled labour				Skilled labour				Agricultural capital				Industrial capital				Land			
	U	T	H	Total	U	T	H	Total	U	T	H	Total	U	T	H	Total	U	T	H	Total
Paddy	11	28	11	17	1	6	3	3	31	34	13	23					32	35	13	23
Other food crops	5	9	20	14	0	2	6	3	10	7	14	11					9	6	13	10
Cash crops	4	17	21	18	0	5	8	5	16	27	36	31					16	29	36	32
Livestock/fisheries	10	16	28	22	0	2	4	2	27	16	27	23					28	15	28	23
Forestry	3	7	5	6	0	2	2	2	16	16	10	13					16	15	10	12
Total agriculture	34	77	84	76	2	18	23	15	100	100	100	100	0	0	0	0	100	100	100	100
Mining	0	0	0	0	0	0	0	0	0	0	0	0	0	0	2	1				
Manufacturing	8	2	1	2	2	3	2	2					18	18	12	16				
Construction	22	8	6	8	1	3	2	2					22	26	28	25				
Gas, electricity, water	1	0	0	0	2	0	0	1					2	1	1	1				
Hotel and restaurant	3	1	0	1	0	0	0	0					4	3	2	3				
Transport/communications	11	4	3	5	4	7	7	6					14	17	21	17				
Trade	2	0	0	0	1	1	1	1					20	12	10	15				
Banking and real estate	14	5	4	5	4	8	7	6					18	21	23	20				
Government services	0	0	0	0	82	56	55	63					0	0	0	0				
Other services	5	2	1	2	3	4	4	3					1	2	2	2				
Total non-agriculture	66	23	16	24	98	82	77	85	0	0	0	0	100	100	100	100	0	0	0	0

Note: U = urban; T = Terai; H = hills and mountains

Table 7.4 Sources of household income by region

	Income shares (%)			Change in factor remuneration rates			Income change		
	U	T	H	U	T	H	U	T	H
Wages									
Unskilled	24.5	33.8	36.1	−2.9	−4.1	−4.3	−0.7	−1.4	−1.6
Skilled	22.0	10.4	9.2	−2.3	−2.3	−2.3	−0.5	−0.2	−0.2
Returns to:									
Agricultural capital	0.4	1.9	1.8	−5.4	−5.1	−4.4	0.0	−0.1	−0.1
Non-agricultural capital	32.5	18.8	11.6	−1.7	−0.6	−0.8	−0.6	−0.1	−0.1
Land	6.2	30.5	34.1	−5.4	−5.1	−4.4	−0.3	−1.6	−1.5
Other income	14.3	4.7	7.1	0.0	0.0	0.0	0.3	0.1	0.1
Total	100.0	100.0	100.0				−1.8	−3.3	3.3

Note: U = urban; T = Terai; H = hills and mountains

regions have a more substantial loss in nominal income than do urban house-holds. Indeed, urban households receive nearly one-third of their income from non-agricultural capital, which experiences the smallest reduction in terms of re-muneration rates.

In summary, on the income side we find that trade liberalisation in Nepal en-courages a reallocation of resources from the agricultural sector, particularly the heavily-protected and inward-oriented paddy and other food crop sectors, to the service and non-manufacturing industrial sector. This, in turn, leads to a fall in the remuneration of land and unskilled labour relative to skilled labour wages and, a fortiori, non-agricultural capital. These changes tend, in turn, to favour urban households over rural households.

Now let us look at how trade liberalisation affects these households on the consumption side (Table 7.5). Sectoral consumer prices reflect changes in import prices (δPM), changes in the prices of local sales by domestic producers (δPD) and the share of imports in local consumption (M/Q). They also reflect the 1.1 per cent uniform consumption tax. We have already seen that initial tariff rates are highest – and, consequently, the fall in import prices is greatest, in the paddy, other food crops, mining and gas/electricity/water sectors. We also saw that import intensities are highest in the manufacturing and transport/communication sectors and how the combination of these factors determines how the domestic producers' local prices evolve. On this basis, it is easy to understand that consumer prices fall most in the initially highly protected agricultural sector and the initially moderately protected but import-intensive manufacturing sector.

While urban households consume a smaller share of agricultural goods than Terai or hill/mountain households (65 per cent vs. 79 per cent), they consume more manufacturing goods (19 per cent vs. 13–15 per cent). Consequently, there

Table 7.5 Effects of trade liberalisation on consumer prices

	δPM	δPD	M/Q	δPC	Urban	Terai	Hills/mtns
Agriculture					65.0	79.2	79.0
Paddy	−11.9	−4.0	0.2	−3.0	14.1	32.1	18.2
Other food crops	−10.9	−4.0	0.6	−3.1	5.9	13.5	18.1
Cash crops	−6.5	−4.3	3.5	−3.4	24.1	24.2	28.8
Livestock/fisheries	−4.2	−4.4	1.2	−3.4	4.4	4.0	5.0
Forestry	0.0	−4.2	0.0	−3.2	16.5	5.4	8.8
Non-agriculture					35.0	20.8	21.0
Mining	−10.9	−2.6	8.6	−2.5	0.0	0.0	0.0
Manufacturing	−7.5	−3.1	47.0	−3.7	19.5	13.2	15.1
Construction	0.0	−2.4	0.0	−1.4	0.0	0.0	0.0
Gas, electricity, water	−9.8	−2.0	2.4	−1.2	0.5	0.1	0.0
Hotel and restaurant	0.0	−2.4	0.0	−1.4	0.3	0.1	0.1
Transport/communications	−5.7	−2.9	13.3	−2.2	2.9	1.1	1.1
Trade	−3.2	−3.1	6.8	−2.1	0.0	0.0	0.0
Banking and real estate	0.0	−2.1	0.0	−1.1	0.2	0.5	0.1
Government services	0.0	−2.5	0.0	−1.4	10.0	5.0	4.0
Other services	0.0	−2.2	0.0	−1.1	1.6	0.8	0.6
Total					100.0	100.0	100.0
Consumer price indices					−3.1	−3.1	−3.2

is practically no difference in the impacts of trade liberalisation on the consumer price indices of households in these three regions. This said, it should be underlined that all households consume almost exclusively the goods that experience the greatest price declines, which implies a strong consumption payoff from trade liberalisation, despite the imposition of a uniform 1.1 per cent consumption tax.

Combining income and consumption effects in equivalent variations, we find that revenue-neutral trade liberalisation has practically no aggregate welfare effects.[13] This is not surprising as we are replacing a moderately distortionary import tariff, varying from 3.4 to 13.5 per cent (Table 7.1), by a uniform consumption tax in a second-best framework where distortionary income and production taxes remain. In terms of its distributive effects, urban households benefit from liberalisation, whereas Terai and hill/mountain households lose out (Table 7.6). This result can be traced to the pro-urban income effects above.

What conclusions can we draw in terms of poverty? If, for example, we consider the urban poor, we might conclude that trade liberalisation is beneficial. However, we saw that the smaller reduction in nominal incomes observed among households in the urban sector was due in large part to their greater endowment of non-agricultural capital and their lesser dependency on income from land and unskilled labour. Yet it is likely that among urban households, the poor are precisely those

Table 7.6 Distribution of income variations and equivalent variations by region

		Income variation	*Equivalent variation*
Urban non-poor	Mean	−1.89	0.39
	s.d.	(5.51)	(2.44)
Urban poor	Mean	−1.42	0.59
	s.d.	(6.02)	(2.08)
Total urban	Mean	−1.81	0.50
	s.d.	(5.61)	(2.25)
Terai non-poor	Mean	−3.33	−0.12
	s.d.	(2.31)	(0.77)
Terai poor	Mean	−2.97	0.06
	s.d.	(1.78)	(0.70)
Total Terai	Mean	−3.32	−0.10
	s.d.	(2.29)	(0.76)
Hills/mountains non-poor	Mean	−3.32	−0.12
	s.d.	(2.23)	(0.83)
Hills/mountains poor	Mean	−3.25	0.00
	s.d.	(1.34)	(0.53)
Total hills/mountains	Mean	−3.32	−0.09
	s.d.	(2.18)	(0.77)

Note: s.d. = standard deviation

households with the least access to capital and the greatest dependency on unskilled wages. We may therefore suspect that households within this region will be affected quite differently. Indeed, when we examine the distribution (standard deviation) of the above nominal income variations and equivalent variations, there is an enormous degree of heterogeneity in the impacts of trade liberalisation among households in each region.

One solution is to disaggregate households in each region into the poor and non-poor with, presumably, quite different factor endowments and consumption patterns. While this may reduce the intra-household heterogeneity, it would be difficult to eliminate heterogeneity altogether in a model with five production factors and 16 consumer goods. When we adopt one-half of the nation-wide median income as the poverty line, we see that the urban poor appear to be affected more favourably than the non-poor. However, there remain substantial differences in the effects of trade liberalisation not only between poor and non-poor within a region, but also within these categories.

An alternative is to assume a fixed income distribution, estimated on the base year data, within each region. However, it is unlikely that the income of all households will increase in the same proportion or in such a way that the income distribution shifts in parallel. In our urban example, it is likely that the increase in the returns to non-agricultural capital relative to unskilled wages will result in an increase in income disparities. We examine these issues as we analyse various poverty and distributional indicators below.

The advantage of the micro-simulation approach is its capacity to incorporate all the heterogeneity of household income sources and consumption patterns directly in the model so that we can model the impacts of trade liberalisation on each individual household. In effect, we use the micro-simulation model to generate the data from a hypothetical new household survey if it were to be executed after trade liberalisation. We then use these data and the base year data (drawn from the NLSS) to calculate and compare standard income-based poverty and distribution indicators before and after the simulation.

We convert all data in terms of individuals, rather than households, using the following standard equivalence scale (*ES*):

$$ES_i = 1 + 0.7(Z_i - 1 - K_i) + 0.5K_i$$

where i is the household index, Z is the number of household members and K is the number of children. Thus the first adult counts as 1, the other adults are each 0.7 and children are 0.5, to take account of scale economies and age.

Foster–Greer–Thorbecke (FGT) indices are the most common poverty indicators:

$$P_\alpha = \frac{1}{Nz^\alpha} \sum_{j=1}^{J} (z - y_j)^\alpha$$

where j is a sub-group of individuals with income below the poverty line (z), J is their total number, N is the total number of individuals in the sample, y_i is the income of individual j and α is a parameter that allows us to distinguish between the alternative FGT poverty indices. When α is equal to 0, the expression simplifies to X/N or the headcount ratio, a measure of the incidence of poverty. Poverty depth is measured by the poverty gap, which is obtained with α equal to 1. The severity of poverty is measured by setting α equal to 2.[14]

We define the poverty line as one-half of the nation-wide median income and thus ours is a measure of relative rather than absolute poverty.[15] Later, we will present FGT poverty curves which map out these results for a wide range of possible values for the poverty line. Our analysis is based on both real income and real consumption data. Post-liberalisation income and consumption data are deflated by household-specific Laspeyres consumer price indices to account for the general fall in these prices.[16]

These results suggest that the impacts of this fiscal reform on poverty are quite small and statistically insignificant (Table 7.7). As we will see, given the substantial heterogeneity of households and individuals within each region, poverty results are extremely sensitive to the choice of poverty line and the use of FGT curves is preferable.

As the choice of poverty line (one-half of median income) is debatable, we present the variation, between the base case and counterfactual equilibria, in the headcount ratios and poverty gaps for a wide range of poverty lines (from zero to twice the median income) in the figures below. The results are highly sensitive to the choice of poverty line. While there is some evidence of a slight reduction

Table 7.7 Normalised FGT poverty indices (%)

Index	All			Urban		
	Before	*After*	*Change*	*Before*	*After*	*Change*
Headcount ratio ($\alpha = 0$)	7.16	7.15	−0.01	3.64	3.57	−0.07
	(0.49)	(0.49)	(0.11)	(1.03)	(1.03)	(0.57)
Poverty gap ($\alpha = 1$)	1.40	1.41	0.01	0.63	0.59	−0.04
	(0.13)	(0.13)	(0.01)	(0.22)	(0.21)	(0.02)
Poverty severity ($\alpha = 2$)	0.45	0.45	−0.00	0.18	0.15	−0.03
	(0.06)	(0.06)	(0.00)	(0.08)	(0.07)	(0.02)
Index	Terai			Hills/mountains		
	Before	*After*	*Change*	*Before*	*After*	*Change*
Headcount ratio ($\alpha = 0$)	6.52	6.33	−0.19	8.21	8.36	0.15
	(0.79)	(0.78)	(0.18)	(0.71)	(0.71)	(0.13)
Poverty gap ($\alpha = 1$)	1.02	1.02	−0.00	1.84	1.86	0.02
	(0.18)	(0.18)	(0.01)	(0.20)	(0.20)	(0.02)
Poverty severity ($\alpha = 2$)	0.26	0.26	−0.00	0.65	0.65	−0.00
	(0.08)	(0.07)	(0.00)	(0.09)	(0.09)	(0.01)

Notes: Standard deviations in parentheses. Poverty line = 0.5*median income of individuals in region.

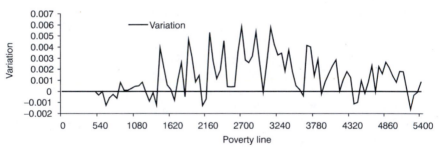

Note: This figure represents the variation in the headcount ratio resulting from trade liberalisation for a whole range of poverty lines.

Figure 7.1 Variation in headcount ratio curves (all regions)

in the number of the very poorest (under 900 rupees, or $US 43, per capita annual income), the number of moderately poor appears to increase as a result of trade liberalisation (Figure 7.1). At the regional level (Figures 7A.1-7A.3 in the Appendix), trade liberalisation appears to reduce the incidence of poverty in urban areas and to increase its incidence in the two rural areas.

Examination of poverty gap curves reinforces the message from the headcount ratio: a slight reduction in the depth of poverty among the very poorest and a clear increase in poverty among the moderately poor (Figure 7.2). Indeed, as we will see later, it appears that the very wealthiest individuals are the main beneficiaries

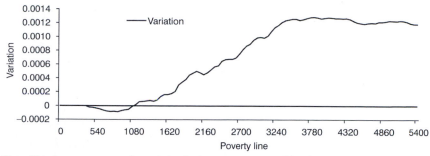

Note: This figure represents the variation in the poverty gap resulting from trade liberalisation for a whole range of poverty lines.

Figure 7.2 Variation in poverty gap curves (all regions)

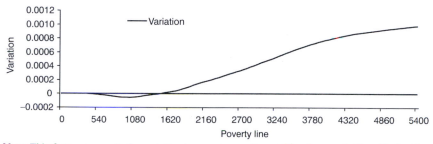

Note: This figure represents the variation in poverty severity resulting from trade liberalisation for a whole range of poverty lines.

Figure 7.3 Variation in poverty severity curves (all regions)

of trade liberalisation. At the regional level, the results contrast dramatically (Figures 7A.4–7A.7 in the Appendix). Urban dwellers are the clear winners, with the exception of a group of moderately poor. In rural areas, the very poorest are relatively unaffected but there is a clear increase in the depth of poverty among the moderately poor.

Similar results are observed when we examine poverty severity (Figure 7.3). Regional results resemble those for the poverty gap and are therefore not presented.

To obtain a broader perspective on the distributive effects of trade liberalisation, we look at changes in the density function for income (Figure 7.4). The density function measures the percentage of individuals with a given income. With some exceptions, there seems to be a movement of individuals from the middle-income brackets (3,000–6,500 rupees annual per capita income) toward lower income brackets (1,000–3,000 rupees). This suggests that further trade liberalisation would increase income disparities in Nepal. There is also a clear urban–rural dichotomy (Figures 7A.7–7A.10 in the Appendix). In urban areas, there is a clear movement of individuals from the lower and middle income brackets (1,000–6,000 rupees) toward the highest income brackets (8,000–15,000 rupees). In contrast, there is an

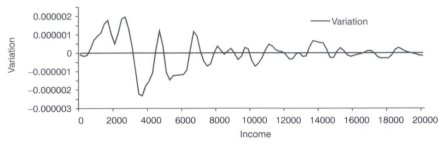

Note: This figure represents the variation in the density function resulting from trade liberalisation for a whole range of poverty lines.

Figure 7.4 Variation in density functions

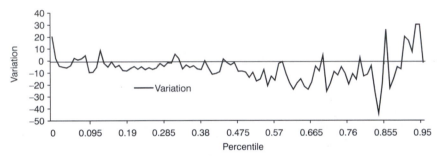

Note: This figure represents the variation in quantile curves resulting from trade liberalisation for a whole range of poverty lines.

Figure 7.5 Variation in quantile curves (all regions)

increase in the density of income among the very poorest (1,000–3,000 rupees) and an increase among the moderately poor (3,000 to 5,000–6,000 rupees).

We can see how income levels change according to income ranking using quantile curves (Figure 7.5). This analysis generates quite striking results. Individuals in most quintiles experience a loss of income as a result of trade liberalisation, with the notable exception of the very richest percentiles. Indeed, we truncated the quantiles at 0.95 as the increases among the highest five percentiles went off the scale. Regional results allow us to see that the gains, in the urban region, tend to increase with the level of income and that the very poorest actually see their incomes fall (Figures 7A.10–7A.12 in the Appendix). In the rural areas, income losses also appear to increase, as does the variability of the impacts of trade liberalisation.

The above results suggest that income inequality may be affected by trade liberalisation. Two popular inequality indicators are the Atkinson and Gini indices. They clearly show that inequality increases as a result of trade liberalisation, primarily in the urban areas but also in the hills and mountains region (Table 7.8).

Table 7.8 Inequality indices

Index	All			Urban		
	Before	*After*	*Change*	*Before*	*After*	*Change*
Atkinson index ($\varepsilon = 0.5$)	13.17	13.31	0.14	19.78	19.96	0.18
	(1.19)	(1.19)	(0.04)	(2.22)	(2.23)	(0.09)
Atkinson index ($\varepsilon = 0.75$)	17.74	17.91	0.17	26.75	26.98	0.23
	(1.40)	(1.40)	(0.04)	(2.65)	(2.66)	(0.13)
Gini index	37.85	38.03	0.18	47.52	47.74	0.23
	(1.38)	(1.38)	(0.04)	(2.63)	(2.63)	(0.13)
	Terai			*Hills/mountains*		
Index	*Before*	*After*	*Change*	*Before*	*After*	*Change*
Atkinson index ($\varepsilon = 0.5$)	6.19	6.18	−0.01	12.65	12.71	0.06
	(0.46)	(0.46)	(0.02)	(2.10)	(2.09)	(0.05)
Atkinson index ($\varepsilon = 0.75$)	8.85	8.83	−0.01	17.19	17.26	0.07
	(0.62)	(0.62)	(0.02)	(2.46)	(2.46)	(0.06)
Gini index	26.99	26.95	−0.04	37.04	37.12	0.08
	(0.93)	(0.93)	(0.04)	(2.43)	(2.42)	(0.06)

Conclusions

We have shown that it is straightforward to adapt a standard CGE model to explicitly integrate a large number of households (over 3,000 in this case). Using data on household income sources and consumption patterns collected in most standard household surveys, we are able to model the impacts of trade liberalisation (or any other macroeconomic shock) on individual households and how these impacts feed back into the general equilibrium of the economy.

Combining household data from the Nepalese Living Standards Survey and a standard CGE model, we are able to simulate the elimination of all tariffs. As the model estimates income for each household, we are able to generate all the data required to carry out standard income-based poverty and income distribution analysis. We conclude that trade liberalisation in Nepal favours urban households as opposed to Terai (fertile plains) and hills/mountain households. This result is traced mainly to the high initial tariffs in agricultural sectors.

However, these average results disguise an enormous variation in the impacts on individuals within each geographic region, even when we separate households into poor and non-poor. In this context, traditional poverty and inequality indicators can be useful to better understand these impacts. Generally speaking, the impacts of trade liberalisation on income distribution appear to be small, however some interesting results emerge.

Urban poverty falls and rural poverty increases, particularly among the moderately poor as opposed to the very poorest. The absolute impact of trade liberalisation, whether it is positive (in the urban areas) or negative (in the rural areas), generally increases with the level of income. Indeed, there appear to be very strong, mostly positive, impacts on the very richest individuals. This explains the increased income inequality found in the urban and hills/mountains regions.

These results have important policy implications. Although trade liberalisation is generally dictated increasingly by international agreements, there may be some scope to tailor these policies in order to ensure a more equitable or, possibly, a more pro-poor outcome. Alternatively, in designing accompanying fiscal policies – with a view to compensating for lost tariff revenue – policymakers can use this tool and the insights it provides to choose among various compensatory taxes (VAT, income tax, production tax, sales tax, etc.) or to design their implementation with a better understanding of the poverty implications. Finally, this type of analysis can help policymakers to design other compensatory policies that target those, particularly among the poor, who are the principal "losers" from trade liberalisation.

We conclude that CGE-based micro-simulations can be constructed with very little technical difficulty and that this type of model is indispensable for studying the poverty/distributional impacts of any macroeconomic policy or shock, such as trade liberalisation, that is likely to have general equilibrium effects. In particular, models such as these can help policymakers to design trade liberalisation, compensatory fiscal policies and other accompanying measures to ensure that all segments of the poor can share in the gains.

Acknowledgements

This chapter is drawn from my DPhil thesis in Economics at Oxford University. I would like to acknowledge financial support from Canada's Social Services and Humanities Research Council (SSHRC) and the International Development Research Centre's (IDRC) Micro Aspects of Macro Adjustment Policies (MIMAP) program. I am grateful to Abdelkrim Araar, Louis-Marie Asselin, Bernard Decaluwé, Véronique Robichaud and Prakash Sapkota for suggestions and assistance. This study builds on research performed by Bernard Decaluwé, Jean-Christophe Dumont and Luc Savard at CREFA (Université Laval). All remaining errors and omissions are my own responsibility.

Notes

1 The Terai region is an area of fertile plains.
2 A number of adjustments were required in the process. Income data in the NLSS were not clearly distinguished between labour (skilled and unskilled) and capital (land, agricultural capital and non-agricultural capital) remuneration. Shares of remuneration of these factors from the base SAM were applied to the NLSS data in order to separate out these sources. Total income data appeared to be under-estimated, as is often observed in household survey data. We first increased all income by a region-specific rate so as to ensure that average regional savings rates were equal to those in the base SAM. Even with this change, total income was not sufficient to cover reported consumption for a large number of households (roughly 30 per cent). We assume that this is due to the failure of the household survey data to capture inter-household transfers. Consequently, we increased the income of these households to equal their reported consumption and compensated this income increase by a reduction in the income of

the other households that was applied at a uniform region-specific rate. As the SAM underlying the CGE model dates to 1986 and the NLSS data concerns 1995, all NLSS income, consumption and savings data were also deflated by a uniform rate so that total household income, summed over the three household categories, is equal to its 1986 value.

3 See Cockburn (2001) for a full description of the model.
4 See Dervis, de Melo and Robinson (1982), Frisch (1959) and Lluch, Powell and Williams (1977).
5 See footnote 2.
6 See Fafchamps and Shilpi (2003) for a discussion of the spatial division of labour in Nepal.
7 The introduction of a migration function would be an interesting extension of the model.
8 Agricultural sectors are: paddy; other food crops; cash crops; livestock and fisheries; forestry.
9 Duclos, Araar and Fortin (2001). DAD is available free with a user's manual at www.mimap.ecn.ulaval.ca.
10 Chan, Ghosh and Whalley (1999) study the consumption effects of trade liberalisation.
11 Variation in value added prices may differ from those of output prices according to the intermediate consumption patterns of each sector. We do not find large differences and so do not present the variations in value added prices.
12 Bernard Decaluwé suggested this decomposition.
13 The equivalent variation measures the amount of money required to allow the individual to attain the same welfare level after trade liberalisation as she/he attained before trade liberalisation.
14 See Ravallion (1994) for a full discussion of poverty indicators.
15 Roughly 1,350 Nepalese rupees (US$65) per person. A common alternative measure of absolute poverty is obtained when the poverty line is defined as the minimum income required to cover "basic needs" (Ravallion, 1994).
16 $CPI_h = \sum_i PC_i CH_{h,i}^0 / \sum_i PC_i^0 CH_{h,i}^0$, where PC_i is the consumer price in sector i, $CH_{h,i}$ is household h's consumption of good i and superscript 0 refers to base year values.

References

Boccanfuso, D., B. Decaluwé, and L. Savard (2004) "Poverty, Income Distribution and CGE Modeling: Does the Functional Form of Distribution Matter?", mimeo, Université Laval.

Bourguignon, F., M. Fournier and M. Gurgand (2000) "Fast Development with a Stable Income Distribution: Taiwan, 1979–1994", Working paper 2000-07, DELTA, Paris.

Chan, Nguyen, M. Ghosh and J. Whalley (1999) "Evaluating Tax Reform in Vietnam Using General Equilibrium Methods", Research Report No. 9906, Department of Economics, University of Western Ontario, London, Canada.

Cockburn, J. (2001) "Trade Liberalisation and Poverty in Nepal: A Computable General Equilibrium Micro Simulation Analysis", Discussion paper 01-18, CREFA, Université Laval, October 2001 (http://www.crefa.ecn.ulaval.ca/cahier/0118.pdf).

Cogneau, D. (1999) "Labour Market, Income Distribution and Poverty in Antananarivo: A General Equilibrium Simulation", mimeo, DIAL, Paris.

Cogneau, D. and A.S. Robillard (2001) "Growth Distribution and Poverty in Madagascar: Learning from a Microsimulation Model in a General Equilibrium Framework", TMD Discussion Paper 61, IFPRI, Washington DC.

Decaluwé, B., J.-C. Dumont and L. Savard (1999) "Measuring Poverty and Inequality in a Computable General Equilibrium Model", Working paper 99-20, CREFA, Université Laval, Quebec.

Decaluwé, B., M.-C. Martin and M. Souissi (1995) "École PARADI de Modélisation des Politiques Économiques de Développement", 3rd edn., Université Laval, Québec.

De Janvry, A., E. Sadoulet and A. Fargeix (1991) "Politically Feasible and Equitable Adjustment: Some Alternatives for Ecuador", *World Development*, 19(11): 1577–1594.

Dervis, K., J. de Melo and S. Robinson (1982) *General Equilibrium Models for Development Policy*, Cambridge: Cambridge University Press, p. 484.

Duclos, J. Y., A. Araar and C. Fortin (2001), "DAD: A Software for Distributional Analysis/Analyse Distributive", MIMAP Programme, International Development Research Centre, Government of Canada and CREFA, Université Laval.

Fafchamps, M. and F. Shilpi (2003) "The Spatial Division of Labour in Nepal", *Journal of Development Studies*, 39(6): 23–66.

Frisch, R. (1959) "A Complete Scheme for Computing All Direct and Cross Demand Elasticities in a Model with Many Sectors", *Econometrica* 27: 177–196.

Lluch, C., A. Powell and R. Williams (1977) *Patterns in Household Demand and Savings*, London: Oxford University Press.

Orcutt, G. (1957) "A New Type of Socio-Economic System", *Review of Economics and Statistics*, 58: 773–797.

Orcutt, G., M. Greenberg, J. Korbel and A. Rivlin (1961) *Microanalysis of Socioeconomic Systems: A Simulation Study*, Washington: Urban Institute Press.

Piggott, J. and J. Whalley (1985) *UK Tax Policy and Applied General Equilibrium Analysis*, Cambridge: Cambridge University Press.

Ravallion, M. (1994) *Poverty Comparisons*, New York: Harwood Academic Publisher.

Sapkota, P.R. (2001) "Regionally Disaggregated Social Accounting Matrices of Nepal, 1986/87", mimeo, Himalayan Institute of Development, Kathmandu, Nepal.

Tongeren, F.W. van (1994), "Microsimulation Versus Applied General Equilibrium Models", mimeo, presented at 5th International Conference on CGE Modeling, October 27–29, University of Waterloo, Canada.

Appendix: regional poverty/distribution indicators

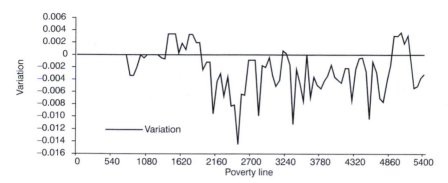

Figure 7A.1 Variation in headcount ratio curves (urban)

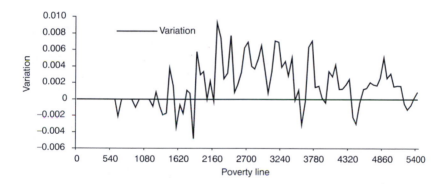

Figure 7A.2 Variation in headcount ratio curves (Terai)

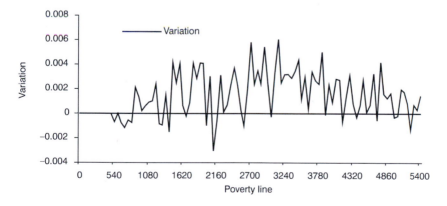

Figure 7A.3 Variation in headcount ratio curves (hills/mountains)

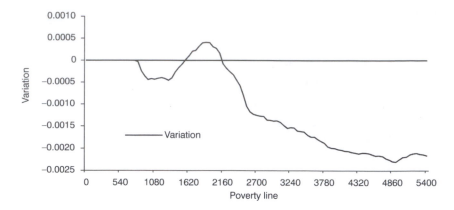

Figure 7A.4 Variation in poverty gap curves (urban)

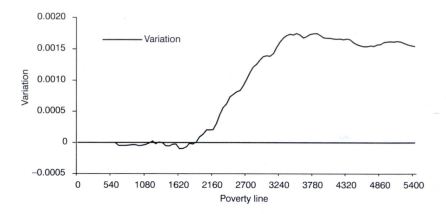

Figure 7A.5 Variation in poverty gap curves (Terai)

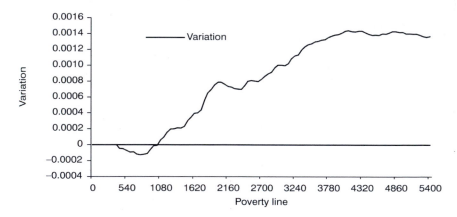

Figure 7A.6 Variation in poverty gap curves (hills/mountains)

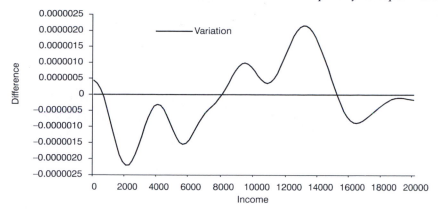

Figure 7A.7 Variation in density functions (urban)

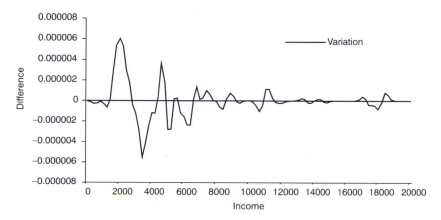

Figure 7A.8 Variation in density functions (Terai)

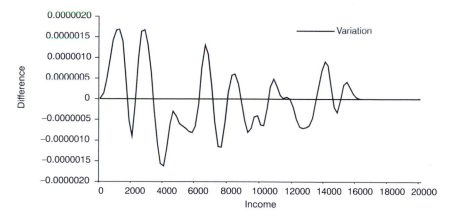

Figure 7A.9 Variation in density functions (hills/mountains)

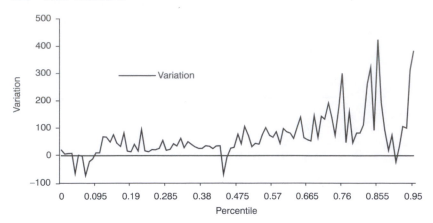

Figure 7A.10 Variation in quantile curves (urban)

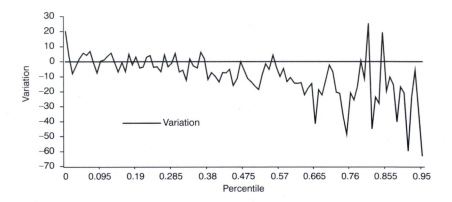

Figure 7A.11 Variation in quantile curves (Terai)

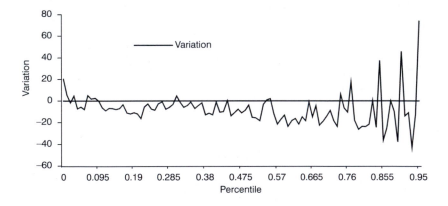

Figure 7A.12 Variation in quantile curves (hills/mountains)

8 Globalisation and poverty changes in Colombia

Maurizio Bussolo and Jann Lay

Introduction

During the last two decades, bilateral and multilateral donors' policy advice to developing countries has been centred on greater market openness and better integration into the global economy. However, this advice has recently been challenged, and the effects of globalisation on poverty are generating growing concern. To address these concerns and, at the same time, to assist in the formulation of better pro-poor policies, a clearer understanding of the complex relationship between globalisation and poverty is needed. The main objective of this chapter is to determine the signs and strength of the effects of trade liberalisation, which is an important globalisation shock on poverty, in the context of Colombia.

Towards the end of the 1980s Colombia abandoned its import substitution industrialisation policy and started a process of trade liberalisation, which culminated with the drastic tariffs cuts of the 1990–91. Colombian trade reform has been one of the most swift import liberalisations in Latin America. Within a few months, tariffs were more than halved and a series of institutions designed to regulate commercial policy had been created or reformed, including the Ministry of Foreign trade. In addition to the trade liberalisation policy, the government implemented a series of other structural reforms ranging from labour market reform and foreign exchange deregulation, to financial markets reforms, including establishing the independence of the central bank, and to the promulgation of a new constitution.

In the same period, poverty showed some improvements in urban areas but stagnated in rural areas, and inequality registered a significant countrywide increase. Identifying the poverty and inequality effects of each of the elements of the reforms, as well as those originating from additional technology and external shocks that affected Colombia in the first half of the 1990s is a complex task, even when two well-conducted household surveys provide data before and after the reform effort, namely for the years 1988 and 1995.

To tackle this task, this chapter follows a quite different approach from that of a large, although not uncontroversial, literature that analyses the links between openness and growth (Rodriguez and Rodrik, 2000, and references cited therein), or from those studies that extend these links to include poverty (Dollar and Kraay, 2000). This literature relies on cross-national regressions and, although they provide some evidence on the positive relationship linking openness to growth and poverty, in the words of Srinivasan and Bhagwati (1999) 'nuanced, in-depth analyses of country experiences [. . .] taking into account numerous country-specific factors' are needed to plausibly appraise the connections between openness and growth. Their arguments apply, even more strongly, to the case of the links between globalisation and poverty. In this case, country-specific characteristics – such as: a) the type and duration of globalisation shocks, b) the structure of the economy, and c) the socio-economic characteristics of the poor – are crucial to assess the final effects of globalisation on poverty.

Single-country studies have their own limitations. They mainly suffer from having too few degrees of freedom, which makes identifying and separating the effects of simultaneous different shocks almost impossible. The use of detailed household surveys reveals many characteristics of income distribution but it is not enough to understand whether trade liberalisation improves or worsens income distribution. Often, alongside tariff abatement, other policy reforms are implemented, and/or there are other shocks that affect income distribution. Multi-year surveys that track households for long periods of time overcome these problems by applying panel data techniques; however, these types of survey are still quite rare for most developing countries.

An alternative method that allows the analysis of single well-identified shocks is represented by numerical simulation models. When a shock is applied to these models, they determine sectoral production changes, resource reallocations, and factor and goods price changes. These macro adjustments can then be *translated* into micro effects at the level of individual and household incomes. This 'translation' normally relies on aggregating households in different groups according to the main sources of income or to other important socioeconomic characteristics of the head of the household. Finally, for each household group, a parametric income distribution is assumed, so that the initial shock is translated into changes of the average income of the household heads of each group, and, through the parametric distribution, the poverty and inequality effects can be assessed.

This method, known in the literature as the representative household group (RHG) approach, can produce insightful results with parsimonious data requirements and straightforward assumptions and it has therefore been applied in numerous cases (Adelman and Robinson, 1978; Bussolo and Round, 2003). However it has two major drawbacks. Firstly, the only endogenously-determined income distribution variations are those due to changes *between* household groups, given that *within* household group variances are fixed. Secondly, the composition of the household income is also fixed, therefore changes of occupational status, for instance, from formal wage-work to informal self-employment of the household head – or even increased labour participation or other important variations in income-generation processes of other non-head members of the households – are not accounted for. Often though, it is the within-group income changes and alterations in the composition of income, such as the dramatic income shift due to a household member finding a job or becoming unemployed, that are the crucial factors explaining poverty and inequality fluctuations.

This chapter, following a pioneering study on Indonesia (Robilliard *et al*., 2002), attempts to get the best of both worlds by using a novel methodology that links the macro numerical simulation model with a micro-simulation model, and thus it can estimate full sample poverty and inequality effects without the drawbacks of the multi-country regressions or RHG single-country approaches.

Beyond implementing these important methodological innovations, this chapter aims at providing policy-relevant results. By clarifying the mechanisms through which important reforms such as trade liberalisation affect income distribution, policy makers can adopt counter-balancing strategies to assist the poorest or to improve their chances of escaping poverty altogether.

Summarising the main results for Colombia, we find that trade liberalisation triggers two types of changes: a) in the labour force composition, moving from self-employment to more wage-employment, and b) in the levels of income, generating an increase of agricultural profits. This latter increase in income is found not to be sufficient to lift the poorest peasants out of poverty, however moving people out of self-employment into much higher remunerated wage-employment may do the job.

Besides these income-related changes, increased openness affects the expenditure side as well by altering the relative prices of consumption goods. Our results point out that the income channel, namely occupational status and factor price fluctuations, is more important for the poor than the expenditure channel, i.e. the change in prices of the goods bought by the poor.

Finally, compared with the full sample approach, we find that the RHG approach does not correctly measure the distributional impact of the income channel. More importantly, the sign of the bias due to the RHG assumption cannot be established ex ante as it leads to an overestimation of poverty effects for some households and an underestimation for others, thus making pro-poor corrective measures very difficult to implement.

Our dual-model methodology clearly illustrates which policy-induced changes are pro-poor, and through which channels the poor are negatively affected. Such detailed insights become essential for a successful pro-poor globalisation strategy.

The chapter is organised as follows. The next section presents the main economic policy reforms and the simultaneous poverty and inequality changes for Colombia at the beginning of the 1990s, then the methodology is discussed in more detail, the results are presented and the final section concludes.

Economic policy, poverty and inequality in Colombia

On the 7 August 1990, Cesar Gaviria was inaugurated as Colombia's constitutional president. During the next eighteen months a set of policies aimed at drastically changing the nature of Colombia's economic structure were put into effect. Even before his election, Gaviria was talking about a 'revolcón' of the economy.[1] Among the various reforms the most relevant were the so-called 'Apertura' or trade liberalisation and the labour market reform.

Colombia's trade reform was announced as a gradual and selective process that should have liberalised imports during a five-year period lasting until the end of

Table 8.1 Trade liberalisation in Colombia

Type of goods/year	Nominal tariff rates %		Effective rates of protection %	
	1990	*1992*	*1990*	*1992*
Consumption goods	53	17	109	37
Intermediate inputs	36	10	61	18
Capital goods	34	10	48	15
Total	39	12	67	22

Source: authors' calculations on the SAM (Bussolo and Correa, 1999).

1994. It is important to notice that Gaviria's strategy for smoothing the adjustments imposed by the liberalisation of imports was to accompany this liberalisation with a monetary policy aimed at a real depreciation of the peso. However, in 1990 the real exchange rate was at its most depreciated level in decades, and efforts towards further depreciation were contrasted by increasing speculations of an appreciation, which were also fuelled by the discovery of new oil fields. Facilitated by the opening of the capital account (another of the structural reforms implemented in that period), large capital inflows and stagnating imports generated a balance of payment surplus that entailed international reserves accumulation. This situation caused increasing difficulties of monetary management and, in September 1991, the government took the brave decision to drastically reduce tariffs almost overnight. Table 8.1 gives some indications of the magnitude of the 'Apertura': in just a few months, nominal average tariffs went from almost 40 per cent to about 10 per cent and the sectoral dispersion of the protection rates also went down as shown by a dramatic reduction of the average effective rate from almost 70 per cent to just 22 per cent. This move finally showed the government's commitment to free trade and imports surged. At a later stage in 1994, vested interests in protected sectors attempted to regroup and change the situation, but they just obtained small exemptions and minor benefits and Colombia's trade liberalisation could not be reversed.

Quantitative restrictions were almost completely eliminated as well. Before Gaviria took office 50 per cent of all imports were subject to import licensing, after one year less than 3 per cent of imports were still under the licensing scheme.[2] As mentioned earlier, trade tax reductions were complemented by other measures including: regulation of trade issues, such as anti-dumping and other unfair competition; institutional reform, such as the creation of a new independent Ministry of Foreign trade; and stipulation of international trade treaties, such as the free trade area (FTA) with Venezuela in 1991, the contemporary reviving of the Andean Pact, another FTA with Chile in 1993, and the Group of three treaty with Mexico and Venezuela in 1994.

The main objectives of the 'Apertura' policy package were to stimulate growth and to improve the distribution of income. A reallocation of resources towards more productive uses accompanied by a weakening of the oligopolistic structure of the domestic industries was expected to create new growth opportunities. These were enhanced by increased private capital inflows. The specialisation towards labour-intensive industries should also have helped the income distribution objective. Besides, a clearer trade policy should have decreased rent-seeking activities and their negative income distribution effects.

The second most relevant policy reform at the beginning of the 1990s was labour market reform and, given that this has strong influences on income distribution, it deserves a brief digression. Colombia's traditional labour legislation was extremely rigid and one of its worst features was represented by the prohibitive severance payments that workers with more than 10 years of continuous employment in the same job were granted. These basically gave automatic tenure to workers with more than 10 years on the job, but also reduced the possibility of a worker to achieve that 10-year limit. In fact it has been calculated that only 2.5 workers out of 100 were continuously employed for more than 10 years. This rigidity created serious employment stability problems in the labour market and was eliminated with the reform. This also regulated more clearly the hiring of temporary workers thereby generating new employment opportunities, especially for unskilled workers. Kugler (1999) and Kugler and Cardenas (1999) provide empirical evidence that this reform increased the Colombian labour market flexibility and its employment turnover.

As already mentioned, the late 1980s and the beginning of the 1990s witnessed a series of other important structural reforms such as those affecting taxes, housing policy, exchange controls, port regulations, central bank independence, financial (de)regulation, decentralisation, social security and privatisation. Additionally, international prices for coffee and oil (the most important exports) fluctuated around a falling trend and other external shocks (mainly capital flow volatility) affected the overall performance of Colombia.

Against this background of economic policy reform and external shocks, the remaining part of this section summarises changes in poverty and inequality. At first sight, economic reforms seem to have brought substantial welfare gains to Colombians. Between 1988 and 1995, mean per capita income had increased at a yearly rate of approximately 2.3 per cent. But this only partially resulted in poverty reduction, since inequality, especially between rural and urban populations, worsened. Whereas urban mean per capita income rose by 3.2 per cent per annum, rural incomes almost stagnated, growing at a rate of less than 1 per cent per annum.[3]

As shown in Table 8.2, a recent World Bank Poverty Report (World Bank, 2002) finds that urban poverty has declined significantly throughout the 1980s and the first half of the 1990s. According to this assessment, rural poverty has remained relatively stable at high levels between 1988 and 1995 after important improvements in the 1980s. A UNDP study (UNDP, 1998) comes to different conclusions. Overall poverty was found to be stable between 1988 and 1995. This stability is mainly due to a slightly improved poverty situation in urban areas, whereas rural poverty increased significantly with a headcount ratio up from 63 to 69 per cent. The World Bank Poverty Report finds that extreme poverty decreases faster than moderate poverty. In both urban and rural areas significant progress can be observed between 1988 and 1995.

Table 8.2 Poverty indicators, Colombia 1988–95

Indicator	World Bank (2002)		UNDP (1998)	
	1988	*1995*	*1988*	*1995*
National values				
Poverty incidence	0.65	0.60	0.54	0.54
Poverty gap	0.32	0.29	0.25	0.23
Extreme poverty incidence	0.29	0.21		
Urban values				
Poverty incidence	0.55	0.48	0.44	0.43
Poverty gap	0.23	0.19	0.15	0.14
Extreme poverty incidence	0.17	0.10		
Rural values				
Poverty incidence	0.80	0.79	0.64	0.69
Poverty gap	0.43	0.40	0.33	0.36
Extreme poverty incidence	0.48	0.37		

Source: World Bank (2002) and UNDP (1998).

With regard to the trends in inequality, the studies came to broadly similar conclusions although the magnitude of observed trends varied significantly.[4] They all noted a significant increase in inequality in the first half of the 1990s. As might be already inferred from the changes in mean per capita incomes discussed above, an important part of the overall deterioration of inequality is due to a widening gap *between* the urban and rural group incomes. Nevertheless, *within*-group inequality remains the most important determinant of income inequality.

All studies confirm opposite trends for *within*-group inequality in urban and rural areas with a decreasing rural inequality and a worsening urban inequality (Table 8.3). Based on generalised Lorenz curve considerations, Vélez *et al.* (2001, p.5) conclude that 'despite income inequality fluctuations, social welfare in urban Colombia improved substantially and unambiguously [. . .] from 1988 to 1995. In rural areas, welfare improvements are [. . .] somewhat ambiguous.'

To sum up, an improvement in urban areas resulted from a decrease of both extreme and moderate poverty, despite increasing inequality. In rural areas, the poverty situation did not change significantly between 1988 and 1995 even though all indicators point to a more even rural income distribution.

The micro–macro modelling framework

The micro-simulation model

In micro-simulation, we model the household income generation process.[5] Individuals make occupational choices and earn wages or profits accordingly. These labour market incomes plus exogenously-determined other incomes, such as transfers and

Table 8.3 Inequality measures, Colombia 1988–95

Indicator	World Bank (2002)		UNDP (1998)		Vélez et al. (2001)	
	1988	*1995*	*1988*	*1995*	*1988*	*1995*
National values						
Gini	0.54	0.56	0.55	0.56		
Theil	0.54	0.57			0.55	0.75
Theil within	0.50	0.59			0.47	0.63
Theil between	0.10	0.11			0.08	0.11
Urban values						
Gini	0.49	0.52	0.49	0.52	0.50	0.54
Theil	0.41	0.48			0.50	0.71
Rural values						
Gini	0.47	0.45	0.51	0.49	0.44	0.41
Theil	0.40	0.36			0.35	0.29

Note: The right-hand panel of the table displays the percentage change of the initial occupational category shares.

Source: authors' calculations on Colombian household surveys.

imputed housing rents, comprise household income. The micro-simulation enables us to take individual and household heterogeneity into account. Individual heterogeneity refers to personal characteristics which influence occupational choices and income generated in the labour market. Occupational choices are subject to a number of factors, which include gender, marital status, and age of children. Important determinants of labour income are education and experience. Household heterogeneity is reflected, for example, in different sources of income and demographic composition. Furthermore, micro-simulation captures some household heterogeneity in terms of expenditure structure. The micro-simulation model used here is based on Colombian household surveys.[6]

Income generation model

The components of the income generation model are an occupational choice model and an earnings model. It is assumed that individual agents can choose between inactivity, wage-employment, and self-employment. In rural areas, there is a fourth option of being both wage-employed and self-employed. The occupational choice model is assumed to be different for household heads, spouses, and other family members. As the possible occupational choices imply, earnings are generated either in the form of wages for employees or as profits for the self-employed. Individuals in rural areas can receive a mixed income from both kinds of activities. But this latter option will be ignored in the following illustration of the model. Being self-employed means being part of what might be called a 'household enterprise'. All self-employed members of a household are assumed to pool their incomes. This pooled income is then called profit. Profit functions in agriculture on the one hand and other activities, such as petty trade, on the other are assumed to be different. Since agriculture plays a negligible role in urban areas, this differentiation is only implemented for rural areas.

The wage-employment market is segmented: the wage-setting mechanisms are assumed to differ between urban and rural areas, between skilled and unskilled labour, and between females and males, which implies that there are eight wage and labour market segments.

Household income comprises the labour income of all active household members plus other income. Wages and profits are thus the endogenous income sources of the household. All other incomes are assumed to be exogenous and constant. The resulting total household income is deflated with a household group-specific price index, which takes into account the differences in budget shares for food and non-food items.

The income-generation process, which consists of the occupational choice and the earnings models, is first estimated using data from the Colombian household survey of 1988.[7] The estimated benchmark coefficients are then employed and adjusted in the micro-simulation.

Links to the computable general equilibrium (CGE) model

The micro-simulation and the CGE models are linked sequentially by a set of aggregate variables. Specifically, firstly, the CGE calculates the new equilibrium for a specific scenario (i.e. an exogenous shock), and from it determines the following aggregate results: the average wage in each labour market segment, the average profits for different activities, the shares of self- and wage-employed for each segment (labour force composition), and the relative price of food and non-food commodities. Then, these aggregate variables are used as targets for the micro-simulation model where individual changes in earnings and labour force composition are computed. These micro changes are obtained by applying coefficients in the occupational choice and the earnings models with adjustment to achieve aggregate consistency.

Elements of the model

The following set of equations describes the model. Household m has k_m members, which are indexed by i.

$$\log w_{mi} = a_{g(mi)} + x_{mi}\beta_{g(mi)} + e_{mi} \tag{8.1}$$

$$\log \pi_m = b_{f(m)} + z_m\delta_{f(m)} + \lambda_{f(m)}N_m + \varepsilon_m \tag{8.2}$$

$$Y_m = \frac{1}{P_m}\left(\sum_{i=1}^{k_m} w_{mi}IW_{mi} + \pi_m \text{ Ind }(N_m > 0) + y_{0m}\right) \tag{8.3}$$

$$P_m = s_{d(m)}P_{\text{f}} + (1 - s_{d(m)})P_{\text{nf}} \tag{8.4}$$

$$IW_{mi} = \text{Ind}\left[c^w_{h(mi)} + z_{mi}\alpha^w_{h(mi)} + u^w_{mi} > \sup\left(0, c^s_{h(mi)} + z_{mi}\alpha^s_{h(mi)} + u^s_{mi}\right)\right] \quad (8.5)$$

$$N_m = \sum_{i=1}^{k_m} \text{Ind}\left[c^s_{h(mi)} + z_{mi}\alpha^s_{h(mi)} + u^s_{mi} \sup\left(0, c^w_{h(mi)} + z_{mi}\alpha^w_{h(mi)} + u^w_{mi}\right)\right] \quad (8.6)$$

The first equation is a Mincerian wage equation, where the log wage of member i of household m, w_{mi}, depends on his/her personal characteristics. The explanatory variables include schooling years, experience, the squared terms of these two variables, and a set of regional dummies. This wage equation is estimated for each of the eight labour market segments. The index function $g(mi)$ assigns individual i in household m to a specific labour market segment. The residual term e_{mi} describes unobserved earnings determinants.[8]

The second equation represents the profit function of household m. Profits are earned if at least one member of the household is self-employed. The profit function is of a Mincer type and includes as explanatory variables the schooling of the household head, her/his experience plus squared terms of the former two variables, and regional dummies. Of course, profits also depend on the number of self-employed in household m, N_m. The residual ε_m captures unobserved effects. The index function $f(m)$ denotes whether a household earns profits in urban or rural areas. Furthermore, different profit functions for agricultural, non-agricultural, and mixed activities are estimated in rural areas.

Family income is defined in equation (8.3). It consists of the wages and profits earned by the family members plus exogenous income y_{0m}. This exogenous income corresponds to 'other income' in the survey and may include government transfers, transfers from abroad, capital income, etc. IW_{mi} is a dummy variable that equals 1 if member i of the household is wage-employed and 0 otherwise. Likewise, profits will only be earned if at least one family member is self-employed ($N_m > 0$). Family income is deflated by a household-specific price index.

This household-specific price index is defined by equation (8.4). The parameter s denotes the expenditure shares for food and non-food. These shares are calculated by household income quintiles. Note that the prices p_f for food and p_{nf} for non-food are generated in the CGE model. The index function $d(m)$ indicates to which of the five income brackets household m belongs and which food expenditure share is assigned to that household.

The fifth equation explains the dummy IW_{mi}. The individual will be wage-employed if the utility associated with wage-employment is higher than the utility of being self-employed or inactive. The utility of being inactive is arbitrarily set to zero, whereas the utilities of the employment options depend on a set of personal and family characteristics, z_{mi}. These characteristics include gender, marital status, education, experience, other income, the educational attainments of other family members, and the number of children. Unobserved determinants of occupational choices are represented by the residuals.

Equation (8.6) gives the number of self-employed. Similar to the choice in equation (8.5), the individual i of household m will prefer self-employment if the associated utility is higher than the utility of inactivity or wage-employment. The self-employed household members form the 'household enterprise' with N_m working members. Thus, the last two equations represent the occupational choices of the household members. The occupational choice model is estimated separately for household heads, spouses, and other family members in urban and rural areas. The index function $h(mi)$ assigns the individual to the corresponding group.

The model just described calculates household income as a non-linear function of individual and household characteristics, unobserved characteristics, and household budget shares. This function depends on three sets of parameters, which are estimated based on the 1988 survey. These parameters include (1) the parameters of the wage equation for each labour market segment, (2) the parameters of the profit function for 'household enterprises' in urban areas and different activities in rural areas, (3) the parameters in the utility associated with different occupational choices for heads, spouses, and other family members. As will be explained later in more detail, some of these parameters are adjusted in order to produce the aggregate results with regard to wages, profits, and employment shares given by the CGE model. The CGE model also gives the price vector, which in a final step is used to deflate family income.

The labour market specification

Some comments are appropriate on the assumptions behind the income-generation model. First of all, despite the availability of data on working time, occupational choice is modelled as a discrete choice.[9] Secondly, our model assumes that the Colombian labour market is segmented. One line of segmentation separates wage-employment from self-employment. In a perfectly competitive labour market, the returns to labour would be equal for these two types of employment. Yet segmentation may be justified because income from self-employment is likely to contain a rent from the use of non-labour assets, and its clearing mechanism may therefore differ from that of wage-employment. Information on non-labour assets, land in rural areas and possibly capital in urban areas, is not available for Colombia, hence distinct equations need to be estimated even if the labour markets were competitive. In addition, even in those cases where information on non-labour assets is available, a segmented labour market can be justified by the fact that wage-employment may be rationed and self-employment thus 'absorbs' those who do not get a job in wage work. Wage work might be preferred because it generates a steadier income stream and/or fringe benefits. Conversely, self-employment might have important externalities, for example for families in which children need care. Self-employment of the household head may also create employment opportunities for other family members.

Further segmentation is also assumed in the wage labour market. The segmentation hypothesis along the lines of different gender, skill, and area is strongly supported by the regression results. The same holds for the estimation of different profit functions for agricultural and non-agricultural activities in rural areas.

Estimation of the occupational choice and earnings equations

As mentioned above, the occupational choice model and the wage and profits equations are estimated as a first step in order to obtain an initial set of coefficients $(a_G, \beta_G, b_F, \delta_F, c_H^w, \alpha_H^w, c_H^s, \alpha_H^s)$ and unobserved characteristics $(e_{mi}, \varepsilon_{mi}, u_{mi}^w, u_{mi}^s)$. Unobserved characteristics say for the wage equation can of course only be obtained for those who are actually wage-employed. For self-employed or inactive individuals the unobserved characteristics in the wage-equation are generated by drawing random numbers from a normal distribution. In the same way, we generate unobserved characteristics for the profit function for households in which nobody is self-employed. As we estimate wage and profit functions using ordinary least squares, we assume these unobserved characteristics to be normally distributed. Additionally, unobserved characteristics need to be generated for the occupational choice model. These residuals are assumed to be distributed according to the double exponential law since we estimate the equation using a multinomial logit model. They were drawn randomly and consistent with the observed occupational choice, i.e. the utility a wage earner relates to wage-employment has to be higher than the utility associated with inactivity or self-employment.

Macro–micro links in more detail

As already mentioned, the micro-simulation and the CGE models are linked in a sequential fashion. In the first stage a shock is applied and simulated in the CGE model and then at the second stage in the micro-simulation model the micro results are adjusted so that values for the aggregate variables are consistent with the CGE macro equilibrium. Consistency requires that across the two models the following items are equal: (1) the changes in average wages in each segment, (2) the changes in average profits in each activity, (3) the changes in employment shares in each segment, i.e. the shares of wage-earners, self-employed, and inactive individuals per segment, and (4) the food and non-food commodities price changes. The CGE model is initially calibrated in such a way that its benchmark data set is consistent with the benchmark micro-simulation data. This benchmark micro-simulation is produced by using the set of initial coefficients and unobserved characteristics obtained through the estimation work just described.[10] Formally, the following constraints describe the consistency requirements.

$$\sum_m \sum_{i,g(mi)=G} \hat{IW}_{mi} =$$

$$\sum_m \sum_{i,g(mi)=G} \text{Ind} \left[\hat{c}_{h(mi)}^w + z_{mi} \hat{\alpha}_{h(mi)}^w + \hat{u}_{mi}^w > \sup \left(0, \hat{c}_{h(mi)}^s + z_{mi} \hat{\alpha}_{h(mi)}^s + \hat{u}_{mi}^s \right) \right] = E_G$$

$$(8.7)$$

$$\sum_m \sum_{i,g(mi)=G} \text{Ind} \left[\hat{c}_{h(mi)}^s + z_{mi} \hat{\alpha}_{h(mi)}^s + \hat{u}_{mi}^s > \sup \left(0, \hat{c}_{h(mi)}^w + z_{mi} \hat{\alpha}_{h(mi)}^w + \hat{u}_{mi}^w \right) \right] = S_G$$

$$(8.8)$$

$$\sum_m \sum_{i,g(mi)=G} \exp\left(\hat{a}_G + x_{mi}\hat{\beta}_G + \hat{e}_{mi}\right) I\hat{W}_{mi} = w_G \tag{8.9}$$

$$\sum_{m,f(m)=F} \exp\left(\hat{b}_G + z_m\hat{\partial}_G + \hat{\varepsilon}_m\right) \text{Ind}\,(N_m > 0) = \pi_F \tag{8.10}$$

Equation (8.7) states that, for each labour market segment, the number of wage-employed individuals in the CGE (E_G) and of micro-simulation systems has to be equal. 'G' stands for the eight labour market segments, i.e. urban male skilled and unskilled, urban female skilled and unskilled, rural male skilled and unskilled, rural female skilled and unskilled labour. The same holds for the number of self-employed in each segment, which is specified in equation (8.8).

Total wages paid in segment G in the CGE, w_G, have to be equal to the sum of wages over families and wage-employed individuals in the micro-simulation, as indicated by equation (8.9). This has to be fulfilled also for the profits in activity F as in equation (8.10). Thus, π_F denotes the total profits for self-employment activity F given by the CGE. The different self-employment activities include urban self-employment, rural agricultural, rural non-agricultural, and rural mixed activities. Note that ^ indicates that the coefficients, residuals, and indicator function values result from the estimation described above.

A globalisation shock produces changes in E_G, the number of wage-employed, S_G, the number of self-employed, w_G, the sum of wages paid in segment G, π_F, the sum of profits paid in activity F, and q, the price vector. The result is a new vector of these variables, which will be identified by an asterisk ($E_G^*, S_G^*, w_G^*, \pi_F^*, q^*$). For the above constraints to hold, an appropriate vector of coefficients and prices $(a_G, \beta_G, b_F, \delta_F, c_H^w, \alpha_H^w, c_H^s, \alpha_H^s, p)$ is needed. For the price vector this is trivial, as p equals q. For the other coefficients, many solutions exist and additional constraints have to be introduced. As in Robilliard *et al.* (2002) our choice is to vary the constants (a_G, b_F, c_H^w, c_H^s) and leave the other coefficients unchanged. Hence we assume that the changes in occupational choices and earnings are dependent on personal and household characteristics only to a limited degree. Changing the intercept in one of the wage equations implies that all individuals in the respective segment experience the same increase in log earnings. This increase does not depend on individual characteristics. The same holds for the profit functions. With regard to the occupational choice, it should be noted that the CGE does not allow for a distinction between the choices of heads, spouses, and others. The changes are thus the same across these groups.

Consistency between the micro-simulation and the CGE results requires the solution of the following system of equations. The right-hand side variables are those through which the macro model communicates with the micro-simulation. Additionally, the prices for food and non-food items are given by the CGE. However, the price vector is only finally applied in order to deflate household income.

$$\sum_{m} \sum_{i,g(mi)=G} I\hat{W}_{m}i =$$

$$\sum_{m} \sum_{i,g(mi)=G} \mathrm{Ind} \left[c_{h(mi)}^{*\mathrm{w}} + z_{mi}\hat{\alpha}_{h(mi)}^{\mathrm{w}} + \hat{u}_{h(mi)}^{\mathrm{w}} > \sup\left(0, c_{h(mi)}^{*\mathrm{s}} + z_{mi}\hat{\alpha}_{h(mi)}^{\mathrm{s}} + \hat{u}_{mi}^{\mathrm{s}}\right) \right] = E_{G}^{*}$$

$$(8.11)$$

$$\sum_{m} \sum_{i,g(mi)=G} \mathrm{Ind} \left[c_{h(mi)}^{*\mathrm{s}} + z_{mi}\hat{\alpha}_{h(mi)}^{\mathrm{s}} + \hat{u}_{mi}^{\mathrm{s}} > \sup\left(0, c_{h(mi)}^{*\mathrm{w}} + z_{mi}\hat{\alpha}_{h(mi)}^{\mathrm{w}} + \hat{u}_{mi}^{\mathrm{w}}\right) \right] = S_{G}^{*}$$

$$(8.12)$$

$$\sum_{m} \sum_{i,g(mi)=G} \exp\left(a_{G}^{*} + x_{mi}\hat{\beta}_{G} + \hat{e}_{mi}\right) I\hat{W}_{mi} = w_{G}^{*} \qquad (8.13)$$

$$\sum_{m,f(m)=F} \exp\left(b_{G}^{*} + z_{m}\hat{\partial}_{G} + \hat{\varepsilon}_{m}\right) \mathrm{Ind}(N_{m} > 0) = \pi_{F}^{*} \qquad (8.14)$$

Equations (8.11) and (8.12) state that the number of self-employed and wage-employed (and both self-employed and wage-employed in rural areas) must be consistent with the CGE results for each of the eight segments (G). This condition also holds for the wage equation for each of the segments and the profit function for each of the four activities, as indicated by equations (8.13) and (8.14). Hence, the above system contains 28 restrictions. The system has eight unknown constants in the wage equations, four in the profit functions, and 16 in the occupational choice model.[11] Thus we have 28 unknown constants and 28 equations. We obtain the solution by applying standard Gauss–Newton techniques.

Solving the above system gives us a new set of constants $(a_{G}^{*}, b_{F}^{*}, c_{H}^{*\mathrm{w}}, c_{H}^{*\mathrm{s}})$, which is then used to compute occupational choices, wages, and profits. The resulting household incomes are deflated by the household group specific price index derived from the CGE results for food and non-food prices.

Linking the CGE and the micro-simulation in the way described above goes beyond simply rescaling various household income sources or re-weighting households according to the occupation of its members, as in the RHG approach. The simulation model takes the different sources of household income into account and mimics individual occupational choices, based on a wide range of individual characteristics, and it is therefore a potentially more accurate method than just rescaling household groups' incomes.

An artificial panel data set?

At first sight, one may be inclined to believe that the simulation method generates a kind of artificial panel, which could be most helpful and interesting from an analytical point of view. If we want to analyse poverty dynamics, we need to trace individuals and households over time. However, to produce a synthetic panel, further assumptions need to be introduced. For brevity, the problems arising are illustrated in the case of the wage equation, but they apply to all the simulated relationships. In a dynamic context, the wage equation contains three components. Wages in period 0 consists of observed permanent earnings, i.e. the share of the earnings that can be explained by our model, unobserved permanent earnings e^p and unobserved transitory earnings e_0^t.

$$\log w_0 = a + x\beta + e = a + x\beta + e^p + e_0^t \qquad (8.15)$$

Moving from period 0 to period 1, the constant a is modified due to the policy change that triggered the changes in the CGE, so that in the next period we have a^*. If we assume that the distribution of the transitory component is the same in both periods, we know that among the people with characteristics x and an unobserved permanent component, e^p, there will be *one* individual with a transitory component equal to e_0^t. Therefore this individual's earnings are given by the following equation.

$$\log w_1 = a^* + x\beta + e = a^* + x\beta + e^p + e_0^t \qquad (8.16)$$

The individual with earnings given by (8.16) is not necessarily the same as the individual whose earnings were represented by (8.15). So we do not generate a synthetic panel, but instead, two cross-sections. Based on two cross-sections it is of course not possible to trace individuals through time. But this is not a problem if we compute aggregate inequality and poverty indicators, which are compared over time. However, in order to study poverty dynamics we would have to make sure that we could identify those individuals of households who cross the poverty line. It is therefore not sufficient to associate somebody with unobserved earnings, but it needs to be a specific individual.

The reason why we cannot simulate a panel arises directly from the fact that we cannot differentiate between two unobserved components. However, the introduction of a set of assumptions helps. First, the transitory component is assumed to be independent and identically distributed across time. Second, an assumption has to be made about the proportions of the variance of the entire residual term e that is due to the respective components. However there are a number of difficulties related to this method, in particular to the specification of the variance proportions. Some estimates of these proportions can be found in Atkinson *et al.* (1992) where a number of empirical studies on earnings mobility are surveyed. They find that the proportions of the three components in an earnings panel model differ substantially across different studies. Of course, the smaller is the total unobserved component the better the model explains log earnings. The proportion of the transitory component in log earnings covariance varies between less than 10 per cent and up to 30 per cent over long time horizons of more than 10 years. We are not aware of empirical work on earnings mobility in developing countries, on which one could analyse these issues in detail. There is scope for further research on earnings mobility as some panel datasets have become available. To assume a small proportion of transitory earnings in developing economies may be justified by a number of arguments. First, social mobility is generally lower in developing countries.[12] From this, we may infer that transitory earnings account for a smaller proportion of earnings. Second, recent research has shown that income shocks have a lasting effect, which also would imply less importance for the transitory component, at least in the short run.[13] On the other hand, the transitory component may be particularly important for small farms, which are exposed to a number of transitory, primarily environmental, risks.

For the purpose of the poverty transition analysis, we simulated a panel based on the aforementioned assumptions. These panel-based results are of a preliminary character and should be treated with caution, as further research in this field is needed. Experimenting with different proportions in the micro-simulation had a substantial impact on the results. Reducing the proportion of the variance of the residual term *e* (which is due to the transitory component) to 10 per cent produced results in the historical simulation which were close to those of the original simulation based on the two cross-sections. Using a higher proportion for the transitory component resulted in considerable increases in inequality indicators. The poverty transition analysis is thus based on the assumption that only 10 per cent of the variance of the unobserved effects is transitory.[14]

The computable general equilibrium model

The 1988 Social Accounting Matrix (SAM) for Colombia has been used as the initial benchmark equilibrium for the CGE model. The SAM, which includes 36 sectors, 20 commodities, 9 factors (8 labour categories and 1 composite capital), 2 types of households (urban and rural), and other accounts (government, savings and investment, and rest of the world), has been assembled from various sources incorporating data from the 1988 Input-Output table, the 1988 households survey and a 1994 SAM.[15]

The CGE model is based on a standard neoclassical general equilibrium model. However, to take into account special features of the Colombian economy, it differs from the typical specification in two important aspects: production sectors are distinguished between formal and informal activities, and the associated labour markets present structural imperfections with different clearing mechanisms for the formal and informal sectors.[16]

Production

Output is determined from a set of nested Constant Elasticity of Substitution (CES) functions that, at the top level, combine intermediate and value-added aggregates. At the second level, on the one hand the intermediate aggregate is obtained by combining all products in fixed proportions (Leontief structure), and, on the other hand value added is obtained by aggregating the nine primary factors. Formal and informal activities differ primarily by employing different labour types, with the former using exclusively wage-workers and the latter using exclusively self-employment. Additionally, informal activities are, on average, less capital intensive. These features, together with the disaggregation of eight labour categories, allow us to model in a more realistic way the segmented Colombian labour markets and to capture the dualistic nature of the economy. On the demand side, each commodity is represented by a composite which includes outputs from formal and informal activities. Imperfect substitutability between formal and informal components of the same commodity is assumed and flexible domestic prices adjust to reach equilibrium between domestic demand and supply.

Income distribution and absorption

Labour income and capital revenues are allocated to households according to fixed proportions derived from the original SAM. Private consumption demand is obtained through the Linear Expenditure System (LES). Household utility is therefore a function of consumption of different goods. Income elasticities are different for each household and product and vary in the range 0.20, for basic products consumed by the household with highest income, to 1.30 for services. Once their total value is determined, government and investment demands[17] are converted into sectoral demands according to fixed coefficient functions.

International trade

In the model we assume imperfect substitution among goods originating in different geographical areas.[18] The demand for imports results from a CES aggregation function of domestic and imported goods. Export supply is symmetrically modelled as a Constant Elasticity of Transformation (CET) function. Producers decide to allocate their output to domestic or foreign markets responding to relative prices. As Colombia is unable to influence world prices, the small country assumption holds, and its imports and exports prices are treated as being exogenous. The assumptions of imperfect substitution and imperfect transformability grant a certain degree of autonomy of domestic prices with respect to foreign prices and prevent the model from generating corner solutions; additionally they also permit to model cross-hauling, a feature normally observed in real economies. The balance of payments equilibrium is determined by the equality of foreign savings (which are exogenously fixed) to the value for the current account. With fixed world prices and fixed capital inflows, all adjustments are accommodated by changes in the real exchange rate. Increased import demand due to trade liberalisation must be financed by increased exports and these can expand owing to the improved resource allocation. Price decreases in importables drive resources towards export sectors and contribute to falling domestic resource costs (or real exchange rate depreciation).

Factor markets

Labour is distinguished by eight categories: urban male skilled, urban male unskilled, urban female skilled, urban female unskilled, rural male skilled, rural male unskilled, rural female skilled, and rural female unskilled. These categories are considered to be imperfectly substitutable inputs in the production process. Additionally, to take into account the fact that the labour market for self-employment and that for wage-employment adjust differently, the model assumes that labour markets are segmented between formal and informal sectors. In particular, given that wage-employment enjoys *formal* protection, such as union wage-setting and minimum wages, a certain degree of formal wage inflexibility is implemented in the model through a wage curve. The equilibrium in the formal market is thus determined by the intersection of the firms' labour demand and this wage curve. The informal labour market adjusts residually so that, for each of the eight mentioned categories, total supply (formal plus informal labour) is kept fixed. Capital is an aggregate factor and includes fixed capital as well as land. Formal sectors show higher capital intensities than informal ones.

To take into account the medium-term horizon of the model, i.e. the time period considered necessary for a trade shock to work through the economy, both labour and capital are perfectly mobile across sectors but their aggregate supplies are fixed.

Model closures

The equilibrium condition on the balance of payments is combined with other closure conditions so that the model can be solved for each period. Firstly consider the government budget. Its surplus is fixed and the household income tax schedule shifts in order to achieve the predetermined net government position. Secondly, investment must equal savings, which originate from households, corporations, government and the rest of the world. Aggregate investment is set equal to aggregate savings, while aggregate government expenditures are exogenously fixed.

Simulations and results

Two main scenarios have been analysed using the methodology described in the previous section: in the first 'historical' scenario, the micro-simulation system, which was estimated on the basis of the 1988 survey, is 'shocked' in such a way that the final aggregate variables for employment composition and wages correspond to the values recorded in the 1995 survey. In this scenario, the CGE model is not used. In the second 'trade liberalisation' scenario, the CGE model is used to simulate tariff abatement and to obtain general equilibrium values for employment and wages, which are then used to shock the micro-simulation model. In this way, two new income distributions are derived: the first includes all the shocks (as reflected in the observed historical changes in *aggregate* employment and wages) that occurred between 1988 and 1995, and the second includes only the shocks directly attributable to trade policy. Before comparing these two new distributions and thus assessing the weight trade shocks have in explaining overall poverty and inequality evolutions, it is useful to take a closer look at the socio-economic characteristics and income sources of the poor, and at the 'historical' and 'trade' shocks on aggregate variables.

Table 8.4 Poverty by occupational choices of household heads, 1988

Occupation of household head	Population shares	Headcount	Contribution to national poverty
Inactive	10	77	10
Wage-employed	48	65	44
Self-employed	40	78	43
Both	3	83	3
Total	100	72	100

Source: authors' calculations based on the Colombian household survey.

Table 8.5 Poverty by labour market segment of the household head, 1988

Segment	Population shares	Headcount	Contribution to national poverty
Urban unskilled male	16	76	17
Urban skilled male	19	46	12
Urban unskilled female	5	76	6
Urban skilled female	4	45	2
Urban segment	43	60	36
Rural unskilled male	43	84	50
Rural skilled male	6	60	5
Rural unskilled female	6	82	7
Rural skilled female	1	57	1
Rural segment	57	81	64
Total	100	72	100

Source: authors' calculations based on Colombian household survey.

The Colombian poor, and the historical and trade shocks

The 1988 Colombia poverty profile corresponds quite closely to that of a typical developing country: the majority of the poor live in rural areas, are either unemployed or, when working, are in the unskilled informal segment of the labour market. To facilitate the interpretation of the micro results of the next sub-section, the poverty data from the 1988 survey have been reorganised to correspond with the labour market specification chosen for our model: Table 8.4 shows the poverty profile according to the occupational choice of the household head, and Table 8.5 considers the rural/urban distribution and the labour market segments.

Table 8.4 highlights the fact that, although the inactive population suffers high poverty incidence, the self-employed (informal) category represents the hard core of the Colombian poor. Finding a job in the formal segment means accessing better remunerated and more secure employment, and most probably as a result, escaping poverty. Assessing the influence of trade reform on this particular channel is scrutinised more closely in the next sub-section.

Table 8.5 shows that the rural poor constitute more than 60 per cent of total poverty; however, with a high incidence (headcount) of 60 per cent, urban poverty should not be overlooked. As long as labour market segments are considered, poverty incidence is higher among households headed by the unskilled. Furthermore, gender differences appear to be of minor importance in urban areas. Conversely, in rural areas, female-headed households seem to be better off. Rural unskilled male-headed households are the largest contributors to overall poverty, given their large share of the total population and high incidence.

Given these occupational choices and labour market segmentation, it should not be surprising that the most important income sources for the poor are wages of the unskilled male and agricultural profits; once again, a significant poverty reduction can be achieved when these types of income are boosted.

The effects of historical and trade scenarios on the *aggregate* employment and income categories are analysed in the remaining part of this section.

The historical scenario

In the historical scenario, the 1988 starting point is compared with 1995. The 1995 survey includes data collected after most of Gaviria's structural reforms had been implemented. As shown in Table 8.6, there are remarkable differences in labour market trends between urban and rural areas.[19] In *urban* areas, self-employment rose substantially across all labour market segments and the share of male wage-workers declined for both unskilled and skilled categories. Female labour market participation increased considerably, especially in self-employment activities. In *rural* areas, females also increased their labour market participation although to a lesser extent and more in wage-work activities than in self-employment. The data suggest that, in rural areas, there was a general trend across almost all segments towards more wage-employment, and in particular for the unskilled. More than

Table 8.6 1988 labour force composition and its recent evolution

	1988 initial shares				1988–95 change in shares			
	Inactive	Wage-work	Self-empl.	Both	Inactive	Wage-work	Self-empl.	Both
Urban unskilled male	6.5	61.2	32.3	−0.5	−12.7	24.2		
Urban skilled male	7.6	72.9	19.5		−6.1	−5.9	24.3	
Urban unskilled female	64.3	21.8	13.9		−8.7	2.6	36.1	
Urban skilled female	48.6	42.1	9.3		−12.8	5.9	40.1	
Total urban	32.5	50.2	17.3	−11.1	−1.6	25.6		
Rural unskilled male	4.7	45.9	45.8	3.6	−6.8	14.2	−13.5	−1.3
Rural skilled male	24.0	47.5	27.8	0.7	2.1	0.1	−3.6	59.2
Rural unskilled female	72.4	6.1	21.2	0.3	−4.8	42.6	3.4	53.9
Rural skilled female	66.9	22.1	10.8	0.2	−9.4	18.4	20.0	39.8
Total rural	39.3	28.7	1.6	−5.9	17.1	−8.6	2.1	

Source: authors' calculations based on Colombian household survey.

Table 8.7 Wages and self-employment income, 1988 and 1988–95 evolution

	Initial values	*1988–95 change (%)*
Wage		
Urban unskilled male	37,185	2.1
Urban skilled male	61,560	7.6
Urban unskilled female	26,784	−4.6
Urban skilled female	45,131	8.3
Rural unskilled male	28,320	−11.3
Rural skilled male	40,311	−4.6
Rural unskilled female	21,591	−8.6
Rural skilled female	36,523	−6.3
Self-employed income		
Urban	40,443	11.4
Rural agricultural	17,628	13.1
Rural non-agricultural	19,969	−6.1
Rural mixed	16,142	8.1

Note: the second column shows percentage changes.

Source: authors' calculations based on Colombian household surveys.

50 per cent of the rural male unskilled labour force was wage-employed in 1995. This implies there was a significant increase in wage employment between 1988 and 1995, whereas self-employment correspondingly declined.[20]

As far as the 1988–95 income changes are concerned, a striking feature in Table 8.7 is the differences across the labour market segments and between wage- and self-employment.

In urban areas, income from self-employment exhibits the highest increase, unskilled wages go down, and skilled wages increase. This is also true for rural areas, where wages seem to decline in all segments, although to a larger degree for the unskilled categories. Self-employment income from agricultural and mixed activities increases significantly, although this may be for seasonal reasons. This is one reason why these results should be interpreted with caution, in particular for rural areas, as they are based on just two surveys.

The trade liberalisation scenario

The 1988–95 historical evolution described above serves as a benchmark against which a trade liberalisation scenario can be compared. As described earlier, the 1988–95 period witnessed numerous policy reforms and several other shocks, so that to identify whether increased openness is pro-poor and improves income distribution a counterfactual scenario that includes just trade policy shocks is needed. Using the CGE model to simulate tariff abatement shown in Table 8.1 provides the basis for this counterfactual scenario.

Table 8.8 summarises the aggregate changes in employment and income levels that result. First of all it can be noticed that wage-employment increases across all segments at the expense of self-employment. This, at first, may seem surprising

Table 8.8 Trade liberalisation induced changes in employment shares and incomes

	Employment		Income	
	Wage-work	Self-employment	Wage	Self-employment
Urban unskilled male	0.5	−1.1	1.1	
Urban skilled male	0.5	−2.6	0.9	
Urban unskilled female	0.3	−0.8	0.5	
Urban skilled female	0.5	−6.1	1.1	
Rural unskilled male	1.7	−0.5	3.4	
Rural skilled male	1.0	−1.8	2.1	
Rural unskilled female	1.2	−0.5	2.4	
Rural skilled female	0.7	−5.4	1.4	
Urban				3.8
Rural agricultural				6.6
Rural non-agricultural				5.1
Rural mixed				5.8

Source: authors' calculations based on Colombian CGE model, percentage changes with respect to base equilibrium.

given that for many models the standard prediction is that trade openness leads to an increase in informal activity. The typical argument to justify this is that when formal sector firms are exposed to increased foreign competition they are forced to release employees, who then move to the informal sector, or they hire temporary workers (coming from the informal sector), or they sub-contract activities to establishments in the informal sector. In all cases, the net effect is that informal employment grows.[21] However, in the present model, a different adjustment mechanism is at work. Formal and informal labour markets adjust to a new equilibrium differently, with the formal sector exhibiting a certain degree of wage rigidity. Accordingly – and, due to the Colombian labour endowment, the initial shares of formality and informality across activities, and their different labour inputs – the trade shock results in a diminishing informal employment. Thus, while both *formal* and *informal* import-competing activities contract to a similar degree, *formal* export-oriented activities expand considerably more than *informal* activities.

Figure 8.1 illustrates the general equilibrium adjustment mechanism at work in the model. The sum of formal (wage-work) and informal (self-employed) labour endowments is assumed fixed and represented by the horizontal segment $O^{nf} - O^f$. Two labour demand curves are depicted for the formal (D^f) and for the informal (D^{nf}) employment and they are negatively sloped with respect to the wages W^f and W^{nf}. The graph also shows two alternative wage curves for the formal market $(S1^f)$ and $(S2^f)$ with different slopes reflecting low and high degrees of stickiness.[22] The initial equilibrium is at point E where wage $w0$ is equal for the formal and informal segments and where formal and informal employments are measured by the distances $O^f - P0$ and $O^{nf} - P0$ respectively. The trade shock is represented by an upward shift of the formal labour demand curve (from D^f to $D^{f\prime}$) and, depending on the rigidity of the formal wage, the new equilibrium can be at points

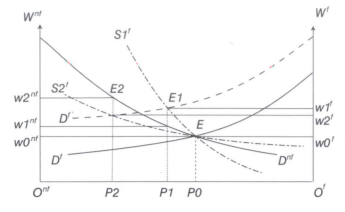

Figure 8.1 Formal and informal labour markets

$E1$ or $E2$. Illustrating the case for $E1$, the new equilibrium of the formal market is found at the intersection of the formal labour demand and the wage curve: the new wage is set at $w1^f$ and formal employment increases from $O^f - P0$ to $O^f - P1$. Informal employment adjusts residually and decreases symmetrically to $O^{nf} - P1$; the informal wage is found on the labour demand (D^{nf}) at $w1^{nf}$. It can finally be noticed that the mechanism just described works in a very similar way to a rural–urban migration framework where, instead of considering movements from one region to another, flows between informal and formal market segments are now taken into account.

The significant increases of wages for unskilled workers (shown in Table 8.8), particularly in the rural areas, and of income levels for rural agricultural self-employed are easily rationalised by the standard comparative advantage theory. Tariff abatement induces resources to move out of contracting import compet-ing sectors and into expanding export-oriented ones. These use intensively the most abundant Colombian resources – unskilled (especially rural) wage- and self-employed workers – which therefore enjoy increasing returns.

In summary, implemented in isolation from any other shocks, the Colom-bian tariff abatement of the beginning of the 1990s would have produced sig-nificant employment gains for wage workers and a slight reduction of informal self-employment. In more detail, these gains would have been greater for the un-skilled categories and more pronounced in rural areas. Correspondingly, wages for these categories would have recorded significant increases. However note that these results rest on two important assumptions: that the formal labour market shows a certain degree of wage rigidity and that labour supplies are fixed.

Income distribution and poverty results

The micro-simulation model maps the above-described aggregate values of em-ployment, wage and income levels of the *historical* and the *trade* scenarios into two new income distributions, so that poverty and inequality micro effects can be carefully assessed.

Table 8.9 Poverty and inequality, percentage changes with respect to 1988 benchmark

	Trade liberalisation			1988–95 historical change		
	Countrywide	*Urban*	*Rural*	*Countrywide*	*Urban*	*Rural*
Per capita income	2.4	1.6	4.0	6.6	9.5	0.6
General entropy (0)	−1.7	0.2	−1.6	0.5	−0.2	−8.7
General entropy (1)	−1.2	0.1	−1.2	5.3	6.7	−6.8
Gini	−0.6	0.1	−0.6	2.0	2.4	−3.6
P0	−1.8	−1.3	−2.1	−3.1	−7.8	−0.2
P1	−2.7	−1.8	−3.1	−3.8	−7.3	−2.2
P2	−3.6	−2.2	−4.1	−4.2	−3.6	−4.4

Source: authors' calculations.

First of all it should be reiterated that the trade shock is of lesser proportion than the historical shock and this explains why it produces smaller effects virtually across the board. However, as shown in Table 8.9, a pure trade shock accounts for a large share of overall poverty reduction. The headcount ($P0$) for the economy as a whole under the trade shock is reduced by 1.8 per cent, accounting for more than half of the total decrease of 3.1 per cent under the historical scenario. Trade seems to be particularly beneficial for the rural poor, given that it reduces the headcount ratio more than in the historical scenario; the reverse is recorded for the urban poor. This should not be too surprising given that trade liberalisation induces specialisation in agricultural exports and other activities requiring rural labour inputs and that this increased demand is reflected in Table 8.8 as increased wage and income levels.

Trade also scores well when the poverty severity ($P2$) index is examined. Even for the urban areas, trade-induced reduction of $P2$ is close to the overall historical reduction.

This positive distributional effect is confirmed by the inequality indicators. The whole population Gini is reduced with the trade shock, whereas it increases under the historical shock. Once again, the standard trade theory embedded in the CGE model can be used to explain this positive effect: unskilled labour, the main income source for the poor, records increased demand and rising wages and this helps to close the gap with higher wage earners. Given that this is more pronounced for the rural than for the urban areas, *between*-groups inequality is also reduced.

Micro-simulation analyses

These trade-related distributional and poverty results, as well as their interpretation may seem somewhat obvious, and one may be tempted to ask why such a complex empirical model needs to be constructed if no original insights are generated. In fact, the micro-simulation approach allows us to analyse income distribution changes empirically and in a much more detailed way than alternative analytical methodologies. To illustrate this further we now examine some analyses exclusive to the micro-simulation approach. In particular, four analyses are considered: a) the increased precision in assessing the poverty and inequality effects of the trade and historical shocks, b) the estimation of the relative weights of multiple poverty-reduction factors (decomposition analysis), c) the identification of determinants of movements in and out of poverty at the individual household level (poverty transition analysis), and d) an appraisal of the expenditure side to assess how important are consumption price changes for the poor.

Precision

Micro-simulation models account for changes in the income distribution at the micro level thus avoiding the drawbacks of other methods that operate at a more aggregate level. Whenever a particular shock implies large adjustments in occupational choices or even changes that are significantly different across income sources, the representative household group (RHG) approach, which classifies households according to the main income source of household heads, will fail to accurately measure poverty and income distribution effects. This is because in the RHG method, the pattern of income sources of all households belonging to a particular group are considered to be identical, thus avoiding the extreme case of a one-to-one income-type to household-category mapping. However, in reality not only do household heads (or other members) change occupation and therefore become members of different groups (in a standard RHG method this 'migration' is not allowed) but also households within the same group may have different income sources, so that, for certain shocks, this may actually determine whether or not they escape poverty.

A direct comparison between the results obtained using the RHG assumption and those of the full sample micro-simulation illustrates these (precision) issues for the Colombian case. It should be stressed that the RHG method applied here takes into account changes in the occupational choice of the household heads and so it is more flexible than is normally the case in a standard RHG application.

In the case of the trade scenario, as shown in Table 8.10, the full sample and RHG approaches produce similar results: changes are of the same sign and similar magnitude. The RHG approach does not account for occupational shifts of spouses (and other non-head household members) from, say, self-employment in subsistence agriculture to highly paid wage-employment. However, given that such shifts are probably of minor importance in the trade scenario, the RHG estimates are not strongly biased. Besides, in the current trade scenario, both wages of the unskilled and agricultural profits register similar increases, and the advantages of accounting for full heterogeneity in sources of income do not matter.

Conversely, important differences between the results of the two methods arise for the historical simulation. In general, one of the reasons for these differences is due to major occupational choice changes, which significantly altered the composition of household income, which resulted in large differences in the relative gains and losses across labour income sources.

Table 8.10 Full sample vs. representative household group

	Full sample			Representative household group (RHG)		
	Countrywide	Urban	Rural	Countrywide	Urban	Rural
Trade liberalisation						
Per capita income	2.4	1.6	4.0	2.7	2.1	3.7
General entropy (0)	−1.7	0.2	−1.6	−1.0	−0.1	−0.7
General entropy (1)	−1.2	0.1	−1.2	−0.8	−0.1	−0.7
Gini	−0.6	0.1	−0.6	−0.4	0.0	−0.3
P0	−1.8	−1.3	−2.1	−1.0	−1.2	−0.9
P1	−2.7	−1.8	−3.1	−2.2	−2.2	−2.2
P2	−3.6	−2.2	−4.1	−3.0	−2.8	−3.1
1988–95 historical change						
Per capita income	6.6	9.5	0.6	7.3	10.3	1.2
General entropy (0)	0.5	−0.2	−8.7	3.3	2.1	−2.8
General entropy (1)	5.3	6.7	−6.8	4.7	2.2	−0.1
Gini	2.0	2.4	−3.6	2.1	1.1	−0.5
P0	−3.1	−7.8	−0.2	−3.0	−7.0	−0.5
P1	−3.8	−7.3	−2.2	−3.6	−9.9	−0.6
P2	−4.2	−3.6	−4.4	−4.5	−12.1	−1.6

Source: authors' calculations.

Now let us consider the comparisons in more detail, and firstly the differences in poverty indicators. Interestingly, as indicated in Table 8.10, the deviations between the two approaches at a countrywide level appear to be minor. However, looking at the comparisons for urban and rural areas separately shows that this is misleading. The reduction in the poverty gap and the poverty severity index are *overestimated* under the RHG approach in urban areas, whereas they are *underestimated* in rural areas. This suggests that the RHG approach introduces neither a systematic upward or downward bias: the sign of the bias is probably 'shock-specific'.

The overestimation of the decrease of the poverty gap and the severity index in urban areas in the RHG method is due to the large increase in self-employment profits. The entire household income rises by more than 10.3 per cent if the household head is self-employed – even if a substantial portion of income is earned by spouses or other household members in wage activities where gains are much smaller.[23]

In rural areas, a movement from self-employment into wage-employment is a major reason for the rise in incomes of the poor as is the substantial increase in agricultural profits. In the RHG approach, even in the flexible version where household-head occupational shifts are accounted for, the full positive impact of changes in employment structure is underestimated.

These few examples show the interplay between occupational choice and labour income changes and their impact on poverty. Depending on the type of shock, the RHG approach might underplay or exaggerate the poverty impact of important labour market developments.

Comparisons

Technically a decomposition analysis consists of applying a shock to the micro-simulation system with only a subset of the target variables. This type of analysis aims at answering questions such as: do occupational changes matter more than wage/profit changes for poverty reduction? Typically, an occupational change, for *any* household member, implies a substantial variation in per capita house-hold income, whereas changes due to wage or profit fluctuations are relatively small. However, this initial answer should be carefully qualified and the following example might illustrate the difficulties involved. In urban areas, average self-employment profits are higher than the average wages of the unskilled. So moving from wage-employment into self-employment implies an average gain. However, when the full heterogeneity across individuals is considered, this *average* gain is not evenly spread across the whole distribution (as it is in the RHG approach) and individuals gain or lose according to their specific characteristics. In this case, much higher returns to education in self-employment compared with wage-employment determine that a well-educated individual typically gains from moving into self-employment, whereas the less-educated individual most likely loses.

These mechanisms explain the results relating to the occupational choice changes for the historical scenario. As shown in the bottom right-hand panel of Table 8.11, in urban areas, poverty indicators worsen substantially despite increasing female labour market participation. The positive effect of increased female participation is outweighed by the negative effect of the massive movement into self-employment. For the poorer and less-educated individuals this occupational switch involves income losses, whereas the more educated gain. In rural areas, the historical occupational shock causes all indicators to improve significantly due to the considerable gains of moving from agricultural self-employment into wage-employment. The occupational choice effects therefore dominate the overall impact on the poor.

As far as the trade scenario is considered, a striking feature highlighted in Table 8.11 is that it is the change in wages and profits that account for most of the poverty and inequality improvements. Changes of occupational choice seem to be of minor importance. It should also be emphasised that increased trade openness does not appear to cause the deterioration of rural poverty observed in the historical scenario. On the contrary, trade seems to be quite helpful in reducing poverty in rural areas due to significant income increases. Additional non-trade-related shocks must therefore explain the worsening situation of the rural population seen in the historical scenario.

Decomposition exercises can be used to analyse the contribution of developments in individual labour market segments to the overall distributional trends and

Table 8.11 Decomposition analysis

	Wage and profit change			Occupational choice change		
	Countrywide	Urban	Rural	Countrywide	Urban	Rural
Trade liberalisation						
Per capita income	2.3	1.7	3.7	0.1	0.1	0.1
General entropy (0)	−1.2	0.1	−0.9	0.3	0.3	0.3
General entropy (1)	−0.8	0.2	−0.6	0.3	0.3	0.3
Gini	−0.4	0.1	−0.3	0.1	0.2	0.2
$P0$	−1.7	−1.4	−1.8	0.0	0.1	0.0
$P1$	−2.5	−2.0	−2.8	0.0	0.1	0.0
$P2$	−3.3	−2.4	−3.6	0.1	0.2	0.1
1988–95 historical change						
Per capita income	2.8	5.7	−3.1	−0.4	−3.3	5.7
General entropy (0)	0.2	−1.3	−7.0	−6.4	−1.3	−6.3
General entropy (1)	2.1	−1.2	−3.2	−2.7	5.6	−7.2
Gini	−0.9	−0.6	−2.3	−1.6	1.9	−3.3
$P0$	−0.9	−4.9	1.5	−0.6	1.7	−2.1
$P1$	−1.4	−7.9	1.6	−2.1	6.6	−6.2
$P2$	−2.5	−9.8	0.3	−2.4	13.5	−8.4

Source: authors' calculations.

this may provide valuable insights to policy makers interested, for example, in the effect of female labour market behaviour.

Poverty transition

As explained earlier, the micro-simulation model was modified to allow individuals to be tracked through time so that poverty transition analyses could be conducted. One of the main advantages of these analyses consists in identifying movements of individuals in and out of poverty (not just the net final effect as described in Table 8.9) so that it becomes possible to study the characteristics of the persistent poor or to understand which factors help particular individuals to escape poverty.

Noting the position of households with respect to the poverty line before and after the shock, households were grouped into four categories: (i) households becoming non-poor, (ii) households falling into poverty, (iii) households remaining poor, and (iv) households remaining non-poor. The first three columns of Table 8.12 show the relative size of these four categories for both the trade liberalisation and the historical shock.

It is noteworthy that the movements out of poverty for the trade shock constitute a large proportion of those movements arising out of the overall shock, but, most

Table 8.12 Poverty transition results

Before shock:	After shock:	Country-wide	Urban	Rural	Country-wide	Urban	Rural	Active hh members/ hh size[3]
		Population shares[1]			Initial distance from z[2]			
Trade liberalisation								
Poor	Non-poor	3.7	4.1	3.3	0.145	0.127	0.162	
Non-poor	Poor	2.6	3.4	1.9	−0.148	−0.149	−0.147	
Poor	Poor	68.0	56.3	77.6	0.544	0.462	0.593	
Non-poor	Non-poor	25.7	36.2	17.2	−1.180	−1.359	−0.869	
Total		100.0	100.0	100.0				
1988–95 historical change								
Poor	Non-poor	5.6	7.8	3.8	0.225	0.195	0.276	11.9
Non-poor	Poor	3.5	3.5	3.5	−0.247	−0.371	−0.145	1.7
Poor	Poor	66.1	52.6	77.2	0.548	0.475	0.589	3.9
Non-poor	Non-poor	24.9	36.1	15.6	−1.203	−1.339	−0.942	2.3
Total		100.0	100.0	100.0				3.5

Notes

1   The first 3 columns show the percentages of the total population for each of the four groups.
2   Initial distance from the poverty line is equal to 1 – household income/poverty line.
3   The last column shows percentage change in the ratio of active household members to total household members.

importantly, it seems that increased openness generates less poverty (i.e. non-poor to poor) than the overall shock, especially in the rural area. Those who remained poor and especially those who are constantly non-poor are of comparable size in the two scenarios. Other characteristics of these groups can be examined, and columns 4, 5, 6 and 7 of the table show some preliminary results in terms of the mean initial poverty gap, i.e. the distance of household incomes from the poverty line, and the mean ratios of active to total household members in each group.

The figures in Table 8.12 show that, in terms of countrywide averages, those escaping from poverty and those falling into poverty appear to experience fairly similar gains and losses. This is true for both scenarios, the only difference being that, given the larger size of the historical shock, the initial distance from the poverty line is larger in that case. Yet, a closer look at the results for urban and rural areas again yields some valuable insights. In the historical simulation, those who become poor in urban areas experience losses that are almost 50 per cent higher than the gains of those who become non-poor. In rural areas, the historical simulation produces the opposite result. So the gains of the 'gainers' are higher than the losses of the 'losers'. Thus the rural–urban disaggregation shows that historically we observe a highly divergent shock. Furthermore, our analysis suggests that trade liberalisation may also contribute to this divergence as it produces similar divergent results, even though they are of much smaller magnitude.

In the historical scenario, a distinguishing feature of those households who escape poverty is the considerable increase in the average number of active members, as shown in the last column. Notice also that increased participation is a common characteristic of all households, but for those falling into poverty the increase in participation is well below the economy-wide average.

Combining poverty transition analysis with decomposition analyses yields an important insight. From the decomposition exercise it can be noted (not shown in Table 8.12) that occupational choice changes are not a major channel through which trade liberalisation affects income distribution. Yet, the poverty transition analysis carried out after applying only the occupational choice changes to the distribution reveals that changes of occupational choice do matter for the poor. Households which become non-poor have more members moving into wage-employment than is the case in other households. As explained before, this is very likely to be beneficial to the poor in both rural and urban areas. Although this result is somewhat tautological, it shows that the income gains large enough to lift people out of poverty are often related to occupational choice changes.

Expenditure side effects

The final point we want to make refers to the expenditure-side effects of the trade and historical scenarios. We should note that expenditure-side modelling is rather rudimentary as no substitution between goods is allowed for. Furthermore, we consider only two price indices based on baskets of food and non-food items and expenditure shares were calculated by income quintiles. In this framework, the relative price changes after trade liberalisation have almost no distributional effect. This is shown in Table 8.13. The historical simulation, which uses historical relative price changes calculated from consumer price indices, indicates that the relative price decrease of food items have worked for the poor. Moreover, it has a favourable effect on the income distribution in general.

Conclusions

This chapter has employed a relatively new methodology, pioneered for Indonesia by Robilliard *et al.* (2002), to study the poverty and inequality consequences of trade liberalisation, a major globalisation shock. This methodology entails combining, sequentially, a numerical simulation general equilibrium macro model with a micro-simulation income distribution model. The former provides counterfactual scenarios and estimates aggregate results, the latter evaluates the poverty and inequality micro impacts due to these scenarios. This approach overcomes the main difficulty of single-country case studies based on a single-year household survey or on multi-year surveys where households cannot be identified through time (i.e. as in a panel). Thus our method allows one to identify the income distribution effects due to a particular shock and to estimate the magnitude of these effects separately from other simultaneous shocks.

Table 8.13 Expenditure side effects

	With relative prices change			No relative prices change		
	Countrywide	Urban	Rural	Countrywide	Urban	Rural
Trade liberalisation						
Per capita income	2.4	1.6	4.0	2.2	1.4	3.8
General entropy (0)	−1.7	0.2	−1.6	−2.0	−0.2	−2.0
General entropy (1)	−1.2	0.1	−1.2	−1.5	−0.3	−1.6
Gini	−0.6	0.1	−0.6	−0.7	−0.1	−0.7
P0	−1.8	−1.3	−2.1	−1.7	−1.2	−2.0
P1	−2.7	−1.8	−3.1	−2.8	−1.9	−3.2
P2	−3.6	−2.2	−4.1	−3.7	−2.5	−4.2
1988–95 Historical change						
Per capita income	6.6	9.5	0.6	7.4	10.4	1.3
General entropy (0)	0.5	−0.2	−8.7	2.1	2.1	−6.8
General entropy (1)	5.3	6.7	−6.8	7.0	8.9	−4.9
Gini	2.0	2.4	−3.6	2.8	3.5	−2.6
P0	−3.1	−7.8	−0.2	−3.3	−7.5	−0.7
P1	−3.8	−7.3	−2.2	−3.5	−6.5	−2.1
P2	−4.2	−3.6	−4.4	−3.5	−2.4	−4.0

Applying this methodology to a trade liberalisation shock in the case of Colombia, the main results and policy conclusions can be summarised as follows. Trade liberalisation appears to contribute substantially to an alleviation of poverty. Abstracting from additional simultaneous shocks and labour supply growth, the beginning of the 1990s tariff abatement seems to have accounted for a very large share of the total reduction in poverty recorded between 1988 and 1995. This holds in particular for rural areas. But the distributional impacts differ fundamentally between rural and urban areas. Structural change and the corresponding occupational choice changes trigger large income gains for the poor in particular. Generating more wage-employment in formal sectors and/or increasing female labour market participation are identified as important sources of higher incomes. Given their divergent performance, an analysis in which rural and urban areas are aggregated would only suggest small net effects and potentially mislead policy decisions.

Finally it should also be emphasised that in the case of trade liberalisation, the income channel, that is employment status and wage levels, appears to be more important to the poor than the expenditure channel, that is the variation in the price of consumption goods.

Acknowledgements

This chapter is a revised version of a paper presented at the World Bank ABCDE Europe Conference, Paris, May 15–16, 2003. We wish to thank François Bourguignon and Anne Sophie Robilliard for inspiring us and guiding us through the research effort behind this chapter; Jaime de Melo and Christian Morrisson for valuable feedback on an earlier draft; and conference participants for their comments. The research was undertaken while the authors worked at the OECD Development Centre. Remaining mistakes are ours alone.

Notes

1 This may be translated as 'major shake-up'.
2 It should be noted that, due to data deficiencies, the abolition of quantitative restrictions is not simulated in the current version of the model. For more details on this sort of policy experiment see Bussolo and Roland-Holst (1999).
3 See World Bank (2002: 13). It should be noted that 1988 was an exceptionally prosperous year for agriculture due to the devaluation and higher coffee production combined with higher coffee prices.
4 See World Bank (2002), Vélez *et al.* (2001), Ocampo *et al.* (2000), and UNDP (1998).
5 The following section borrows from Robilliard *et al.* (2002). A more detailed discussion of a similar labour market specification can be found in Alatas and Bourguignon (2000).
6 The household survey used for estimation of the micro-simulation parameters is the Colombian Encuesta Nacional de Hogares from 1988 (EH61). After the removal of outliers, removal of individuals with top-coded earnings, and observations with missing data, the survey covers 29,729 individuals living in 12,092 households in urban areas, and 15,006 individuals in 5,384 households in rural areas. The expenditure shares are calculated from an income and expenditure survey and matched with the EH61 based on household groups. For the problems of these datasets see Núñez and Jiménez (1997).
7 The occupational choice model was estimated using a multinomial logit. The wage equations were estimated by Ordinary Least Squares. Correcting for selection bias in these equations did not lead to major changes in the results and was hence dropped. In the estimation of the profit functions, the number of self-employed was instrumented. For a more detailed discussion of the estimation methods see Alatas and Bourguignon (2000).
8 It is important to note that the micro-simulation as specified here does not generate a synthetic panel. It rather produces a second cross-section. As will be explained later in more detail, we need to differentiate between permanent and transitory components of the residual in order to analyse income mobility or poverty transitions.
9 However, estimating wage equations based on hourly wages did not make a major difference in the coefficients.
10 By doing this, we simply reproduce the original dataset.
11 Note that the constants of the occupational choice model – though estimated separately for heads, spouses, and others – are changed separately across the eight labour market segments. Therefore, we have 16 unknown constants in the occupational choice model, two occupational choices in each of the four urban labour market segments, and three in each of the four rural segments.
12 For social mobility in Latin America see Andersen (2000).
13 See Newhouse (2001) who studies the persistence of transient income shocks to farm households in rural Indonesia. He finds, for example that 'about 40 per cent of household income shocks remain after four years'.
14 As mentioned before, aggregate inequality indicators increased under the synthetic panel approach. This increase was more pronounced the higher the share of the transitory component. We thus 'redistribute' income from the poor to the rich if we substitute the unobserved earnings or a portion of it by generated normally distributed unobserved earnings, thereby increasing inequality.

15 For more details on the SAM see Bussolo and Correa (1999).
16 The CGE model used here is the result of merging the CGE model built for Colombia and described in Bussolo *et al.* (1998), and that constructed for the Indonesia case study mentioned in Robilliard *et al.* (2002) and more fully discussed in Löfgren *et al.* (2001).
17 Aggregate investment is set equal to aggregate savings, while aggregate government expenditures are exogenously fixed.
18 See Armington (1969) for details.
19 Our results are consistent with former studies, although comparability is limited due to the different segmentation choices. For an overview of labour market indicators for 1988 and 1995 see Vélez *et al.* (2001). Ocampo *et al.* (2000) additionally consider the sectoral composition of employment.
20 As the occupational choice of being *both* self- and wage-employed in rural areas is of minor importance, we do comment on it.
21 An alternative approach explaining the link between trade liberalisation and increasing informality is presented by Goldberg and Pavcnik (2003).
22 Wage curves in the figure represent labour supply behaviour.
23 Notice that, in urban areas, an additional effect is at work and not considered by the RHG approach: increased non-head female labour market participation. If it had not been for the large increase in self-employment income, the RHG would have underestimated, instead of overestimated, the decrease in poverty.

References

Adelman, I. and S. Robinson (1978) *Income Distribution Policy in Developing Countries: A Case Study of Korea*, Oxford University Press, New York.

Alatas, V. and F. Bourguignon (2000) 'The Evolution of the Distribution of Income During Indonesian Fast Growth: 1980–96', mimeo, Princeton University.

Andersen, L. E. (2000) 'Social Mobility in Latin America', IISEC Working Paper.

Armington, P. (1969) 'A Theory of Demand for Products Distinguished by Place of Production', IMF Staff Papers, 16: 159–178.

Atkinson, A. B., F. Bourguignon, and C. Morrisson (1992) *Empirical Studies of Earnings Mobility*, Fundamentals of Pure and Applied Economics 52, Harwood Academic Publishers, Chur, Switzerland.

Bussolo, M. and R. Correa (1999) 'A 1994 Detailed Social Accounting Matrix for Colombia', Technical Paper no. 5, Fedesarrollo. Bogotá .

Bussolo, M. and D. Roland-Holst (1999) 'Colombia and the NAFTA', *Integration and Trade*, September–December 99, INTAL, Washington, DC.

Bussolo, M. and J. I. Round (2003) 'Poverty Reduction Strategies in a Budget-Constrained Economy: The Case of Ghana', Paper presented at the OECD Development Centre Conference on Globalisation and Poverty, December.

Bussolo, M., D. Roland-Holst, and D. van der Mensbrugghe (1998) 'The Technical Specification of FEDESARROLLO's Long Run General Equilibrium Model', Technical Paper no. 4. Fedesarrollo. Bogotá.

Dollar, D. and A. Kraay (2000) 'Trade, Growth, and Poverty', World Bank Policy Research Working Paper no. 2615.

Goldberg, P. K. and N. Pavcnik (2003) 'The Response of the Informal Sector to Trade Liberalisation', NBER Working Paper no. 9443.

Kugler, A. (1999) 'The Impact of Firing Costs on Turnover and Unemployment: Evidence from The Colombian Labour Market Reform', *International Tax and Public Finance*, 6(3): 389–410.

Kugler, A. and M. Cardenas (1999) 'The Incidence of Job Security Regulation on Labour Market Flexibility and Compliance in Colombia', mimeo, World Bank, Washington, DC.

Löfgren, H., R. L. Harris and S. Robinson (2001) 'A Standard Computable General Equilibrium Model in GAMS', Trade and Macroeconomics Division Discussion Paper no. 75, IFPRI, Washington, DC.

Newhouse, D. (2001) 'Do Negative Income Shocks Last Longer, and Do They Hurt the Poor More? Evidence from Rural Indonesia', mimeo, Cornell University, Itahca, NY.

Núñez, J. A. and J. A. Jiménez (1997) 'Correcciones a los Ingresos de la Encuestas de Hogares y Distributcion del IngresoUrbano en Colomia', mimeo, República de Colombia, Departamento de Planeación.

Ocampo, J. A., F. Sánchez and C. E. Tovar (2000) 'Mercado Laboural y Distribución del Ingreso en Colombia en los Años Noventa', Revista de la CEPAL, No. 72.

Robilliard, A.-S., F. Bourguignon, and S. Robinson (2002) 'Examining the Social Impact of the Indonesian Financial Crisis Using a Micro–Macro Model', mimeo, World Bank, Washington, DC.

Rodriguez, F. and D. Rodrik (2000) 'Trade Policy and Economic Growth: A Skeptic's Guide to the Cross-National Evidence', in B. Bernanke and K. S. Rogoff (eds), *NBER Macro Annual 2000*, NBER, Cambridge, MA.

Srinivasan, T.N. and J. Bhagwati (1999) 'Outward-Orientation and Development: Are Revisionists Right?' mimeo, Yale University, New Haven, CT .

UNDP (1998) 'Informe de Desarrollo Humano para Colombia – 1998', United Nations Development Programme.

Vélez, C. E., J. Leibovich, A. Kugler, C. Bouillón, and J. Núñez (2001) 'The Reversal of Inequality Trends in Colombia 1978–1995: A Combination of Persistent and Fluctuating Forces', mimeo, World Bank, Washington, DC.

World Bank (2002) *Colombia Poverty Report*, World Bank, Washington, DC.

Index